CONSUMED

CONSUMED

HOW SHOPPING FED
THE CLASS SYSTEM

HARRY WALLOP

Collins

First published in 2013 by Collins

An imprint of HarperCollins*Publishers*
77–85 Fulham Palace Road
London W6 8JB

www.harpercollins.co.uk

1 3 5 7 9 10 8 6 4 2

Text © Harry Wallop 2013

A catalogue record for this book is
available from the British Library

ISBN: 978-0-00-745708-3

Printed and bound in Great Britain by
Clays Ltd, St Ives plc

MIX
Paper from
responsible sources
FSC
www.fsc.org   FSC C007454

FSC™ is a non-profit international organisation established to promote
the responsible management of the world's forests. Products carrying the
FSC label are independently certified to assure consumers that they come
from forests that are managed to meet the social, economic and
ecological needs of present and future generations,
and other controlled sources.

Find out more about HarperCollins and the environment at
www.harpercollins.co.uk/green

CONTENTS

INTRODUCTION

'We are all middle class now,' said John Prescott to howls of derision in 1997, in the run-up to the general election that swept Tony Blair into power.

Prescott was, of course, Blair's bruising, working-class side-kick who had gone to sea at the age of 16 and worked his way up the ranks of P&O. With his pugnacious beliefs and mangled English, he was wheeled out to persuade old Labour voters that Blair, the first prime minister since Sir Alec Douglas-Home to attend a public school, understood their concerns. The idea that Prescott was middle class seemed as likely as finding caviar in Asda.

But 15 years on his astute comment has been proved correct, with the great majority of us considering ourselves middle class. Meanwhile he's sitting in the House of Lords, the ultimate sanctuary of the ruling elite of Britain, and Asda sells John West lumpfish caviar. Yours for £2.48 for a 50g tin.

The election was held on 1 May 1997. It was, I remember, a very warm day, and in glorious sunshine I cast my ballot for regime change, as nearly all students that day did. It was the summer of my finals at Oxford, and for a generation who had only ever known Margaret Thatcher and John Major things really could only get better, as D:Ream sang. My vote was not really political; it was generational.

That evening I went down to London to attend the dinner to celebrate my cousin's 21st birthday. It was being held at White's, the smartest of all London's gentlemen's clubs, a glorious early Georgian building on St James's, which had once served as the unofficial headquarters of the Tory party and where the Prince of Wales had his stag night. The dress code, as it is always at gentlemen's clubs, come rain or stifling heat, was jacket and tie. I turned up in a three-piece tweed suit. Nowadays I would call it vintage. Then, it was charity shop chic, bought in a second-hand outlet in Oxford for a student Chekhov play. It was, in reality, a 1950s garment, but accessorised correctly I was sort of passable as a turn-of-the-century Russian doctor hanging out near a cherry orchard. I thought I looked pretty stylish.

My father thought otherwise. Possibly the mildest mannered man you could imagine, he exploded with ill-concealed contempt, ending with the immortal lines uttered without any hint of irony: 'Gentlemen do not wear tweed after six o'clock in London.'

Behind this temper was, I knew, a deep-seated disappointment that I had let him down. My entire upbringing had been an extended lesson in the British class system, and its tiny invisible rules, a living out of Nancy Mitford's list of 'U and non-U' words to ensure my vocabulary did not embarrass any of the guests for tea. Debrett's was occasionally brought down from the shelf to teach me how to address envelopes correctly to the assorted earls, countesses and viscounts from whom I had received Christmas presents. Mostly these were aunts and cousins. How to curtsy to royalty, eat asparagus and artichokes, pluck a pheasant, tip a gamekeeper, when to leave the room, what one wore – this was not some parlour game, this was just how I was brought up in west London in the 1970s and 80s. These rules were never drilled into me, they were merely taught alongside tying one's shoelaces, riding a bicycle and asking to get down from the table. It seemed, as it always does for any child, normality itself. Whether one wore tweed after six, brown in town, if one called it 'pudding' or 'dessert' were things I was just meant to know. If I wanted to look like a tramp in my student flat, fine, but please God, not in White's.

I had got it wrong and my father believed I had done so on purpose as some sort of silent political protest – though it was clearly laughable to suggest that wearing tweed in the grandest of all St James's clubs was an act of solidarity with John Prescott.

I spent the entire evening fuming, as the grandees around me fumed too about how the incoming government was going to ruin Britain. The votes had yet to be counted, but the landslide was already inevitable. Change was in the air, but not in this privileged corner of SW1. Surely, I argued, in the summer of 1997 such niceties of class and of what gentlemen did or did not do were not just a decade out of joint, but a full century? Apparently not.

And 15 years later the niceties are still very much alive – just in a different form. Class has never gone away. Even after the years of never having it so good, the white heat of technology, the no turning back, 13 years of New Labour and, now, of being all in it together. If anything, it is more prevalent than it has ever been and it touches nearly everyone, including millions who consider class an irrelevant anachronism. John Major promised a classless society by the end of the 1990s, Tony Blair said that the old establishment was being replaced by a new, larger, more meritocratic middle class, Gordon Brown vowed to create a generation that would build a Britain where the 'talent you had mattered more than the title you held'. But for all the pronouncements from various different governments, the country is obsessed as much as ever about class. When the chief whip Andrew Mitchell reportedly hurled abuse at a Downing Street policeman, he was mostly criticised not for his appalling manners, but for his alleged use of the word 'pleb', confirming in the eyes of the critics of the Government such as Polly Toynbee that 'the social class of Cameron's crew ... rule for their own ruling class'.[1]

A whole host of activities and institutions are attacked for being 'too middle class' – the Church of England, English Heritage, Girl Guides, tennis, BBC sitcoms, the Labour party. Various broadcasters, the Chelsea Flower Show, the Royal Opera House and the entire cabinet are derided for being 'too posh'; rows over the education system are almost entirely centred around how to ensure more working-class children get better grades and places at university; hands are wrung about how nearly every Bafta winner and top-40 musician went to private school, and why a disproportionate number of white working-class boys end up out of work, out of a job, out of luck.

It's not just the press which casts so much of what they write about in the molten, malleable language of class – 'Are your neighbours middle-class cocaine addicts like me?'[2] is a recent headline in the *Daily Mail*. Policy makers too increasingly see class as the cause of so many of Britain's economic and social woes. The Office for National Statistics, and a dazzling array of think tanks and research houses, publish almost weekly data to show that social inequality continues to widen in Britain – your health, your wealth, your happiness are all related to the social class you belong to. An astonishing amount of time and money is spent measuring and defining the socio-economic groups that make up modern Britain: C1, D, Class 1, managerial, semi-routine sales occupation, intermediate clerical. These groups are meant to be as objective and statistically robust as possible. And all serve to help the Government and its agencies attempt to improve 'social mobility' – the ultimate goal of so many in charge.

But the dry statistics relating to the upper deciles, the long-term economically inactive, the 'discouraged' and higher managerial classifications are not a true reflection of class in Britain today. Class has never been simply about whether you were rich or poor, whether you were the boss or the worker, or if you paid for your education or not. It was more than that. Class was always a subjective, loaded term, one that implied judgement. It used to be about a thousand little rules designed to trip up those not in the inner circle – what time you ate your evening meal, phoning for the fish knives, how you pronounced Cholmondeley and Featherstonehaugh Ukridge, which day to wear an old school tie. Much of it was knowledge, wrapped up in a secret language and accent, and was a way that social superiors knew to assert their superiority. It was tricky (though not impossible) to fake, and it was designed, so it seemed to those not in the inner circle, to keep outsiders in their place. When Brian Winterflood started a job at the London Stock Exchange in 1951 he wore brown shoes to work, only to be greeted on his first day with shouts, running around the exchange, of 'Brown boots, brown boots!' He quickly scuttled off to find a pair of black shoes. 'And I've always worn black ever since.' Hardly anyone remembers these rules now. Brown shoes are a common sight in the City, while accents have become blurred, with the public school drawl edging ever closer to the Essex twang. Even Prince Harry's speech is peppered with glottal stops.

Class has changed, as Britain has changed, and its populace have been faced with an ever wider array of choices. Class used to be about your position in life; now it appears to be increasingly about lifestyle. This is a term that only took hold in the 1950s when there started to be enough money around to furnish a lifestyle with more than a scuttle of coal and a week's holiday in a boarding house at Blackpool. And it took off in the 1960s with the glossy Sunday newspaper magazines that chronicled the swinging consumerism of the era.

This book is an attempt to map some of those changes and to find out what class means in Britain today. It is about the habits and lifestyles of millions of households and families who grew up on salad cream and ended up using balsamic glaze from Morrisons on their monkfish fillets. Of how holidays hop picking in Kent turned into flights to Disney World and cruises around the Canaries, and how tables bought on tick from the Co-op became adorned with Jo Malone smelly candles and an orchid from M&S.

This makes no claim to being a history book, but it does have a nominal starting point: 1954, a year of British triumph, when the first sub-four-minute mile was run, the year after Everest had been conquered and the structure of DNA established, the early years of the new Elizabethan era when it seemed after two decades of deprivation and war that anything was possible. Importantly, for millions of households, 1954 was the year when meat rationing was lifted, the last of the restrictions to be scrapped and an end to 14 years of continually having to check your pocket book before you calculated what you could buy. Families finally had the freedom to spend their weekly pay packet as they saw fit. It kick-started six decades of conspicuous consumption, which have culminated in people scanning their iPhones for Wagamama discount vouchers and supermarket delivery vans ferrying jars of anchovies and espresso pods at ten o'clock at night around the streets of Britain. An era which now looks under threat from the dramatic and almost unprecedented collapse in disposable income for many families – a phenomenon that did not happen in such a sustained way during the recessions of the 1950s, 60s, 70s, 80s and 90s.

It has been six decades of radical change. 1954 also saw the first purpose-built comprehensive school, an attempt to give equal opportunities to the children of Britain, regardless of where or to whom they were born; the release of Bill Haley's 'Rock around the Clock', the first cultural event to give a voice to teenagers; the very first Wimpy bar, bringing the concept of 'jet-age eating' to the masses; and the first package holidays to Benidorm, giving ordinary workers a taste of the sun-kissed beaches that only their betters had enjoyed a generation before.

During this second Elizabethan era there have been plenty of seismic changes and many things that have not really moved on at all. Class manages to straddle both camps. In the last 60 years there has been the almost complete destruction of the upper classes, the substantial dismantling of the working classes and the enormous, remorseless rise of the middle classes.

The landed aristocracy who owned Britain and ruled Britain have, save for a few notable exceptions, been forced to either sell off or open up their family homes to the public and vacate their comfortable benches in the House of Lords. Meanwhile, millions of manual workers who were paid decently for a hard day's work have ended up jobless or in call centres, while the unions and working men's clubs, organisations that gave so many working communities their backbone, appear to be in terminal decline.

The population of Britain has not got smaller; far from it. Those at the top and the bottom have not disappeared – they have merely moved class. Millions have left the ranks of the working classes and joined the ranks of the middle classes, while hundreds of thousands of those at the top have taken a step down. In the mid-1950s various surveys suggested that about a quarter of the population considered themselves 'middle class'; that figure now is consistently 70 per cent. The rest say they are working class. No one openly admits to being upper class.

But even if seven in ten people *are* middle class, that does not mean they all share the same lifestyle. There has certainly been some blurring of once strict boundaries of taste and consumption patterns. The majority of people own their own homes, and some of those a place in the sun too. Even more own a car. Prime ministers wear trainers, royal princesses pop into Topshop to buy skirts, sushi is so commonplace that commuters can pick it up with their pint of milk at the station, and Iceland can sell you frozen chicken Kievs. Sky satellite dishes, formerly a sign of 'council house culture', are now found on the side of Belgravia maisonettes. What was once recherché is now quotidian, products and decorations that used to be strictly for the working class are now symbols of distinction. Politicians rush to Greggs to scoff sausage rolls and pasties in an attempt to prove how 'in touch' they are with 'ordinary' voters, while chipped and rough kitchen utensils that their grandparents would have been thrilled to have thrown out are now snapped up by their wealthier descendants as 'vintage'.

Despite the severe recession, most of us enjoy a lifestyle of what seems – in comparison with 1954 – unbridled luxury: flights to Thailand, 47-inch televisions, food blenders, bread makers, steak on sale at the local supermarket (open till 10 o'clock at night), fashions that can be replenished every season, olives served alongside chilled chardonnay at your local pub. We are, in consumption terms, nearly all middle class. The white-goods revolution that started under Harold Macmillan, along with the white heat one under another Harold, not only put gadgets into consumers' hands, it freed millions of women from the drudgery of housework, allowing them to join the ranks of the salariat. Washing machines, freezers and micro-waves replaced domestic servants, and in so doing played their part both in creating two-income households and, in turn, a society with enough disposable income for status-defining trips to Itsu and days out at Blenheim Palace, where they can buy the 'Below Stairs' range of House Maid's scrubbing brushes and Butler's champagne openers.

Even as early as 1960 David Marquand, the academic and future Labour MP, declared that – superficially at least – 'the class war appears to be over, its warriors drowned in a sea of consumer durables. The working class itself is rapidly adopting middle-class standards, middle-class values and a middle-class style of life. Marks and Spencer dress every shopgirl like a débutante, hire purchase equips working-class kitchens with gadgets which would once have made the middle classes gasp with envy; night after night telly erodes what cultural barriers still remain to divide one class from another. These changes may disconcert the intellectual and appal the nostalgic, but the onward rush of modern industry continues undismayed, slowly transforming the most class-conscious country in the world into "one nation".'[3]

But 50 years on new gulfs have opened up within that 'one nation' of shoppers. Do you buy your meat wrapped in waxed paper from a farmers' market, from Tesco or from Asda? Is your holiday a trip to Butlins in Bognor or via Ryanair to Rimini? Is your electrical gadget a Roberts Radio from John Lewis or a James Martin spice grinder from Argos? These may seem trivialities that can only concern a society corrupted by consumerism. But they matter to an awful lot of people – even if they don't realise it. One of the women I interviewed for this book, Hayleigh, a mother of three who was brought up in a council house, is accused by her mother of 'shooting above her station' because she owns a Sainsbury's hessian bag-for-life. 'She says I've forgotten where I came from.' Hayleigh uses that same bag for life if she should ever pop to Iceland to buy her food – too embarrassed to be seen carrying Iceland plastic carrier bags.

Snobbism was never confined to ducal palaces, and certainly didn't die out when the Queen stopped débutantes ('debs') being presented at court in 1958. It is a powerful social force and has a major influence on how we spend our money. This, particularly in an era when there is less cash about, is now more important, when it comes to deciding status, than how we earn that money, I argue. If everyone around you professes to be of the same class, or even classless, then the battle to assert one's position comes down to what you consume rather than what you produce. It is about the little things – where you buy your jeans, the thickness of froth on your coffee, the thinness of your bresaola. The food, the clothes, the holidays, the homes, the culture, the furnishings we choose to spend our money on – even the plastic sacks we choose to carry those purchases around in.

This book tries to decipher all these products and work out what they say about us. Spending is more than just a frivolous matter of bags and burgers. It is, for some, a cause of great social anxiety as well as financial hardship and starts when they are in the womb – whether they were born in a private hospital or not, and whether their parents paid for a classified to announce their birth in the pages of a broadsheet newspaper or bought a Burberry sleepsuit and a Juicy Couture buggy to welcome them into the world.

I am aware that a book on class, which ignores the old pillars of social status – family, education, work – is one that only tells half the story, so I have attempted to tackle these topics as well, though even here, I argue, consumption plays a significant part in determining status. There are not many children that made it to Oxford whose parents never spent a penny on a tutor, music class or educational trip out.

It is all these consumer decisions that help separate the 'middle classes' that somehow include the Duchess of Cambridge – in her Le Chameau green wellies, Zara tops and Boden skirts – from the 'middle classes' that include Asda Mums, living off tinned food just before pay day. With a dazzlingly varied array of shops, brands and products available to furnish our lifestyles, there are many different types of middle class. This book attempts to categorise these different middle classes along patterns of consumption and explain why some brands remain exclusive and desired and others succumb to 'prole drift', why Iceland is despised by so many while Aldi is worshipped, why holidaying in Norfolk in a tent is so much more high class than in a hotel in Florida. For ease of reference I have given all these groups labels, many of them a bit flippant. Despite the stereotypes, we are not as a nation easily split into discrete groups, and I realise many of the labels are far from perfect.

There are the Portland Privateers, high earners and high spenders, who stamp their status (often newly won) onto their children before they have even been born by booking into the private maternity unit, preferably the Portland Hospital in London. They are some of the key supporters of a number of successful high-end, high-visibility brands that have flourished even in the economic downturn: Mulberry, Belstaff, Smythson. To the untrained eye they may appear similar to the Rockabillies. This lot is a broad church of consumers, but they have very much a rural attitude to life, even if they live in Fulham rather than Fairford. They are often wealthy individuals, sometimes not at all, whose defining feature is holidaying at home, ideally at the resort of Rock in Cornwall, where they can mingle with fellow Prosecco-sipping holidaymakers in their Jack Wills hoodies and Boden swimming trunks, red trousers, whipping up a Jamie Oliver recipe on the barbecue.

Similar in attitude to the Portland Privateers, but a million miles away from them in terms of income, are the Hyphen-Leighs – acutely aware of the power of brands and labels and keen to assert their status through spending. Their ability to latch onto the latest fashions and make them their own stretches even to the naming of their children – invariably double barrelled and unusually spelt. Paul's Boutique and Sports Direct are their natural high street habitats, places where smart casual takes on a whole new meaning.

Sun Skittlers couldn't really give two hoots about whether their polo shirt has a penguin in a top hat, a crocodile, a polo player or a hippo in a bath on the front. Money is spent on leisure, not fashion – from a 40p copy of the *Sun* to a game of skittles down at their local working men's club. None of them defines themselves as middle class, but they are fully paid up members of the modern consumer class who despite fairly low incomes are usually home owners, sun seekers and season ticket holders.

The Middleton classes, named in honour of Carole, rather than Catherine, started off life in almost an identical situation to the Sun Skittlers, but have spent many of their waking hours escaping from their red-top, blue-collar, hire-purchase background. They too embraced all the opportunities that consumer Britain threw at them but they wanted more; and trips to Torremolinos were upgraded to Tuscany, the *Daily Herald* was swapped for the *Daily Mail*, the Co-op meat counter for M&S ready meals. This does not make them traitors to their roots; they are the golden generation that helped drive post-war Britain out of austerity and are proud to declare themselves 'middle class'.

Asda Mums, mostly on low incomes, shy away from defining themselves as middle class. But their subtle understanding of status and brands, their insistence that their babies are given organic Ella's Kitchen mango pouches (while the older one gets a McDonald's as a treat), their championing of Pampers and Thorpe Park, prove that so much of modern consumption is driven by parents buying for their children. No more so than with this group.

Then there are the Wood Burning Stovers, the descendants of the original Habitat shopping generation. A well-turned garlic press and a wood burning stove, rather than an electric whisk and a large TV, is what gives them pleasure – you can spot them with their Daunt book bags tripping their way to pick up a box of yellow courgettes from their farmers' market in their Birkenstock sandals, trying not to look too smug.

These groups are introduced throughout the book, and will I hope shed a little light on the country we are. Of course many people straddle more than one group and throughout their life have travelled through different classes. I am already on about my third class, having strived to squash my pheasant-plucking background ever since I was at school. I now fall mostly within the Wood Burning Stove category, which is not something I feel particularly comfortable with. No one likes to be pigeon-holed; we all understandably believe that our consumption patterns are unique. But, as the book explains, the consumer companies that supply us with our food, drink, leisure and clothes spend a considerably amount of time categorising us. We might as well try to beat them at their own game.

There are a small number of consumers who claim, with some legitimacy, to be entirely outside the consumer society – to never shop at a supermarket, to never fly abroad and to take great pleasure in shredding the Argos catalogue onto their compost heap. But these too are defined just as much by their opposition to the branded, consumer world as those who shop at JD Sports. And you'll find a fair few of them happily scouring the John Lewis kitchen department or their local car boot fair and picking up a cut-price smoked salmon at Aldi.

Crucially, I hope to explain why this ability to define ourselves through what we buy or don't buy is partly out of our control. Many of our choices have already been 'edited' by the shop, the restaurant, the food manufacturer, the holiday company. Sir Terence Conran – one of the towering figures in the rise of the consumer classes – was always very firm in refuting the idea that he 'instructed' people how to live their lives, that his restaurants and shops somehow imposed on us a manual for middle-class living. But though he was never as crass as to tell people that the only route to happiness was sipping an espresso or snuggling under a duvet, his 'philosophy' was choice editing. 'I want to show people things they may not have seen before. After all, people can only buy what they are offered and what I want to do is offer them things in as honest and genuine way as I can manage; offer things that people may not have known they might want.'[4]

Over the last two generations one of the triumphs of capitalism has been consumer companies' ability to anticipate what their customers wanted, or thought they wanted, and provide it for them. They have done this through relentless analysis of their customers, where they live, what they buy, when they shop. Supermarkets have been at the forefront of this trend, but others have learnt to be just as adept and spend millions of pounds every year to refine their marketing, their choice of stock and where they site shops. Often what you put into your basket or which outlet you visit is determined not by you, but by the company, many of whom have worked out exactly who they want through their doors. And who they don't.

I too have tried to mine the data and find out more about these different middle classes – and indeed about those that are still outside the 70 per cent. From toffs to chavs, from posh wankers to gyppos. The class system still throws up terms of abuse with a vitriol that would be unacceptable when describing race, sex or age. Working class is only occasionally heard as a straight description; it is usually as a nostalgic badge of honour worn by those who have made it to the House of Lords. Instead we have the underclass, the benefits spongers, the feckless, the scroungers. What's left of the upper classes, too, come in for an equally rough ride. Posh, public-school toffs are to be laughed at, in their 'Look at my fucking red trousers' and appearances in the pages of *Tatler*. The middle classes, in becoming ever wider, have pushed those outside of its ranks to the margin, so far away from normal life as to be comic-book creations fit only for 'scripted reality' shows.

* * *

Although this book is mostly concerned with products, shops and brands, it is really about people, all of them in some way members of the modern British consumer classes. Class does not reside in products, it only takes shape in ownership of those things or rejection of them. I hope their stories, and my story too, will explain a little bit about where we have ended up in Britain today.

CHAPTER 1

FOOD

*How did something as innocent as a lunchtime sandwich
or morning coffee become the cause of social anxiety?
Here we meet the Asda Mums.*

The ready meal was nothing new in 1979. TV dinners were in existence before the advent of colour television, and Fray Bentos pies had long been available to consumers unwilling or unable to take the time to cook their own evening meal.

But in 1979, the year Margaret Thatcher swept to power promising to bring harmony to the discordant classes, the ready meal went upmarket, thanks to Cathy Chapman, then 24-year-old head of poultry development at Marks & Spencer. She had already enjoyed success thanks to the simple, though radical for the time, idea of removing first the skin from a chicken breast, and then the bone from a thigh. The following year the breast became coated in Japanese breadcrumbs – crunchier, denser breadcrumbs than a home cook could ever produce from a stale piece of sliced white. Her next product, however, took it to another level.

It was the chicken Kiev. Now, for some, an object of derision, as naff as a tie-dye shirt or snowball cocktail, then, a sophisticated bistro dish that had been appearing on the menus of London restaurants for a few years. It was the first 'middle-class' ready meal and helped pave the way for the produce we see on our supermarket shelves today: everything from cheese and ham chicken Kievs from Iceland (£1 for 2) to Charlie Bigham's Moroccan chicken tagine from Waitrose (£5.99). The ready meal industry is now worth £1.22 billion every year and is at the front line of a never-ending class war over food. Mealtimes have always been fraught, but over the last genera-tion as our diets have become ever more varied, exotic and full of choices, the opportunities to feel bad about what you have put on your plate have been been greater than ever.

Back in 1979, when most people probably thought a Moroccan tagine was something you either smoked or sat on, high-quality cuisine meant French cuisine. Chapman lived in Islington, north London, just 400 yards from Robert Carrier, a restaurant in Camden Passage named after its owner, by then a television star, best-selling cookery writer, innovator of the wipe-clean recipe cards, and proud owner of two Michelin stars. In 1975 the restaurant had hosted dinner for the Queen Mother and Lord Grimthorpe, the first time Her Majesty had dined out in a public restaurant since before her marriage in 1923.[1] Chapman was encouraged by her bosses at M&S to eat at the best restaurants, and it was at Carrier that she first tried chicken Kiev.

'Yes, I liked it. What's not to like? Butter, garlic and a crisp outside,' she recalls. Her taste of crispy, buttery heaven coin-cided with the rise of an entrepreneur called John Docker, 'who believed this kind of food – chicken Kiev, prawn cocktail, duck à l'orange – could and should be available to a wider audi-ence,' explains Chapman. He set up a factory and staffed it with professional chefs who would then sell their pre-prepared meals for restaurants to re-heat. But he had ambitions for families at home also to enjoy this sophistication. And when he showed the dish to M&S Chapman and her team decided Britain was ready for the first-ever chilled ready meal.

This is what made it different. It was not a boil-in-the-bag meal that you bought from the freezer cabinet, or a dismal pie in a tin. This was a dish presented in an aluminium tray, in the chiller cabinet of a supermarket, still a relatively small area dedicated to dairy products. It was protected by a cardboard box, with a glossy photograph on the front, and sold for £1.99 – the equivalent of about £8 in today's money, a premium price for a premium product. They even, in the early days, came with a little paper chef's hat on the sprig bone that protruded from the meat to make it look worthy of a magazine photo shoot. 'It was really upmarket, fresh prepared food, the first time we'd done restaurant quality meals. It was a very big launch.' This was food for the middle classes, and the upper middle classes at that.

Like all big launches for M&S it had to be approved by the board of directors. At this point the Kiev was nearly torpedoed. 'My boss at the time, the head of food, said when he tasted it, "It's got garlic in. I don't like garlic, people don't like garlic" – and said it shouldn't be put on the shelves.' This was not an uncommon view at the time. But with six weeks to go before launch it was too late to back out. With all the boxes printed, Chapman was forced to persuade the director he was wrong, and a Kiev without garlic was pointless.

She was right. It was an immediate hit. The dish was the height of sophistication, with its very name evoking exotic, Cold War Russia (*Tinker Tailor Soldier Spy* was one of television's hits of 1979), while the oozing, melting, garlicky butter hinted at a continental elegance that most people in winter-of-discontent Britain could only dream of. The first weekend, £10,000-worth was sold, and they ran out; production was immediately doubled. Within four weeks this one dish was bringing £50,000 a week into the M&S tills. 'The sales were phenomenal and it became a talking point at the time. People would have dinner parties and serve it, saying, "Here's one I made earlier," and it wasn't; it was one they'd bought at the end of the road.' To this day, Marks & Spencer, despite its food sales being one-tenth the size of Tesco, sells more chilled ready meals than any other retailer in Britain[2] and its dine-in-for-£10 meal deal during the recent recession was the salvation for many Portland Privateers and Middleton class people who had been forced to cut back on eating out at their local restaurant.

M&S's timing was impeccable and Chapman's persistence was prescient. Ever since Tetley introduced the tea bag in 1953, convenience food had been growing more sophisticated, but it had never really won over either gourmets or the upper middle classes, the customers that had helped M&S become Britain's biggest clothing retailer. There was always a fear that processed food was either a bit gimmicky, or frankly just a little common, especially when it was frozen or dehydrated. Fresh ready meals that could be passed off as restaurant-quality dishes you had magically whipped up in your kitchen were a salvation for a generation of women, who were now out during the day working, and didn't have the time to slave over a stove as their mothers had done.

But though the Kiev was a hit, and helped encourage all the other supermarkets to launch chilled ready meals – in turn fuelling their amazing success at grabbing more of consumers' disposable income – it exposed class divides when it came to eating, divides that are now deeper than ever before. Greggs versus Pret à Manger, McDonald's versus Wagamama, frozen chicken dippers versus *sous-vide* smoked duck. Something as innocent as a slice of white bread may have had the salt content reduced, but it has never been so loaded with social anxieties. It used to be about whether you asked Norman to phone for the fish knives, and whether you called it tea, supper or dinner (or even 'country supper' if you are in the Chipping Norton set). Those old-fashioned distinctions about terminology and cutlery still exist to some extent, but the deeper divides are about what you put in your mouth and sip from your morning cup.

Some people not only turn down but actively despise certain meals because they are 'for chavs and idiots' and refuse to step inside particular food shops. Food writers are both worshipped – Delia, Jamie, Nigella all so famous they go by first names only – but also reviled for promoting an unobtainable, Wood Burning Stover lifestyle, where the windowsill always has fresh basil, the sausages are always organic and the olive oil is always Fair Trade, and preferably Palestinian too.

Indeed, one's supermarket of choice has now become almost a short-hand for what socio-economic group you belong to – are you an Asda Mum or Tescopoly drone? A Waitrose deli-counter devotee, an Aldi acolyte or a member of the Farmfoods underclass? Which one are you?

*   *   *

It was all so different back in 1954, when food rationing finally ended with the lifting of meat restrictions. Ration books were burnt in celebration and Smithfield market opened at midnight for the first time since before the war. It had been a slow process allowing Britons unfettered access to food. Indeed, food rationing had been in place for nearly half of the period between 1954 and the end of the First World War.

In an age when sushi is so ubiquitous that Marks & Spencer sells enough seaweed to wrap around the M25 every year[3] it is hard to imagine quite how dismal the diet of most families was. As the 1950s were about to start, the weekly ration for a man was 13 ounces of meat, 8 ounces of sugar, 6 ounces of butter or margarine, 2 pints of milk, 1.5 ounces of cheese, 1 ounce of cooking fat and 1 egg.[4] It was just not possible to have a food revolution on those provisions. Or even a particularly tasty meal. Of course the rich, as always, enjoyed some immunity because they could afford to eat in restaurants, which were free from rationing – though certain limitations were in place, such as meat and fish not being allowed to be served at the same sitting.

Even when eating out, however, the options were limited. Before the war, most food eaten out of the home was consumed, if not in a work canteen, either in a fish and chip shop, a tea room or department store café at one end of the scale, or in an intimidating hotel restaurant at the other end. Outside London, the idea of a reasonably priced, unpretentious restaurant where a working-class family could enjoy a meal was almost unheard of. The most popular option was Lyons corner houses, a chain that had dominated the eating-out market for decades, which made a fortune for its founders, the Jewish immigrant Salmon family (Nigella Lawson is one of the heiresses). Hot meals were served, and some were waitress service, but it was hardly sophisticated fare.

The first (1951) edition of *The Good Food Guide*, produced by an army of amateur reviewers (a full half-century before Tripadvisor), lays bare quite how uncosmopolitan the British restaurant scene was. Of the 484 restaurants and pubs reviewed outside London, only 11 served primarily foreign food, and of those ten were European, with just one Chinese included.[5] The idea of the guide came from Raymond Postgate, who had been a founding member of the British Communist party. Though by the 1950s he had put aside Marxism, he took a militant approach to eating out. He believed that diners had a duty to approach their Dover soles or brandy snaps with a certain hostility if they were to ensure they were not to be diddled by the owners of the means of production. 'On sitting down at the table polish the cutlery and glasses with your napkin. Don't do this ostentatiously or with an annoyed expression, do it casually. You wish to give the impression not that you are angry with this particular restaurant, but that you are suspicious, after a lifetime of suffering.' He deserves credit just as much as Elizabeth David, the ground-breaking food writer, for freeing the British from brown meat and browner sauces.

The old hotel dining rooms were crucibles of class. Intimidating, and so often depressing, they were a test for most families eating out. Cutlery, china, wine lists and waiters – all were traps to trip you up and make you feel a fool. My father-in-law can remember clearly the tension in the house as his own father prepared to go off on a trip down from their home town, Workington, to London to represent his union at a dinner. The dinner was to be a formal one at a big West End hotel. So, his father was sat down at the 'best kitchen' table (what most working-class people would have called the parlour) and given a tutorial by his wife about the arcane rules of fish knives, soup spoons and which glass to touch first. She had been in service and knew the pitfalls and was determined that he wouldn't let the side down.

As a family they never ate out, except for when they went on a trip to the department store in Carlisle or Newcastle. 'Department stores had quite nice restaurants in those days. The prices in Binns [now owned by House of Fraser] were quite reasonable. We'd have fish and chips or a pie, nothing spectacular. Certainly no coffee.

'But we would never have eaten out in Workington. There was a chap called Walter Archer, who had a bakery and confectionery business, who opened a café in one of his shops, which survived no more than a year or so. He told us that the trouble with the people of Workington is that the moment they're within five miles of home they don't see the point of eating out. He was right.' And if a café or tea room was considered a wasteful luxury, the restaurant at one of the town's two hotels was out of the question.

The playwright Alan Bennett, a butcher's son who won a scholarship to Oxford, recalls the horror of his parents visiting him at university and the trip to the hotel. The waiter came with the menu. 'Mam would say the dread words, "Do you do a poached egg on toast?" and we'd slink from the dining room, the only family in England not to have its dinner at night.' They were also befuddled by the wine list. But then, as Bennett asks plaintively, 'What kind of wine goes with spaghetti on toast?'[6]

This partly explains why Britain, more than any other country outside America, was to embrace fast food. It offered the promise of being classless. No waiters, no wine list, no pretentious French terms, no embarrassment about the bill. The first in Britain, opening the year that food rationing ended, was Wimpy. Within a few years it was already starting to change the face of Britain's high streets and diets, as the *Observer* reported at the end of the decade: 'Dirty and lethargic cafés with fly-blown sandwiches and antique sausage rolls have given way to mechanised eating places, though the staff have not always kept pace with jet-age eating.'

Each table came with a wipe-clean menu and the Wimpy signature condiment: a ketchup bottle in the form of a plastic, squeezy tomato; and burgers cost just one shilling and sixpence, the equivalent of a cinema ticket or three loaves of bread – more expensive than it is now in relative terms, but considerably cheaper than a café meal.

The concept, American of course, was brought to Britain by Lyons. In 1958, 5.5 million burgers were sold, enough for one in ten of the population to have eaten a Wimpy that year. What was their success? the newspaper asked. 'For the customer, particularly the all-important teenager, they are quick, simple and classless. A Wimpy can be eaten in less than ten minutes, leaving the rest of a lunch hour for shop gazing, flirting or jazz.' Sadly, the nearest today's office workers get to flirting and jazz at lunchtime is a quick trawl on Facebook.

'The Wimpy bars, with their bright layout and glass fronts, are inviting and casual, with none of the inhibiting air of posher places. In contrast to the working-class egg-and-chip cafés or middle-class ABCs [Aerated Bread Company tea rooms] the Wimpy bars have the same kind of American class neutrality as TV or Espresso bars.'[7]

Of course eating out in fast food places, or indeed any places, never became a classless activity. As with so many exciting, new, American activities that hit Britain in this period – pop music, jeans, frozen fish – classless merely became a euphemism for working class. No more so than with fast food, which over time took on a demonic quality, at least in the eyes of those who refused to eat it. Junk food for the junk classes.

This demonisation was mostly peddled by the Wood Burning Stovers, who as time went on were more than happy to have someone else cook their meal in bistros, trattorie and pho noodle bars – but not if it was 'mechanised', nor if it was American. McDonald's, by the sheer force of being successful and American, became the whipping boy. By the mid-1980s, a decade after it arrived in Britain, it was expanding fast, rapidly taking market share from Wimpy and Wendy's, another chain, and the company wanted to open an outlet in Hampstead, invariably described in tabloid newspapers as 'leafy'. It is a particularly charming borough of north London, whose heath has majestic views down to the City and Westminster. Home of Keats, Sidney Webb, D.H. Lawrence and Edith Sitwell, it was, in its own estimation, a cut above McDonald's. There proceeded an almighty 12-year-long row that ended up in the High Court.

'The last rampart has fallen,' *The Times* declared in 1992 when the burger chain finally won the right to open – on the site, symbolically, of a disused bookshop. Everyone quietly forgot that prior to that it had been occupied by a branch of Woolworths. The Hampstead residents, led by local MP Glenda Jackson, the only elected member of parliament to have won an Oscar, and author Margaret Drabble, insisted they were neither being snobs nor prejudiced against burger bars, they just didn't like the idea of extra traffic and litter. The Heath and Old Hampstead Society said the result would be a rash of copy-cat chains, low-grade boutiques instead of proper shops 'where one could buy a reel of cotton'.

The true feelings of residents, however, were revealed in a letter to Camden Council, which complained about an influx of 'noisy undesirables', while the actor Tom Conti said,

'McDonald's is sensationally ugly.' As the *Washington Post* rather neatly put it, Hampstead was not so much a village, more a rather smug state of mind. The residents of Hampstead always have been Wood Burning Stovers to a man, Radio 4 devotees, owners of Ottolenghi cookbooks, recipients of organic food boxes. They sip flat white coffees from their local Ginger & White café (slogan: 'We don't do Grandes'), which offer organic marmite and soldiers for toddlers who have learnt to order a babycino before they can wipe their own nose.

The article in *The Times* reporting on the chain's final victory in NW3 could not hide its outright snobbery: 'The most valid objection to [McDonald's] is in fact their ubiquity and the fact that they have done so much in 18 years to debase the act of eating. Many customers are already excavating their purchases as they walk away from the counter, smearing ketchup around their mouths and grabbing handfuls of the deep-fried tooth-picks that are parodies of the honest British "chip".'[8]

McDonald's has undergone something of a transformation in the last six or seven years, particularly in Britain. There was certainly a time when I would never have taken my children into one of their outlets, partly because I disapproved of the food's unhealthiness, partly because I am a reluctant owner of a wood burning stove and quite like a flat white coffee – and with that comes a fairly large dollop of snobbism. Putting aside the issue of the food, most outlets just weren't very nice, with harsh strip-lighting, sweaty formica tables and even less healthy-looking customers.

But the McDonald's of the 1980s and 90s is no more. Partly spurred on by an alarming slippage in profits, partly thanks to a boss in Britain determined to tackle the hostility towards the brand, the restaurants started to go upmarket. The décor in all 1,200 branches was spruced up. Some now even have flowers on the table. The milk went organic, the eggs became free-range. Free WiFi was introduced, when this was an expensive luxury, and espresso and lattes started to be served. Then the recession came along, and it won over hundreds of thousands of new customers determined to continue enjoying a weekly meal out, or a morning cup of coffee on the way in to work, but keen to save money. Eight out of ten families in Britain with children visit at least once a year. My family is now one of those, though that horrifies some fellow north London parents.

There is still an astonishing level of animosity felt towards the golden arches, with much of it class based more than anything else. I interviewed the new British boss, Jill McDonald (no relation), who perhaps rather provocatively compared the burger chain to John Lewis, the epitome of understated Middleton taste on the high street. 'You get the white van man in the morning stopping in for his egg McMuffin and you get the guy who has stopped off before his meeting with his laptop. There's not that snobbishness about our brand any more,' she said.

The reaction to the interview proved that there was still some way to go. 'Only idiots and chavs go to McDonald's ... nobody but them would take their children there,' said one online reader, responding to her comments. Another said: 'I take one look at the customers inside with their noisy and totally uncontrolled offspring and back off quickly. Am I being snobbish? Probably, but I do not want to eat near that lot, nor do I want to walk about the street eating one of their products.'

Despite its move upmarket and its broad appeal to most of the country, McDonald's will never really win over the Wood Burning Stovers, who like to think the food-on-the-go that they eat is individual, authentic and preferably 'artisanal'. The fact that it is prepared in a big industrial kitchen on a trading estate in Park Royal, before being shipped out to their local gastro pub or sushi bar, is something they don't consider. McDonald's key demographic is Asda Mums – a large swathe of the population who straddle what some would call the lower middle class and the upper working class, but now defined in these recessionary times by their loyalty to the cheapest of Britain's big four supermarkets. Food for Asda Mums is mostly fuel, not a statement of status. Their presiding concern is that their children are well fed, which means nutritiously so (they fret about the sugar content in Fruit Shoots), but that also means generously so. McDonald's brilliantly supplies that need – and it is a fortnightly treat, and a guilt-free one at that, for many Asda Mums.

The company assiduously targets Asda Mums, through its advertising but also its associations, with its support of football, and tie-ups with Disney and other mass-popular movements. In a study by the think-tank Britain Thinks, undertaken during the summer of 2011, McDonald's came third in a list of 'the most working-class brands' behind the *Sun* and Iceland and above KFC and Asda. It is revealing that four out of the five brands are food-related.

McDonald's and KFC owe their place in this list partly to price, but partly to the ideals introduced by Wimpy back in 1954 – fast, quick service of a commoditised food. No one can ever feel as if they are going to be caught out either by their table manners, their pronunciation of a product or the arrival of a shockingly large bill at the end. Tipping and a wine list, two of the most anxiety-inducing social phenomena, are categorically absent from fast food.

The boss may be wrong about the snobs, but she is correct when she asserts that it is a 'democratising' brand, a term that Sir Terence Conran used in the 1960s to describe Habitat, his home furnishings shop. Thanks to fast food, eating out was no longer a social minefield.

If Asda Mums are the bedrock on which McDonald's builds its success, then it is the Hyphen-Leighs who have turned Greggs into the country's biggest fast food chain – with more outlets than anyone else. Based in Newcastle, Greggs has a range of nice bread, perfectly decent sandwiches and a selection of savoury pastries, selling an amazing 140 million sausage rolls every year – that is 800 every minute. But no food item in Britain, not even a Big Mac, has been the object of so much class debate in the last year. This came about when the Chancellor tried to close a long-standing (and complex) loophole that meant hot pasties, steak bakes and sausage rolls, as sold by Greggs, avoided VAT.

The political elite, many of them Wood Burning Stovers, mocked Gideon 'George' Osborne, son of a baronet and owner of a £3 million Notting Hill house, for failing to understand the diet of the hard-pressed working classes. Osborne's critics had us believe that millions of Britons breakfasted, lunched and dined on pasties, rolls and onion bakes. Cheryl Cole, the Hyphen-Leighs' pin-up of choice, was wheeled out to invoke the spirit of Oliver Twist, saying: 'I would have been penniless as a teenager – and hungry – if I'd been taxed every time I had a hot pasty. Pasties, pizza, McDonald's – we didn't have a clue about nutrition. It was tasty and it was what we could afford.'

Just as bad was the sight of senior members of the shadow cabinet, including Ed Balls, trying to out-prole Osborne by sauntering into a Greggs (camera crew in tow) and casually ordering some pasties. Until Osborne made Greggs and its customers class martyrs – helped by the chain being championed by the *Sun* – it was widely derided, particularly by the likes of Asda Mums, for providing the lower orders with fatty, cheap pap. A 'Greggs dummy' was a phrase often used in the north east to refer to the sausage roll given to toddlers in their buggies to keep them quiet.

Of course selling £700 million worth of food every year means its customer base is extremely broad. Indeed, a cousin of mine who is an earl is so partial to a Greggs sausage roll that he invested some of the family fortune in the company's shares. But then many of Britain's aristocracy have always preferred nursery food over a *ballotine de volaille* and saffron infusions.

Even within something as seemingly innocuous as the lunchtime sandwich there are clear social distinctions, as evidenced in my own defiantly white-collar office. A fast-food burger or Greggs pasty is clearly unacceptable and only to be eaten ironically when suffering from a hangover. The Boots Shapers meal deal is for secretaries and junior staff in the advertising department only; the M&S sandwich, Pret à Manger wrap the safe option for the mass of mid-ranking reporters; while a box of Itsu sushi or Leon beetroot and horseradish soup is verging on ostentatious and suggests that office work is a tedious impediment to furthering one's gourmet credentials. Columnists and those on the Arts Desk can get away with that. News editors show off by going to the local Italian delicatessen which whips up an overpriced, rather dry prosciutto and rocket ciabatta, but it comes wrapped in tasteful waxed paper. Of course, the really smart Wood Burning Stovers bring in their own sandwiches, ideally on home-made bread – or, better still, left-overs heated up in a wide-necked thermos flask. Perhaps Ottolenghi's spiced winter couscous.

One colleague, with quiet pride, brought in home-cured bresaola. I was well and truly trumped and went back to munching on my re-heated mushroom risotto out of the Tupperware box.

These variations all occur within a very tight-knit group of (mostly) graduates, a fair few Oxbridge ones at that, working within a single office. Lunchtime choices are small, subtle public acts that allow you to set yourself apart within the restrictive office environment. Class has never been all about money. The cost of these lunches varies just a little, but the differing messages they send out are loud and clear. The home-made chorizo soup is less expensive than the Subway sandwich, but one is 'middle class' and one is not. If we are all middle class now, then we need to strive to distinguish ourselves from the ranks. Tucking into a sandwich from the country's biggest eating-out operator just fails the test. Your lunch has to come from a more exclusive brand, or better still be completely unbranded.

Portland Privateers, in contrast, would rather slash the tyres on their BMW X5 than be spotted bringing a cellophane-wrapped home-made sandwich into their Mayfair office. They are remarkably unfussy about lunch, as long as it is a reputable brand. Most of them send out their secretary, or the work experience kid, for Itsu sushi or Birley sandwiches. Or they have miserable 'water lunch meetings' to prove how macho they are. This consists of bottled water and nothing else.

Finding unbranded food outlets in modern Britain can be a challenge. Expensive high street rents, cautious landlords, unimaginative town planners all conspire to encourage a familiar name over the door. But one of the reasons has been the relentless rise of the Middleton classes, those millions of families who within a generation have navigated their way through the choppy waters to end up at the front of the great class flotilla. If one of the abiding aspects of climbing up the social ladder is a fear of being found out, there is safety in clinging to an established name, a proven formula. The Berni Inns (founded in 1955), and all the chains that came after, allowed people to eat out, to enjoy a dash of glamour with scampi in a basket or lemongrass in the soup, but never be made a fool of. As people holidayed abroad and consumed hours of cookery programmes, restaurants became less daunting and visiting a chain outlet provided you with a failsafe option, whatever town you visited.

Berni's place as a staging post on the climb upwards was taken by Browns, All Bar One, Pizza Express, Chez Gerard and Loch Fyne. In recent years we've reached the sunny uplands of Strada, Wagamama, Ping Pong, Yo! Sushi and Starbucks – all offering a bowl, or cup, of something exotic, all with unpronounceable names, all with strange, almost masonic rituals of how one orders and eats. But once we've cracked the formula, we have made it. The insouciance with which one mixes the wasabi into the dish of soy sauce, or orders a skinny Frappuccino, proves that you are a person who knows their mind and won't be intimidated by any waiter or waitress – even if they have swapped their 1950s bow tie and pinafore for an attitude T-shirt and stud in their nose.

The majority are unable to afford or are too intimidated to eat at the Ivy or Claridges – venues reserved for the Portland Privateers, who like nothing more than a restaurant where a member of the paparazzi waits outside every evening: The Wolseley, Heston Blumenthal's Fat Duck, anything associated with Gordon Ramsay (both a Portland Privateer and an Asda Mum pin-up), or Panacea in Alderley Edge.

But high street, upmarket, branded dining chains are the economy-class ticket to a more sophisticated life, burnishing their customers with the vocabulary and grammar of cuisine. They are aspiration on a plate, and a public one at that. This explains why sellers of daily cups of frothy coffee – logically the first little luxury that should have been ditched when money is tight – in fact remained buoyant in the recession, even though this extravagance totals for many people well in excess of £1,000 a year. It is the most public symbol of having made it, a little paper clutch of success.

If eating out is all about public displays of aspiration, then surely within the privacy of one's own fridge and store cupboard class should be totally absent. But this is not so. Soups: fresh chilled, canned or, heaven forfend, dried. Mustard: Colmans, Maille, French's, out of a squeezy yellow bottle, or Pommery moutarde de Meaux out of an earthenware jar. Breakfast cereals, breakfast bars, 99 calorie bars, dried mangoes, unsulphurised dried apricots, Medjool dates, bejewelled dates, star anise, sumac and saffron. Rice: American long-grain, basmati, Arborio – 'Oh, but carnaroli is essential for risottos.' Table salt, rock salt, sea salt, natural Halen Môn Anglesey sea salt with organic celery seed or just plain old Maldon; black pepper, white pepper, crushed pepper, never, never powdered pepper. The tyranny of choice. Waitrose has

47 different types of salt and pepper, Asda has 68 different varieties of mayonnaise or – drum roll – salad cream. Christmas 2011 saw Tesco sell 23 different types of Christmas pudding, from a 98p Tesco Value version to a £16 number topped with 24-carat gold leaf.

Coffee, however, tops them all, with the ownership of a cafetière once considered as much proof of membership of the middle classes as a reserved parking space at the golf club. But even with 'proper' coffee there are gradations of snobbery. The Portland Privateers have a Nespresso machine – electronic, showy, but neatly packaged, and it turns out a cup of coffee that looks classy. Mainstream Wood Burning Stovers and Rockabillies use a cafetière but the smugger WBS brigade use a Moka pot, one of those Italian metal stove-top devices that are a nightmare to wash up. Everyone else, at least in their own kitchen, uses instant. Curiously, Elizabeth David, the arbiter of so much culinary taste, herself hated real coffee and always preferred granules – a fact my wife trots out when the north London nespressorati arch their eyebrows on being asked for something out of a jar.

There are three main reasons for this staggering array of choice. First, and foremost, it is the result of the relentless mechanisation of food production combined with an unparalleled half-decade of growth in disposable income. Farmers and food factories have been able to make food cheaper than ever before at the same time as customers have had the money to spend.

Second, it is the culmination of 60 years of experimentation – of freeing up the taste buds – that the end of food rationing and Elizabeth David and Raymond Postgate helped awaken and which took flight along with the first foreign holidays.

David was the first of what would become a long line of cookery writers who not only provided recipes, but – in a strangely prescriptive fashion – laid down what was good food and what was not. A deb, who had been presented at court, she had the confidence to state categorically that the ideal was 'sober, well-balanced, middle-class French cookery, carried out with care and skill'. Most working-class people from the provinces had just never been exposed to the Mediterranean produce she demanded – garlic, bay leaves, aubergines, courgettes and wine. Wine was something that was never drunk in the great majority of households. My father-in-law was typical of millions of working-class households in the 1950s in never drinking alcohol at home, save a toast on high days and holidays – and certainly never wine. He can remember the first time a bottle of 'champagne' came into the house – a present brought in by an uncle, who worked at the docks. A great hush descended as the family gathered around and opened the bottle. As a boy, he was aware of the disappointment from all the adults that there was no pop as the cork came out. They then quietly sipped their strangely dark and pungent liquid. It was, it turned out, Cognac Grande Champagne – a brandy, made from champagne grapes – but no one dared say anything that might suggest they had got it wrong. It seems inconceivable now, in a day when champagne is sold at £10 a bottle at Morrisons, that any family could have so little knowledge of what champagne looked or smelt like. Britain now consumes 35 million bottles of the fizzy stuff a year, enough for every household in the country to have one and a half bottles.

And thirdly, this bewildering choice in our kitchens has been driven by class divisions. Whereas once it was all about keeping up with the Joneses, now it is about differentiating ourselves from the Joneses. And helping us in this mission, indeed driving this project, is the world's most sophisticated and powerful supermarket industry. Supermarkets not only have pioneered the cheap distribution of food, but they have also been at the cutting edge of social research, endlessly analysing who their customers are, and encouraging them to trade up – or sometimes down.

Now, about 80 per cent of all our food shopping is done in supermarkets. They didn't even exist in 1954. Well, not in the way we would recognise them. Grocery shops were often fairly formal places, where you would be served by an apron-wearing assistant, who would stand behind a counter. The Co-op, at this stage the country's largest food chain, had tried out 'pay as you go out' sections in its shops in the 1940s, but they had never taken off. It was left to Sainsbury's to pioneer what was known back then as self-service with 'Q-less shopping'. The company had converted a shop in Croydon in 1950 and cleverly used tough, unbreakable Perspex left over from wartime bombers as a means of protecting fresh food displays. By 1956 there were 3,000 self-service shops in Britain.

There are now well over 55,000 supermarkets, and with their growth has come the alarming decline of butchers, bakers and fishmongers. This rapid decline of the independents and rise of the supermarkets is often seen as a wholly bad thing. But the rise of large retailers, and their corresponding ability to negotiate hard with suppliers (because they were buying in such volumes), allowed us to eat more cheaply than we had ever done before. Back in 1957 a family had to spend on average more than a third of their disposable income on food and non-alcoholic drink. Despite recent food inflation spikes, this figure has fallen dramatically since the 1950s and now stands at only at 17 per cent. Food is still cheap in relative terms.

Most of us can now easily afford to buy all the calories we need, with spare change left over to spend on the fripperies, herbs, spices and exotica that mark us out as sophisticates. Nowadays, that may mean aioli from Tesco's deli counter or samphire from Morrison's vegetable section. We have come a long, long way. It was not until 1970 that Sainsbury's first sold pasta. It really was that exotic just a generation ago, and didn't make it into the Office for National Statistics annual basket of goods (used to measure inflation) until 1987. Prior to the 1970s it was the preserve of specialist delicatessens, of which there were plenty in London, Edinburgh and wealthy market towns, but none at all in many working-class areas. That was why, on 1 April 1957, so many people were fooled by the spoof *Panorama* documentary that purported to show spaghetti growing on trees. Sainsbury's now sells more than 70 different types of pasta, from wholewheat organic conchiglie to fresh walnut and gorgonzola tortellini. In 2011 the final triumph of continental over British eating habits, of Elizabeth David over luncheon meat, occurred when trade figures showed that, as a nation, we bought more olives than peanuts. The trendy wine bar had overtaken the pub.

The rise of the supermarkets and the rise of the middle classes went hand in hand with the rise of working women. Not only did this post-war phenomenon create a double-income household with the means to enjoy the finer things in life, it involved the woman of the household spending less time in the kitchen – for many a liberating experience their mothers could only have dreamed of. But this was only possible with the supermarket, selling frozen and processed food.

In the early days it was the brands that led the way. They were the ones to hold the hand of the nervous consumer having a go at cooking a cake from a pre-prepared mix, or serving up a TV dinner. And the well-trusted names of Flora, Birds Eye, Heinz, Fry's, Batchelors, Cookeen, Vesta and Crosse & Blackwell introduced housewives and their families to not just a host of new flavours, but also endless short-cuts. Brands, invariably slightly more expensive than cooking from scratch, were mostly looked up to as an affordable luxury at this stage.

Frozen food could only become part of people's lives once they had a freezer, which started to happen in the 1950s. By the end of the decade about 20 per cent of households had a freezer, and sales of frozen food doubled between 1955 and 1957.[9] Birds Eye even opened their own chain of shops, and when frozen peas first became available there were queues out of the door in Kendal, such was the interest and hype surrounding these amazing things. Birds Eye frozen peas were also the first brand ever to be advertised in colour on British television.

But though owning a freezer was considered a major achievement for many families, frozen food after a while took on the air of inauthenticity, of food without distinction. And fish fingers, introduced in 1955, became the primary villain. The story goes that they were going to be called 'frozen cod pieces', until just a few weeks before the launch and someone pointed out how foolish Birds Eye would look. Children loved them. Thick Japanese-style breadcrumbs (the secret to the M&S Kiev) and an unthreatening-shaped piece of cod were promoted aggressively by television advertising – a primary black mark for many foods in a Wood Burning Stove household. Linda Shanovitch, revising for her 11+ exam as a north

London schoolgirl in the 1960s, recalled: 'My parents were frightfully middle class so it would have been a disaster not to pass the 11 plus. I was terrified of failing. I remember on the day of the exam I got home and for a special treat my mother let me have fish fingers, which I was usually never allowed as she saw them as working-class food. All of my friends were working class, so I always wanted fish fingers. As it turned out I passed the exam and did really well.'[10] When Elizabeth David revised her epic of French provincial cooking in 1977, she listed the deep freeze and prefabricated sauces as two of the evils of modern cooking.

After a washing machine and a television, a separate freezer was the most likely of all durable goods to be owned by a household headed up by an unskilled manual worker by the mid-1990s.[11] Easy access to frozen pizzas, ready meals and ice cream was considered at the time a higher priority than even a telephone or video recorder.

Today's fish fingers are Cheese Strings, Cocoa Pop Mega Munchers, Fruit Shoots – all highly processed, heavily advertised foods aimed at children and jeered at by the those who email the *You and Yours* programme on Radio 4. Sunny Delight was briefly catapulted into the position of Britain's third most popular drink (behind Coke and Pepsi) after a relentless TV campaign. But after reports suggesting it turned toddlers orange it became so vilified that it has all but disappeared from view.

All of these products may be detested by Wood Burning Stovers, but they are a godsend for Asda Mums, who have an instinctive trust in big brands and a willingness to succumb to the pester power of advertising, while also managing to fret about the nutritional content of their children's food. Asda

Mums are one of those rare demographic groups that were invented by marketing executives but took on a life of their own. Originally brought together by the supermarket's own PR team in the run-up to the 2010 election, they were latched onto by the politicians – becoming the heirs to Mondeo Man and Worcester Woman, these mythical hard-working, aspirational, floating voters that had swung it for both Margaret Thatcher and Tony Blair. Both Cameron and Gordon Brown were persuaded to record special video messages for Asda Mums, along with famously taking part in biscuit-based webchats on Mumsnet.

Asda Mums now live on in the form of focus groups that the supermarket convenes to help it understand its customers better. I met some of them in Bootle, Liverpool, one of the poorest areas of the country, where the shiny new Asda stands across the road from the bleak Strand shopping centre, forever etched into the national consciousness as the setting of a grainy ten-second CCTV film – showing the last recorded moments of James Bulger's life.

Asda attracts 18 million shoppers through its doors every week, so it is ludicrous to suggest its customers are one particular type. But Asda Mums are a particular sub-section and are more definable. They are mostly council house tenants, relentless about finding bargains and cutting down on food bills for themselves, but keen to give their children lunch-box treats of packaged goodies such as Dairylea Dunkers or Rice Krispie Squares. The name of a big, highly advertised manufacturer on the package makes them confident rather than sceptical about the wisdom of their purchase. And their anxiety about providing good food translates into buying a surprisingly large amount of organic food for their toddlers even though they know it costs more and is probably no better than standard. Again, it is the label rather than the content that gives reassurance. Strawberries are another popular snack among Asda Mums – further proof that this particular fruit has become so mass-market that it has lost all snob value. Raspberries are much smarter, but Rockabillies know that the only truly posh summer fruit to impress your guests with at a dinner party are gooseberries – preferably picked from your own garden.

Asda Mums, of course, can be found not just in Asda, but also in Tesco, Morrisons, Iceland and even Sainsbury's. The key defining factor is not the name above the supermarket door as much as the attitude towards what they put in their basket. Despite their need and desire to keep their shopping bills down, they are curiously attracted to premium brands, with many of them unwilling to buy Smart Price goods. This is Asda's range of own-label value food. One said: 'I don't know why I wouldn't, I just presume it wouldn't taste as good. There's got to be a reason why it's so cheap, and it's not just the advertising. The quality would not be as good.' Another said: 'Two days before pay day, I would have nothing in the house, I would buy Smart Price. But I wouldn't get Smart Price meat. I just wouldn't buy Smart Price ham. Think of the tubes.'

Smart Price is at the bottom of Asda's little ladder of brands, with Asda Chosen by You in the middle and Asda Extra Special at the top. Asda Mums know their place – firmly in the middle, and only reluctantly slipping down to the bottom when circumstances force them to.

This is in sharp contrast to Rockabillies, who don't give two hoots about food brand, as long as it tastes nice and isn't too expensive (in their eyes). They are happy to pop into Tesco or Asda without any hint of condescension; Sainsbury's is their default supermarket but they would prefer Waitrose if one was available. This explains the success of the Waitrose Essential range of food. Waitrose is clearly at the top of the supermarket tree – it has been the champion of the Prince of Wales's Duchy Originals produce, and seller of Charlie Bigham's steak and ale pies which come in their own porcelain ramekins. The charity shops of Swaffham and Uckfield are awash with these little cast-off dishes. Stacked on a kitchen table, they are as obvious a trophy for a Waitrose shopper as a stolen Quaglino ashtray was for a Portland Privateer back in the early 1990s. Which other supermarket stocked £412 bottles of Château Mouton Rothschild? But during the recession of 2009 it started to lose customers, not just to Tesco but also to Aldi and Lidl. In response it brought out a value range called Waitrose Essential, which many thought would be a disaster – if you need to save money, stop shopping at Waitrose. Except it wasn't really value at all. In fact, 1,200 of the 1,400 in the range were exactly the same – and the same price – as previous Waitrose own-brand products, but just repackaged in basic, white labels, I was told by the supermarket. It was all about kidding the customers that Waitrose wasn't as expensive as they thought it was. When I asked, at the time, wouldn't the well-heeled customers feel a little embarrassed about being seen popping a value range into their basket, the commercial director told me: 'Far from it. We have found some customers putting their Waitrose goods in Tesco bags, because they are nervous that their neighbours will think they are decadent for shopping at Waitrose.'[12] Rockabillies hate showiness when it comes to food, but quite like the good things in life, so they had found a brand just for them. Waitrose Essentials just a few years down the line sells more than £1 billion every year. That's the power of reverse snobbism.

These clever sub-brands within supermarkets were the brainchild of Tesco – as so many supermarket innovations are – and were a response to another recession. It was its way of competing with the European supermarket companies known as 'hard discounters' coming to Britain in the early 1990s. They included Aldi and Netto, who, along with Kwik Save, started a major supermarket price war. This was the era of the 7p loaf of bread and the absurd situation of the 3p tin of baked beans – priced at less than the cost of the aluminium and beans themselves, let alone the cost of transporting the cans to store.

Tesco decided to make the price war permanent by launching Tesco Value. This would not just be a short-term promotion selling bargain beans, it would be a whole range of groceries packaged in utilitarian white, red and blue labels that shouted: cheap. Loo roll, washing-up liquid, digestive biscuits, bacon, bread ... it offered an entire weekly shop on a cut-price budget. But what made Tesco such a pioneer was that it started to analyse customer data in astonishing levels of detail thanks to its Tesco Club Card, which had been launched in 1995. It had on file the postcode, date of birth and detailed spending patterns of millions of its customers. What day of the week you bought Tesco Value cheddar, when you splashed out on Brie, where you filled up with petrol, when you bought a pregnancy kit and even whether it had been positive (all those vitamin pills, and a drop in sales of white wine). The company was sitting on a database more valuable than the Office for National Statistics.

This data was initially used to help it be more accurate when it mailed out certain offers – there was no point posting a 10p-off voucher for nappies to a pensioner or sending a two-for-one beer offer to a teetotaller. The ultimate use of the data was in developing a strategy, which has now been adopted by almost all major retailers aiming at the mass market. They called it 'good, better, best'. The Tesco Value line was good; their normal Tesco-branded products were 'better'; and in 1995 it launched Tesco Finest, its 'best'. At the time Tesco's marketing director said the company's ambition was to be 'classless ... to be the natural choice of the middle market'. But by segmenting and introducing Finest the company was able to attract a whole swathe of Middleton classes, those who might feel uncomfortable upgrading to Waitrose (or who don't have one nearby) but keen to assert their superior status, while still keeping Asda (or Tesco) Mums happy. This segmentation can be seen at Sainsbury's, with its Basics, By Sainsbury's and Taste the Difference, and at Asda, with its Smart Price, Asda Chosen by You and Extra Special. But it is also a tactic used by other shops including Marks & Spencer, B&Q and Homebase. It is now standard procedure among these big chains to analyse the customer base intensely and offer them within one shop an entirely different selection of products based on their socio-economic category. This gives customers the tantalising option of 'trading up' as well as the face-saving option of 'trading down' if they are short of cash but unwilling to suffer the shame of going to a more downmarket supermarket.

You might be one of 33 million shoppers who shop each week at Tesco, but by buying Finest you are in a separate class. Upgrade to Organic and you're home and dry.

The real battleground was our old friend the ready meal. It was here that it was easiest to segment, to 'add value', as the jargon went, and indeed to strip out costs. M&S pioneered the concept, but as the microwave took off during the 1980s and 90s other supermarkets were able develop a whole range of packaged and processed meals designed for customers who were working longer hours, and had the desire for more sophisticated food, but lacked the skill or inclination to cook it themselves.

By 1994, two-thirds of households for the first time had a microwave, and the ready meal had become part of the landscape. The Kievs of this world were put in supermarkets' 'best' ranges, but the supermarkets were also keen to attract working-class consumers to the booming ready meal category. Cut-price lasagnes, curries and stir-fries were developed. So, within one supermarket, Tesco, you can now buy 44p tinned Value meatballs in tomato sauce; treat yourself to a microwavable spaghetti and meatball ready meal, costing £1.87; or you can splash out on a dish of Finest classic Moroccan spiced lamb meatballs for £5.80, to be lovingly heated in the Aga. This allows shoppers to both look down on and envy the choices being made by fellow shoppers right in front of their eyes. With a supermarket ready meal, with the merest glance at the packaging one can immediately start to judge. The top-of-the-range ready meals, such as the ones promoted by Marks & Spencer as part of their recession-busting Dine in for £10 promotion, are deemed smart or even luxuriant. But the 'good' ranges – basic, value, budget, in their white boxes and tin foil devoid of any descriptive words – are demonised as the worst of all modern products: inauthentic, processed, and ruinous to the environment and your family's health.

Or course, both are invariably made in the same factory by the same supplier using more or less the same ingredients. The difference lies in some flavourings, a bit more generous use of the main protein, and crucially the packaging and marketing. White space on the ready meal box is not a cost-cutting measure by the supermarket but used as a signifier – a quick way, in the 2.3 seconds in which a customer makes up their mind to buy a product, to shout 'cheap'. On a price per calorie basis, the difference is often not that enormous. And often the discount ranges were put in the freezer, in a further prompt to their low-class status.

This schizophrenia about ready meals came to head in 2004 when Jamie Oliver's television programme *Jamie's School Dinners* led to very public soul-searching, led by the Wood Burning Stovers. A petition with 300,000 signatories was presented to Downing Street. Processed, frozen food was for ill-educated, obese parents who wanted to kill their children, or, as Jamie put it, 'what we have learnt to call "white trash"'.

Iceland, despite a brief (and disastrous) experiment to become the only national retailer of 100 per cent organic food, has become the main lightning conductor for this hatred. One quite reputable online chat room had a forum by the title: Is Iceland Food Chav Cuisine?[13] One poster said: 'Have you seen the sort of crap they are doing now! Prawns that come on their own spoons, is that meant to be some sort of chavvy amuse bouche?' Another was more direct: 'I would rather lick the bottom of a tramp's ageing sandals than be seen dead in Iceland. If the likes of Kerry Ketamine Katona and bloody Coleen Nolan are associated with the establishment it just makes me turn to trusty old Tesco (and its more civilised clientele).'

This of course was another key factor in how Iceland set itself apart from the discounters – it used a series of low-class celebrities in its adverts. First was Kerry Katona, a former member of Atomic Kitten, who later kept the flickering candle of fame alight by being a runner-up in *Celebrity Big Brother* and starring in a reality television show about her addiction to cocaine. Then there was Stacey Solomon, former *X Factor* contestant, who was vilified for being caught smoking while pregnant. These stars were aspirational, but only to the Hyphen-Leighs. The cherry on top of the frozen black forest gateau was when Iceland signed a tie-up with Greggs, which paid to install branded freezers stocked with the full range of pasties, steak bakes and sausage rolls for its customers to cook at home.

Iceland's rock-bottom image is not something that particularly bothers the company – it helps reinforce its role as supplier of choice to a very specific demographic. In recent years it has flourished more than almost any other supermarket apart from Waitrose.

* * *

My nearest park in north London recently spent a lot of money improving the facilities. A new playground was built, the pond was dredged and the café – located inside an old house in the park – was refurbished. It appeared to have gone smoothly, but then the local paper reported: 'Class war has erupted over Clissold Park's newly opened café with complaints it's too snooty and expensive and doesn't serve up chips. Instead the caf promotes healthy living – and has the likes of cumin, roast carrot, couscous and spiced nut salad and beetroot cake on the menu.' In a bid to win plaudits from the numerous Wood Burning Stovers in the area, the new management had alienated the equally large number of Asda Mums who used to eat there. This was not, however, just a little mischief-making in the local paper. Action groups were formed, petitions signed, rabbles roused. The leader of the movement said he objected to the café being centred around 'the most self-conscious of the middle class'.

Twenty years after battles against McDonald's, consumers were fighting for the right to eat chips, and against cumin. Down with Indian spices! Death to root vegetables! All these flavours and cuisines we have been exposed to over the last 60 years should have freed us from rows over restaurant menus, from being embarrassed to serve your guests something, from trying to hide products in your supermarket shopping basket. But the millions of choices in the supermarket have not wiped out the class divisions, merely reinforced them, because even the simplest decision – of what sandwich to have for your lunch, or coffee to have in the morning – is about status.

The café war was won by the protesters. Beetroot and watercress on focaccia has been struck off the menu.

CHAPTER 2

FAMILY

How important are your birth certificate and maternity ward in deciding what class you end up in? Here we meet the Portland Privateers and the Middleton classes.

2011 was acknowledged to be an abnormally busy year for news. A devastating earthquake and tsunami in Japan, the Arab Spring, bogeymen Bin Laden and Gaddafi both killed in a violent and dramatic way, the *News of the World* shut down by scandal, the worst riots on Britain's streets in a generation – all events that demanded acres of coverage and analysis. But there was one story, above all, that obsessed the British press: the wedding of Prince William to Kate Middleton. This was partly because there had not been a royal wedding on a large scale since 1986 (you need to discount the low-key second marriage of the Prince of Wales and any event involving the Earl and Countess of Wessex); partly because they looked like two attractive young adults genuinely pleased to be tying the knot; partly because many of us love a soldier in uniform, and the Household Cavalry in their pomp, because the sun shone and we were a granted an extra bank holiday. But more than anything it was the story of how not just Kate, but also her parents, Carole and Mike, had ended up on the Buckingham

Palace balcony sharing the limelight with Britain's premier family. It was, in some ways, a modern wedding embraced by the YouTube and Twitter generation – the wedding was, up to that point, the most streamed event on the internet. However, at its heart was an old-fashioned story about class, and it was the Middleton family's very particular status and position which appeared to inject the necessary 'fairy-tale' element into the big day.

The *Daily Express* described the engagement thus: 'From Pit to Palace; the Middletons used to be miners, now they can boast a future queen.' The *Daily Mail*'s take was 'From Pit to Palace, the first steps in a very upwardly mobile family.' *The Times* went with 'From Pit to Princess, the long journey of the Middleton family.' Even the *Guardian*, many of whose readers are of a republican bent, wrote in its leader: 'Hats off to the prince and commoner Kate.' The coverage was unequivocal and curiously old-fashioned: not only was there a unanimous belief that the class system very much existed in Britain – and their readers immediately understood the terms and conditions – but that social mobility was also alive and well. During the week of Kate's engagement, 192 newspaper articles mentioned her family's class. Apparently it was impossible to mention the Middletons without reference to their supposedly humble background. Kate's story was one that confirmed there was hope for us all. However miserably horny-handed and proletarian we may be, we could one day end up a Royal Highness waving to the adoring crowd. Karl Marx's belief was that one day we would become a classless society, but that was not the lesson of the Middleton family – they appeared to prove the triumph of the lower orders' ability to climb up the ladder, not to dispense with the ladder altogether.

In this regard, the attention was focused not really on Kate, nor on her Royal Hotness Pippa, but on Carole Middleton, the mother of the bride. It was her family history which gave the story its potency. Kate herself was already in an elite of sorts, just one of the 7 per cent to be educated privately, and at Marlborough, a top boarding school, at that. Michael Middleton, Kate's father, came from a long line of respectable and successful county solicitors, was privately educated and had been a senior employee at British Airways. Carole, by contrast, was not just a former air stewardess but the daughter of a lorry driver turned builder and the granddaughter of a miner. Within one generation she had travelled from a council house in Southall, west London, to stand next to the Queen in front of a million cheering people. The journalist Amanda Platell, in what was meant to be a hymn of praise for Mrs Middleton's poise and elegant dress on the wedding day, couldn't halt a tide of class-based judgements in the pages of the *Daily Mail*. 'The woman from the council estate, whose daughter was once pursued by taunts of "doors to manual" by William's toff friends because her mother had been an air hostess, was about to watch her daughter marry the future King of England. Who could deny her a wry smile of satisfaction? She may be a social climber, her daughters may be called the "Wisteria sisters" for their ability to climb and cling on so tenaciously, but the Middleton women on this day triumphed. The bride, the mother of the bride and the maid of honour – all of them middle-class Middletons and proud of it. Kate had got her man.'

This social mobility exercised by Carole was achieved by a combination of hard work, the accumulation of wealth, ingenuity and education – the traditional routes up the class ladder

– and the oldest of them all: marriage. You may be born into a certain class, but you can marry out of it.

It is often assumed that before the war the class system was as rigid as a coronet. If you were born into a family of coal miners, you were destined to be sent down the pit yourself. If your birth was ushered in with a courtesy title and trees planted in your honour, you would always reside in the upper classes. This was true for many, possibly most. But long before the war social mobility was very much part of British life, thanks in part to the grammar school system, which catapulted many into university, enabling millions to leap-frog their parents. And the Establishment had always welcomed plutocrats, public servants and political fighters to its ranks, not least by creating hereditary peerages for many of them. Arguably, Harold Macmillan, in creating the concept of a life peer – and the resulting complete decline in the creation of hereditary peers (Macmillan himself was one of only three non-Royal hereditary peers created since 1965) – was instrumental in kicking away one of the ladders up which people could climb.

But beyond industry and education, marriage was always the quickest guarantee of ensuring that your children began life in a different class from the one in which you did. While that is spectacularly so with any children that the Duchess of Cambridge may have – among them the future monarch of the Commonwealth realms – it is also just as much the case with Carole Middleton herself. She gave birth to three children who have ended up in a dramatically higher class than she was, principally thanks to her marriage to Michael Middleton.

It can work the other way too, of course. And at this point I should explain my family and how my four children have ended up as a triumphant product of the fluidity and perversity of the British class system. My children were born into a distinctly lower class than one of their grandfathers, my father, and an assuredly higher one than their other grandfather, my father-in-law. My own father was born in the nursery of the house that had been in the Wallop family since Elizabethan times, and as a son of an Earl was immediately granted a title. If we are being honest, it's about the lowliest one there is: The Honourable. Five rungs on the ladder below a standard Duke, six below a royal Duke and waving rights on the Buckingham Palace balcony. Though, according to comically intricate rules of precedence, if he should ever be invited to a State Banquet he gets to sit closer to the Queen than any Knight and he trumps the Chancellor of the Exchequer. Take that, Gideon. He started life as unambiguously posh. Of course that's a word the posh never use. They say 'smart'. Nurses, cooks, monogrammed linen, a house with a sprung ballroom, 'map room' and library, shooting, fishing, a few thousand acres of Hampshire farmland to explore. It was all his.

But despite the silver spoon, the history, the entry in *Burke's Peerage*, the enormous advantages that were bestowed on him on his birth, he was always destined to end up in a lower class than his own father. The die was cast by the mere fact that my father was born after his older brother. He would never become an Earl, never inherit a prime dairy herd, never sit in the House of Lords. That is how primogeniture works, and one of the principal reasons for the enormous power the aristocracy held in Britain for about 900 years – their estates and wealth were not divided up between all their children, as happened on the Continent. They became concentrated in one individual. Among the über-aristocracy there are enough subsidiary estates to fund all the children into a life of luxury. Not so with the

Earldom of Portsmouth, which was never awash with cash, but fell into impoverishment after the war. My cousin and I, himself a younger son of a different Earl (the aristocracy tend to attract each other and two of my father's sisters married into grander families), joked as children about how we could mastermind a *Kind Hearts and Coronets* style plot to leap up the social ladder. How many murders and poisons before we got our hands on the prize? Yes, it is possible to have an inferiority complex as an Honourable. In fact, it is probably a prerequisite.

So my father, without the prospect of land and peerage, became the first Wallop in the twentieth century to seek regular employment and – gasp – one in trade too. This may have been a blow to his ego, but he did what all shabbistocrats do when low on income and prospects: marry well. Of course, I would say that because she's my mother. But he went down the classic route of finding a bride with money and beauty. My mother was the granddaughter of Sir Montague Burton, a man who arrived in Britain in the first year of the twentieth century from modern-day Lithuania as a penniless Jew. He started off peddling shoe laces around the slums of Leeds and ended up with a tailoring business that clothed much of the British Empire. In doing so he accumulated, and gave away, mountains of cash, much of it to good causes. And a small but meaningful amount ended up in our household. I was acutely aware that all of the comforts in my life as a child – holidays, a private education – were not because of the posh lot from Hampshire but thanks to the enterprise and chutzpah of a Jewish immigrant. If in any doubt, it would be drummed into me every September, when I went to get school uniform from Debenhams (then part of the Burton empire), and I'd suffer the embarrassment of my mother whipping out a staff discount card and the check-out girl invariably asking which branch she worked in. She would quietly, but politely, tell the white lie: 'head office'. I would squirm. Why couldn't we just go to John Lewis, like all my classmates?

My childhood in 1970s and 1980s west London was utterly unremarkable to me at the time, as it always is for children. I knew, because I was told so and because I sensed it clearly, that I was very lucky. But we were far from grand. We had a live-in nanny – but so did many of our friends – and a 'daily', but no other staff. There were occasional shafts of light that illuminated the slightly abnormal privilege – the Christmas drinks parties at St James's Palace, where my aunt and uncle lived in a grace and favour flat; the play dates at Kensington Palace, where a school friend, the heir to a Royal Dukedom, lived; the knowledge from an early age of how to tip a gamekeeper correctly (note folded up small, passed over with a firm handshake and with no reference at all to the money, but a hearty quip about the crosswinds on the final drive); the black tie dinner parties my parents would hold where the women really would retire to let the men smoke cigars and discuss affairs of state. Even at a young age, I knew this was not what most children did. But they were rare moments, and for most of the time it was a quotidian cycle of normality: *The Times* and the *Daily Express*, the *Beano*, homework, *Saturday Morning Swapshop*, Sunday School, walking the dog (a golden retriever, of course) in Hyde Park, Wagon Wheels and Findus Crispy pancakes, Action Man and Lego, dread of Wednesday afternoon swimming, washing the Ford Granada, perfecting a John McEnroe impression, waiting for Abba on *Top of the Pops*, filling in Royal Wedding scrapbooks.

I always knew exactly where I fitted in. I always have done. I am not sure how this was achieved. But I knew exactly how 'smart' we were, and I knew, as a result, that despite the flashes of proper, undiluted privilege, many of my classmates and cousins were considerably grander. I knew that we were 'smart', mostly on account of my father's side, and that we were 'comfortable', thanks to my mother's side. In short, I knew we were upper class. Just. Hanging on to the coat-tails of aristocracy by our fingertips, though hoping we didn't look too desperate as we got caught up in the slipstream.

My children have been born middle class. Or, if we are being more accurate, Class A in the National Readership Survey category: born to a share-owning, broadsheet-reading professional in the 40 per cent tax bracket. Or, if we are being more up-to-date, using the Office for National Statistics' most recent classifications for socio-economic groups, introduced in 2000, they live in an L3.1 household, fourth placed in a list of 17 different gradings. I am a traditional employee in a professional organisation. Or, if we are being even more specific, in category 18 of 56 Acorn socio-economic classifications: 'multi-ethnic, young, converted flats', where the *Guardian* is likely to be the newspaper of choice, and the householders visit the cinema far more regularly than most people, while having a strong propensity to buy their groceries online, but an above-average experience of having had their mobile phone stolen.

Confused? Trying to be specific about your class is like trying to nail jelly to a fast-moving Mondeo Man.

My children are not aristocrats, certainly. Neither are they Rockabillies with a tendency towards the scruffy and occasionally expensive country tastes and habits of old Britain. That's because I have spent most of my adult life, indeed from adolescence onwards, trying – not always successfully – to edge away from the class I was born into, while retaining some of its habits and even maintaining a quiet affection for it. Indeed, I am probably onto at least my third class, even though I am (I hope) less than half way through my life. The process has been accelerated by marrying out of my class.

And this is where I need to explain my father-in-law's class. He was born resolutely in the working classes but ended up assuredly in the middle classes. He, indeed, is a triumphant member of the Middleton classes, because for every Carole there are many millions of others who in the space of one lifetime climbed up from the bottom of the ladder to pretty much the top. Money is important but not really the key. What matters is assimilation – the ability innately, or through careful consideration, to make the right choices in order to furnish themselves with the lifestyle and habits of the class above them. And to then feel comfortable, confident even, to continue upwards.

He was born in Workington, now a sad and depressing town on the wrong side of the Lake District. His actual father was a 'wrong 'un' who never featured in his life, so he was brought up by his mother and grandparents. His grandfather, whom he always referred to as 'Dad', was a blast furnaceman at the Oldside iron works, a dirty, dangerous and physically demanding job. His grandmother was a maid in service, though not for a grand family. It was a home financed by and in the shadow of the great factory. In the days before the Welfare State and the widespread building of council houses, there were many millions who lived in a factory or pit house on a peppercorn rent. It was a proudly working-class household, and a respectable one at that. The man he called Dad was a union man and a member of the Co-operative; bills were paid from the jar of savings, the *New Gresham Encyclopaedia* was on the book-shelf, the *Daily Herald* on the kitchen table.

He passed the 11-plus exam, unimaginable to 'Dad' who'd started work at the iron works at the age of 13, and this was the first rung up the ladder, as it was for countless members of the Middleton class. University, however, was denied to him by lack of money. To escape national service, he opted to join the merchant navy. Caked in oil and sweat in the engine room, it might have looked as though he'd done no better than his own father, but it was skilled labour of a kind that only an engineer who'd trained as an apprentice could undertake. In the evening he'd wear his white mess uniform and host a table in first class, and it made him realise that the luxury the passengers at his table were enjoying was something worth aiming for. Back on land, he used his savings to open a ten-room hotel in Workington designed for travelling salesmen; his mother did the cooking in the kitchen. It was a success, and was expanded. Eventually he built the biggest hotel in town, with crêpes suzette on the menu and rotary club dances in the ballroom. Golf was learnt, the *Telegraph* was taken, and savings were used to send the children to private school. Holidays were initially in Bournemouth, but as the years rolled on they ventured first to the Costa Brava, later to Normandy, eventually to Tuscany. In 1980 the Queen visited the hotel, where she was served roast saddle of Lamb Henry IV (with artichokes, a bewildering array of tubers: Parisienne Potatoes & Bernaise Sauce, Delmonico Potatoes, New Potatoes, and Bouquetière of Vegetables). It was his Carole Middleton-on-Buckingham-Palace-balcony moment. 'It was a huge thing, huge,' he remembers.

Whether or not your family ends up defining you until the day you die has to do with the choices made along the way. Not all of them are choices governed by economics, and not all of them are choices you can make. Some of the most important ones are made for you by your parents, who can purposefully or unwittingly set you on a path very different from the one down which they travelled. The most important choice, in many ways, is the first one: your name. Before you have even left the womb you have already been allotted a very specific socio-economic class thanks to a (frequently idiotic) decision made by your parents. And the divisions have increased along with the proliferation of names. Last year 6,039 boys' names were registered by the Office for National Statistics along with 7,395 girls' names – a bewildering choice.

It used to be the case, in the main, that you named your child after either a monarch or a saint. My parents played it straight – as most people did in the 1970s, be they Rockabillies, the Middleton classes or Asda Mums. I was Harry, my sister was Victoria. Simple. Solid. Classy but classless. Shakespearean Prince Harry or Cockney Harry Palmer: names back then just didn't carry that much baggage. There were a handful of names such as Sharon, Tracey, Wayne or Kevin that were a little downmarket for children born in the 1970s, and Quentin and Rupert were certainly quite upmarket, but the class issue has become far more stark as more and more people – regardless of which class they come from – attempt to find something a little bit special. It's another example of how consumers since the 1950s have striven to assert their individuality through the choices they make – it just happens, in this case, to be a deci-sion as long-lasting as a tattoo on your ankle. And even though it costs nothing, it can carry as much metaphorical baggage as a Louis Vuitton suitcase.

Casper or Casey? One is posh, one is not. Jayden is unequivocally low class. Artemis and Arthur are for the type who think slumming it is buying Waitrose Essentials ratatouille. Acorn, the data company that splits the country up into 62 different socio-economic groups on behalf of consumer companies and government agencies, can immediately categorise you by your name. It has 51 million individuals on its database by name, and statistically if you are a Crispian, Greville, Lysbeth or Penelope you are about 200 times more likely to be in the 'wealthy executive' top class than in the 'inner-city adversity' bottom one. Seaneen, Terriann, Sammy-Jo, Jamielee, Kayliegh and Codie are the six names most disproportionately skewed towards the 'struggling families' category, a group of people Acorn works out as most likely to live in social rented accommodation, work in a routine occupation, read the *Sun* newspaper and play bingo.

If in doubt about how class determines baby names, just spend a minute scanning the Births announcement column in the *Daily Telegraph* – a group which is immediately self-selecting. Not only are they readers of the most upmarket national paper in Britain, but they are a niche category within that, happy to spend upwards of £150 on an announcement and keen to make public the joy of their child's birth along with a sense of pride in the wisdom of their choice of names. 'A son, Zebedee Ebenezer Jay, a brother for Badger, Clementine and Florence' is a particular favourite of mine. So too: 'Sybella, a sister for Freddy, Hugo, Oscar and Rex' and 'Lysander, a brother for Ottilie and Rafferty'. These all appeared over the last year.

The truly grand have no need to be so showy. When the 15th Duke and Duchess of Bedford had their first child in 2005 – a son and heir, Henry Robin Charles Russell, born already bearing the title Marquess of Tavistock – the following announcement appeared in the *Daily Telegraph*: 'Bedford – On June 7th, to Louise and Andrew, a son.' That was it.

The *Telegraph*'s top ten names for girls in 2011 were Florence, Isabella, Charlotte, Alice, Isla, Jemima, Daisy, Matilda, Olivia and Emilia. Just two of those names appear in the Office for National Statistics' top ten list of all baby names registered that year. You will not find many Jemimas or Florences shopping in Brighthouse, visiting a bookmaker's or claiming housing benefit. Just compare this list of names to those of some who were convicted during the riots that erupted during the summer of 2011: Shonola, Ellese, Aaron, Reece, Kieron and Wayne. The difference between the two is as great as the gulf between Gieves & Hawkes and Primark and, more importantly, it is immediately apparent to anyone hearing those names.

Much of this class divide in names is because of the proliferation of new names appearing in recent decades. The most famous example of these is Kayleigh, which came into existence thanks to the neo-prog rock band Marillion, who had a number two hit with a single of this name in 1985. It was almost unheard of before the song. But since then it has taken hold, especially with parents who grew up with a love of long-haired bouffant power ballads. And it is exclusively a lower-class name, as most newly invented names are. The Jemima class are happy to dredge up an obscure family name, and have no fear of calling their child after an animal (I was at school with both a Beetle and a Frog), but the invention of entirely made-up names is reserved for those lower down the social scale. Some are remarkably imaginative. I know of both a Meta-Angel (her mother 'met an angel' on the way to the abortion clinic who told her to keep the child) and a Taome (it stands for 'the apple of my eye').

A few years ago Kayleigh made it to the 30th most popular girl's name in Britain, and it remains popular: 267 children were given it last year. And as I've mentioned, the version spelt Kayliegh is one of the five names most heavily skewed towards Acorn Group N, made up of 'low-income families living on traditional low-rise estates, where unemployment is high'. Kayleigh has spawned a bewildering subset of names, nearly all of which are unrelentingly bizarre. There were 101 Demi-Leighs born last year, seven Chelsea-Leighs, six Tia-Leighs (which could be a liqueur), five Everleighs (a retirement home?), three each of Honey-Leigh and Kaydie-Leigh and even a trio called Lilleigh, which sounds like a sanitary product. In total there were 128 different iterations of 'Leigh'. These children were born with that name and have no control over what class they have begun life in; but the Hyphen-Leighs represent a group all of their own: children of parents desperate to assert their individuality, regardless of income, housing or education. They do it through a series of public actions, from the naming of their child to their choice of clothes brands. These youngsters were born after Princess Diana stumbled over her wedding vows in St Paul's Cathedral, but they are as steeped in class as Charles Philip Arthur George. Even the use of a hyphen – a hijacking of what was once the preserve of the upper classes – is a tacit attempt to assert their status, to prove they are not part of the masses. But this has been done on such a scale that those who have done it have become a whole new class.

The Hypen-Leighs are the main supporters of certain fashion chains, and we meet them again in the clothing chapter. As with their appropriation of upper-class punctuation, they are the most agile at spotting high-status brands and making them, or cut-price versions of them, their own, be it Burberry, Blackberry, Barbour or Uggs. They are as central to this book as the Middleton classes. They both, in their own way, revel in the status they have gained through the choices they have made.

One of the other key class markers when it comes to children's names is the number of them. It used to be simply that the more you had, the posher you were. It was a way for the Rockabillies who sent their children off to boarding school to help keep Cash's nametape company in business. I was given two middle names along with my Christian name and was baffled when I met someone at my prep school called just Leo. He had fewer characters in his name than I had initials. The 12th Duke of Manchester, who has spent three years in jail for fraud, called his son, who had the courtesy title Lord Kimbolton, the following jumble of names, all high ranking on the *Telegraph* list: Alexander Michael Charles David Francis George Edward William Kimble Drogo Montagu. That's ten pre-names plus the family name Montagu – enough for a cricket team. My father-in-law was embarrassed when he made it to grammar school that he was just 'John' and had no middle name – this became apparent when the team sheet for the cricket XI was posted on the school noticeboard. He proceeded to tell the cricket master that his initials were 'T.G.J.' – a complete lie, but one that was believed. It was his silent little joke; only he knew that T.G. stood for The Great.

The Hyphen-Leighs have proved that double-barrelling is no longer the preserve of the upper classes, which used the technique as modern companies do with corporate mergers. Families into which they married, and which frequently injected the upper classes with a shot of money or strong genes, were rewarded with being added to the surname. It was briefly thought that Prince William might marry Isabella Anstruther-Gough-Calthorpe, but he ended up with Miss Middleton. Who knows? Maybe he thought it might damage the Windsor brand to associate it with a triple barrel.

The method of your birth is another key marker of class, though again it reflects far more on the parents than on the babies, who clearly couldn't care two hoots if they were born at home with a doula, in a busy NHS hospital or in a thick-carpeted private one. But, boy, does it matter to the small number that avoid the NHS option. A mere 0.5 per cent of the population is born in a private hospital, and it is almost entirely for the status-enhancing comfort that it brings to the parents. The two most famous options are the Portland, a private hospital in London, where all of the Spice Girls, Jemima Khan and the Duchess of York had their respective children, and the Lindo Wing of St Mary's Paddington, where Princes William and Harry were born. Only a handful of parents announcing the birth of their children in *The Times* or *Telegraph* waste precious words (you pay by the word) on detailing the location of the delivery. But a disproportionate number of those giving birth in the Lindo Wing or the Portland like to tell you so. I suppose if you have spent many thousands on a private birth, what's an extra £20 on telling the world about it? And indeed the Portland offers you a 50 per cent discount on placing a birth announcement in *The Times* as part of the package, though the choice of name is as much a giveaway as the consultant's invoice. Hermione, Zander, Honor, Felix, Oscar,

Freya, Walter, Amalfi Cordelia and Cosima Celery are just a small selection of the names of the children born in these places.

The statistics support the cliché that the Portland really is the first choice for those too posh to push. Of the 2,232 births that took place there in 2011, 53 per cent were Caesarean sections, more than double the UK average of 24 per cent. Those that come here to give birth are the real elite in Britain. The babies born at the Portland are, of course, at that moment of naked, mewling innocence no different from those born a quarter of a mile down the road at University College Hospital, but they are born into a world absurdly different, and some might say grotesquely privileged. A simple birth costs £5,900, an elective Caesarean costs £8,200 – though you need to add £890 for an epidural. And all of these fees must be added to the consultant's bill, which starts at £5,000 a baby. But it is not the cost that marks out the Portland Privateers as Britain's über-elite. It is the added extras that come as part of the package. Along with the discount for announcing the birth in *The Times*, Sky television, a hair dryer and complimentary toiletries from Molton Brown, there are discounts for certain nanny agencies and an extensive menu for you to enjoy during your stay (£1,750 for each extra night after your first day). I know of a couple, both City lawyers, who chose the Portland over the Lindo Wing purely on the basis of the wine list. I kid you not. Perrier-Jouët, chilled, will set you back £70 a bottle.

The great majority of the Portland Privateers easily fall into the legendary '1 per cent', so despised by politicians as being the venal, blood-sucking, corporate-raiding section of society, earning over £150,000 a year. But they can be surprisingly insecure about their status, with most of them recent arrivals into the Club Class lounge. They have enough money to buy almost any comfort, but they do not feel it. Over-taxed and under-loved, they seek comfort in various brands and labels that offer them the reassurance that their sacrifice of working ludicrous hours and rarely seeing their children is all worth while. Most of them are successful enough professionally – as lawyers, accountants, investment bankers, consultants, fund managers, designers – to have rubbed shoulders with the mega-rich, the 0.1 per cent, the 'have yachts', the servant-employers, and to know that their own wealth is but small change for the international plutocracy who mostly pay their wages. And despite earning five times or more the national average salary, their disposable income is not that huge once they have paid for what they consider key outgoings: private medical insurance, nannies, private school fees, a cleaner, gym membership, weekly frothy coffee and dry cleaning bills. What defines them is their separateness, from Britain and from the other classes that make up Britain. They are almost uniformly Londoners, or live in the commuter towns around the capital, while a handful can be found in Cheshire, and they reside within certain very specific postcodes within those areas, sometimes even choosing the gated community option. While private births make up just 0.5 per cent of the national figure, they are as high as 33 per cent in certain wards in Kensington & Chelsea in London. They will at every opportunity choose private over state, believing – with some justification – that the Welfare State was never designed for them. They have a sense of community, but it is unrelated to their neighbours; it almost entirely derives from fellow parents at their children's private school and work colleagues. Unlike the Middleton classes, they have no desire to assimilate if that means they have to wait for a dentist's appointment, swim at their local council-run pool, shop at Asda and eat at La Tasca. Without the support of the Portland Privateers a whole host of very successful brands would not thrive as they do. We will come across some of them in later chapters, but they include Smythson iPad covers, By Nord bed linen, Jo Loves smelly candles, Mulberry handbags, Louboutin shoes, Hermès ties, Bugaboo buggies, Emile et Rose and Marie Chantal baby clothes, Beulah London (Lady Natasha Rufus's ethical clothing line), Emu furry boots, anything from Daylesford Organic, the Chewton Glen hotel in Hampshire and the Harbour Club gym chain: all brands that defiantly cater to the affluent bubble floating above the rest.

Many of the Wood Burning Stovers would love to go private, but don't dare face the opprobrium of their friends for buying their way to a room and a midwife all to themselves. The Rockabillies, who have fewer scruples but often less money, pretend they adore the NHS, but can't wait to get home to the comforts of the au pair. The solution for the WBS crowd is to go for a home birth, with a doula, a Birkenstock-wearing hand-holder, who can help you deliver your baby with the same stamp of exclusivity that a box of Abel & Cole organic vegetables brings.

After the birth, there is the delicate matter of circumcision. This is now seen as a barbaric act to perform on a young child and one only practised by orthodox Jews and Muslims. Not true. It is, or was until really quite recently, common practice among the upper classes, all the way down to Rockabillies, but no further. The most recent figures suggest just 3.8 per cent of male babies are circumcised, with the rates lowest in the white working-class districts of Liverpool, specifically the Bootle area, as medical opposition to the act takes hold. But it was as high as 20 per cent during the 1950s, with those at the upper echelons the most likely to do it. My father reckons that 95 per cent of his school contemporaries were done. In my prep school changing rooms you could tell who was really smart by their lack of foreskin. Mine was lopped off, when I was one week old, at home, by a rabbi called Jacob Snowman, who performed the procedure on Prince Charles. His name was shared around the upper classes of 1970s London in the way the Portland Privateers now divulge the name of their plastic surgeon. When my mother asked if he needed anything, expecting an answer such as 'some hot water', he replied, 'A glass of red wine would be nice.'

Breast-feeding, too, is still widely a class issue. Your willingness to expose yourself to feed Clemency during lunch at Leon says as much about you as your ironing board cover or newspaper of choice. An academic study of thousands of mothers found that 86 per cent of the top class, as defined by job status, initiated breast feeding when the baby was born. Only half of the lowest class did so. By the time babies were four months old the discrepancy was even more stark: half the top class were still exclusively breastfeeding, but just one in five of the lowest class were.

From life-changing events to tiny immaterial items, class is everywhere when it comes to babies. Even nappies. There is a clear hierarchy, with Pampers the smart option. Huggies are low class. The really chic choice is any of those supposedly eco ones such as Nature Babycare. Only a handful of self-flagellating Wood Burning Stovers attempt washable nappies. If you think it is only the higher echelons of the modern middle classes that obsess about such ludicrous things, think again. Asda Mums are defined by their children almost as much as their supermarket of choice. Vikki, a dental receptionist, is typical of many in her careful choosing of brands. Little Angels nappies, the supermarket's own brand, are acknowledged by many of its customers to be excellent. 'I haven't tried them,' says Vikki. 'I just think they wouldn't be the same quality. I feel bad that I haven't tried them. It sounds awful, but I'd feel bad sending the baby to nursery wearing Little Angels. I'd be embarrassed.' Her baby is nine months old, but already wearing a brand that ensures she is a cut above.

After the name and location of birth, the number of children is the next clear marker of class. How many children do you have? For, make no mistake, the number of mouths you have to feed is driven just as much by class as it is by religion or money. The 2.4 children that British families had on average in the 1960s has shrunk to 1.7 children – freeing up a significant amount of income to be spent on life's little luxuries that lend status and class, be it a side-return conversion or a cruise through the Panama Canal. But whether you are under or over the average, that's a class issue.

In the 1950s the received wisdom was that having plenty of children was one of the most socially useful things the swelling middle classes could achieve. Britain needed not just New Towns for its returning heroes, but young people to grow up and fund their pensions. The Archbishop of Canterbury, Geoffrey Fisher, told the Mothers Union in 1952 that 'a family only truly begins with three children'. But public opinion was moving quickly away from big families. A Gallup poll in 1957 found that most people wanted just two children.[1] And the average size of the British family continued to shrink, with two key exceptions – the top end and bottom end of society.

70

The Portland Privateers breed prodigiously. Children, with their exotic names and scaled-down designer clothes (Burberry even call their children's department in their flagship Regent Street store in London the 'mini me' section), are the ultimate status symbol. Again, look at the birth announcements of those born in the Lindo Wing or the Portland – frequently the sprog is one of four, five or even six children. Tana Ramsay, Jools Oliver, Nicola 'supermum' Horlick – all birthing machines, proving that a large horde is as much a class delineator as a Garrick club tie. Judith Woods, writing in the *Daily Telegraph* in 2011 after David and Victoria Beckham said they were going to have a fourth child, expressed the horror that many Middleton classes felt: 'The Beckhams are reproducing in a way that, were they members of the underclass, would be regarded as not quite responsible. The only couples who have four children these days aren't really couples at all. Either they're brands, selling thousands of cookbooks faster than you can boil an egg, or they're people who resemble the cast of *Shameless* and don't stay together long enough properly to qualify as couples.'[2]

While the Portland privateers and the über-rich are surveyed with wry amusement for collecting children like Swarovski crystal animals, having four children or more if you are a member of the Hyphen-Leighs is seen as deserving of scorn. The Joseph Rowntree Foundation has done extensive research into child poverty and found that, at the lower end of the scale, large families are closely associated with deprivation. A child in a family of five or more children is almost four times more likely to be poor than a child in a one-child family.

Scorn for large lower-class families has always been doled out, even in the early days of the Welfare State. Mass

Observation diaries from the early 1950s bring out the fear among some middle-class people about the dirtiness and lack of self-control of the working classes. Gladys Langford, a retired schoolteacher, wrote after visiting Chapel Street Market in Islington: 'It was very crowded. Nearly every woman of child-bearing age was pregnant and many were pushing prams as well and these often had more than one infant in them already. It was shocking to see how many of these women were very dirty ... their eyes were gummy, their necks and ears were dirty and their bare legs grimy. These are the people who are multiplying so fast and whereas once a number of their children would have died, now, thanks to pre-natal and post-natal clinics, most of their children will live – and will choose those who are to govern us. Anyhow I shall safely be dead by then.'[3]

Anna Woodthorpe Brown, mother of two, and daughter of Irish working-class parents, who was educated at a Roman Catholic comprehensive and brought up on a council estate and who defined herself as 'middle class', was interviewed in the *Observer* for a feature on class in 1993, a few years after John Major promised a classless society. 'My big thing is people not being able to control their reproductive parts. I just get irritated people aren't in control of the number of people living around them that are dependent on them. They moan about it, and they whinge about the fact they don't have enough facilities to take care of those people they've reproduced.'

This hostility towards people at the bottom end of the socio-economic scale having lots of children has only intensified as the era of austerity has taken hold, and the Coalition government has vowed to cut back on benefit payments. A small number of people who have undoubtedly abused the system,

by using children to get higher up on the council homes waiting list, has tarnished the reputation of all who chose for whatever reason to have a large family. The prejudice is deeply held
by many. John Ward, a councillor, said during the Shannon
Matthews farrago, when a woman from West Yorkshire
kidnapped her own child in an attempt to win reward money:
'There is a strong case for compulsory sterilisation of all those
who have had a second child, or third, or whatever while living
off state benefits.'⁴ Louise Casey, the head of the Government's
troubled families unit, said in the summer of 2012 that struggling mothers with lots of children, who are a drain on social
workers' resources, should be 'ashamed' of the damage they
inflict on society.

＊　＊　＊

My mother was born too late to be presented at court to the
Queen, a practice which ended in 1958, but she was unequivocally a 'deb', with a coming-out ball and the strict expectation
she would marry someone she met in this tight group of people.
The archaic tradition of debs and 'the Season' served a most
definite purpose for the aristocrats and Portland Privateers of
their day, many of whom didn't go to university or work in a
bustling office – it provided a forum in which to meet a spouse.
It was also a way for their parents to assert their status. The
Season limped on for many years and still exists in a truncated
and rather commercial form to this day. I was surprised one
summer holiday, in the mid-1990s while I was at university, to
suddenly receive a number of invitations to parties from people
I'd never heard of. When I mentioned this to my mother she
explained I must have made it onto Peter Townend's list of
'debs' delights'. Townend was the idiosyncratic, amusing if

oleaginous, borderline alcoholic, 'confirmed bachelor' editor of the Bystander column in *Tatler* magazine, who single-handedly managed to keep the season alive after the Queen stopped presentations. It was he, with his encyclopaedic knowledge of the gentry and squirearchy of Britain (he was a one-time editor of *Burke's Peerage*, which he kept by his hospital bed as he lay dying) and an insatiable appetite for cocktail parties, who drew up the list of debs. He was a one-man arbiter of who was upper class. Each spring he would send 200 letters to mothers in his extravagant turquoise handwriting inviting them (you could never apply) to submit their daughters. My sister was persuaded by my mother to partake, and found the whole experience a painful one.

I too thought Townend's puppet-master act bizarre and ever so slightly creepy. Despite the allure of free champagne and vol-au-vents, I was happy to turn down the invitations to stand awkwardly in a room with people I'd never met – even if that was how my parents had found each other, both of whom loved the whole process. It just wasn't for me. I knew instinctively that anyone whose mother thought I was a debs' delight was not going to make future wife material. I ended up marrying outside my class. This sounds an absurd statement to write, but back in the 1950s, or even the 1960s when my mother and father met, this was still a radical idea. When Princess Margaret broke off her relationship with divorcé Peter Townsend (not to be confused with Tatler man Townend) in 1955, it was widely seen as a class issue rather than a religious one, with many unhappy that she wanted to marry an untitled commoner. It prompted a thunderous letter to the *Daily Express* written by a number of angry young men, including the cartoonist Ronald Searle, the public school film-maker Lindsay Anderson and

Kenneth Tynan, who said: 'It has revived the old issue of class distinctions in public life.'[5]

Fifty-five years later nearly all applauded William's marriage to Kate Middleton. Only pockets of 1950s-style resistance remained. A letter to the *Telegraph* from a James Lewis, in Wembley, said: 'SIR – I don't doubt that middle-class Miss Middleton is just what "The Firm" needs. However, that is not what royalty is all about. The Royal family is by definition above us all. You cannot have an institution that is bowed to, sung to in anthems, privileged and exalted in history, and then say it needs penetrating by the middle class.' No one outside of hard-core *Telegraph* letter writers seriously questioned the appropriateness of the marriage. Most immediately recognised that they came from two very different classes, but the idea that this meant they could not form a successful union was not seriously entertained.

If you accept that people come from different classes, you have to also accept that the act of marriage allows one member of the partnership, or both, to alter their class. It sounds feudal, but it is a simple act that still transforms many families' sense of position. The choice of whom you marry remains one of the surest ways for people to leave the class into which they are born, and possibly more importantly it ensures that their children have a different sense of their status than they do – a process that continues with endless little acts of consumption from the moment they leave the womb.

Carole Middleton, born in 1955, arguably represents the golden generation of social mobility. Statistics show that of those people born into the poorest families in 1958, fewer than one in three was still poor three decades later. Most had moved up the ladder – impressively, almost one in five had reached the highest income bracket.[6] Much of their journey upwards was thanks to Britons enjoying significant amounts of disposable income during this period, allowing them to make purchases and choices that were just not available to the previous generation. The affluent, consumer society not only offered Britons a wide array of choices, from the supermarket they frequented to the clothes they wore and the holidays they took, but also engendered an attitude that you did not have to ape your parents. You could choose to break out of their social circle. You could even marry outside it.

And of all the consumer purchases available to these New Elizabethans, none was bigger than buying your own home.

CHAPTER 3

PROPERTY

Our home is the most expensive consumer product most of us will ever buy. But is home ownership an essential requirement for 'middle-class' status? Here we meet the old-fashioned aristocrats, and the Sun Skittlers.

When the 12th Duke of Bedford, Hastings 'Spinach' Russell, died in a mysterious shooting accident in 1953 on his estate in Devon, it appeared to be the final straw for one of Britain's premier aristocratic families. His son had to find £4.5 million to pay the Treasury in death duties. A sale of 200 Dutch and Flemish paintings, most of them masterpieces, had failed to raise enough money. The trustees of the estate – whose jewel was Woburn Abbey in Bedfordshire, but which sprawled across several counties – urged the 13th Duke to sell up, give the Abbey to the National Trust and live off the proceeds of the rents from Covent Garden, the prime piece of real estate in central London that the family owned.

But the 13th Duke, John Russell, who at the time was a fruit farmer in South Africa, was determined that Woburn, given to his ancestors by Henry VIII on the dissolution of the monasteries, would stay in the family and not be sold. 'Once that happens, then your roots have gone, and if a place like Woburn means anything in terms of history and tradition, then it is only because of the personal identification with the family that has built it up,' he said.

The Abbey, with its 120 rooms, then cost some £300,000 a year to maintain, with a heating bill alone of £5,000. It had not been lived in for decades, the paintwork was peeling off the walls, and furniture was stacked up as if in an antiques warehouse. The annual running costs were the equivalent of well over £6 million in today's money. It seemed impossible that it could continue. Its perilous position echoed that of thousands of other country houses and estates that were beset after the war by a new, higher level of death duty and the unwillingness of servants to go back to their former jobs after fighting or working in factories. Family after family found it easier to sell up, hand over the estate to the National Trust or – scandalously – demolish the buildings, an act of vandalism that was perfectly legal then. In 1955, country houses were being destroyed at a rate of one every five days.[1]

It seemed that the war, and the subsequent years of austerity and the Welfare State, had driven the final nail into the coffin of the British aristocracy and their landholdings, from which flowed not just their wealth, but their prestige and power. For centuries those that physically owned Britain – its farmland, rivers, forests and cities – had run Britain. It was as simple as that; and it looked as if they would no longer have any basis for their assertion of superiority. As Sir Ian Anstruther, the 13th Baronet, lamented: 'The upper classes are not wanted.' My own grandfather, the 9th Earl of Portsmouth, was one of many to despair about the new era of the Welfare State, high taxes and his lack of purpose. The family home – an 11-bedroom house which he described as a 'modest mansion for 20th-century living' and which had been in Wallop hands since Elizabethan times – was leased to a prep school as he decided to start a new life in Africa. 'All was drab, alas too drab, in England. The motto of the new democracy seemed to be … "the greatest misery to the greatest number",' he said.

Marx's great prediction of a 'classless society' had come true, albeit 100 years later than he predicted: the middle classes had won. The stranglehold of a very small number of families on the assets of the country was being loosened. Britain was free to finally become a proper democracy, free from the shackles of inherited positions.

But John, the new Duke of Bedford, was made of stern stuff. He'd suffered from an eccentric and deeply loveless childhood which had seen him at times forced to steal the food left out for his father's beloved parrots. As a young adult, living off an allowance of £98 a year, he became an estate agent in the East End of London and was so hard up that at one point his friends had to club together to buy him an overcoat. On inheriting the estate he set about trying to save it – and decided the only option was to open it to the public.

As he himself pointed out, he was not the first to do so. After the war both the Marquess of Bath, with the 118-room Longleat, and Lord Montagu of Beaulieu had opened their homes to the public, charging them for the privilege. But Bedford should take credit for pioneering the very concept of 'stately homes' – vast, aristocratic piles not just open for the occasional bank holiday visit, but aggressively marketed for 'half-crown' coach trips and unashamedly commercial. His methods, which involved him appearing countless times on television, especially in America, as well as manning the tills in the souvenir shop – 'whenever I do the selling, the turnover goes up by 50 per cent' – was frowned upon by many fellow peers. He marketed ashtrays with the family crest, allowed a nudist film to be made on the estate and installed a cappuccino machine and a juke box in the 'milk bar'. He was instrumental in ensuring some of the Hollywood glamour of the 1950s and 60s and the emerging celebrity culture rubbed off on Britain's original stars of gossip columns, the aristocracy, making guest appearances at the 1959 Ideal Home Exhibition, for instance, testing out Europe's first-ever automatic dishwasher.[2] Most shockingly of all, he welcomed complete strangers into his home as house guests, touting Woburn, so his fellow aristos believed, as little more than an upmarket B&B. 'Dinner with a Duke', hugely popular with American tourists, set you back £90 (an eye-watering £1,600 in today's money), but secured you a four-course meal in the Canaletto dining room, full English breakfast served in bed, and a guided tour and banter – over the coffees and digestifs – with their Graces. Bedford said: 'I do not relish the scorn of the peerage, but it is better to be looked down on than overlooked.'[3]

His commercial tactics worked. In the first year 180,000 visitors came to the Abbey. Within a few years the figure was over a million. By 1958 the souvenir shop alone had a turnover of £180,000 a year (well over £3 million in today's money). Then in 1974 the 13th Duke retired in rather a rush to Spain – rumours among his friends suggested that he was the master-mind behind the Great Train Robbery and he wanted to put distance between himself and Scotland Yard. The project was taken on by his son, who built golf courses and allowed Neil Diamond to stage concerts in front of the house. The estate is now in rude financial health, one of many such stately homes that provide the middle classes with a bit of culture along with an expensive cream tea.

The 13th Duke's success helped save a small part of the landed gentry from losing their estates. And, just as interestingly, his methods kept the aristocracy in the public eye and part of the national debate at a time when it looked as if they were a complete irrelevance and would disappear from sight for ever. Various surveys suggest that not a single person in Britain would describe themselves as upper class. Well, a number do in private – they just don't answer emails from market research companies. My cousin, the current 11th Earl of Portsmouth, says: 'What class am I in? Well, I am a toff, aren't I?' There may only be about 1,000 hereditary peers left in Britain, but nearly all are honest enough to admit they are still upper class. He and his fellow aristocrats owe a debt of thanks to Bedford. A small number of über-aristos still own an astonishingly large proportion of the country, with estates that cover everything from hundreds of thousands of acres of Scottish highlands to central London office blocks. The fact that titled blondes and aquiline-nosed Viscounts still appear prominently in the gossip columns, news pages, advertising campaigns of designer labels, as public guardians of a traditional version of Britain, has something to do with the fightback in the early 1950s by Bedford *et al.*

More than anything, however, the 13th Duke's crisis and the resulting solution underlined the country's obsession with property, an obsession that has become all the more potent in the last half-century. He neatly expressed his fear of losing Woburn: 'I do not know any great family that has survived the loss of its house,'[4] he said. It is a sentiment not exclusive to the aristocracy. It is not living in a nice property *per se*, but the ownership of it which has become the touchstone of the middle classes since the 1950s.

* * *

Woburn's great feat of survival coincided with an era which suddenly saw an increase in property values, after a 70-year slump that had started in the Victorian age. This increase in house prices continued unabated with only short-term blips until 2007. In the process it created vast amounts of wealth for home owners as they re-mortgaged their properties and used the billions on holidays, cars, luxuries – products to furnish their newly found middle-class lifestyles. Property ownership became a national habit, as increasing millions of people bought their biggest ever consumer purchase either as an investment, or just a safe roof over their heads. It is only in the last couple of years that the property crash, which was the first sign of the impending financial meltdown, has proved to be more than the usual short-term 'correction'. The middle-class shibboleth of property ownership has finally been called into question. The tap of seemingly endless cheap credit has been turned off, in the process squeezing the middle, as Ed Miliband has put it.

Squeezed or not, property has possibly been the most defining feature of the modern class system. In simple terms, the rise of the middle classes exactly mirrors the rise of home ownership. The terms home owner and middle class are, in most instances, synonymous. But it is, of course, more complex than that. Even if you do own your home, how big is it? Does it have wooden sash or UPVC windows? Is it a whopping great Abbey, a late-Victorian terrace with a side-return, a three-bed semi in a 1990s cul-de-sac, or in a 1960s tower block?

Most important of all, where is it? Location, location, location is not just the mantra of estate agents, it is the subject of an increasingly sophisticated science called geodemographics. The principle is that where you live – down to which particular end of a particular street – helps determine the supermarket you use, the type of clothes you wear, even your favourite brand of wine. Whether you are a 'Wealthy Achiever', a 'Post-Industrial Family' or classified as 'High Rise Hardship', much is determined by postcode. But more of this later.

It is perhaps not that surprising that in a slew of surveys, undertaken over the last couple of years asking people to define what class they themselves fitted into, nearly always 70 per cent have said they were 'middle class', a percentage that almost exactly mirrors the percentage of home owners in Britain. Back in 1950, just 27 per cent of households were occupied by home owners – again a figure which correlated almost exactly with the 28 per cent who said they were middle class in a 1951 survey. So, in the last two-thirds of a century home ownership has nearly tripled, along with the size of the self-defined middle classes. Recently, Britain Thinks, having found that 71 per cent of people defined themselves as middle class, asked some to come to a focus group and bring with them an object that most accurately summed up what made them middle class. Along with a Cath Kidston ironing board cover, a golf ball and numerous cafetières that were brought along, there was one object that was hard to argue with: one person brought the keys to her flat.

The biggest catalysts to the growth in home ownership were two Tory prime ministers. The first was Harold Macmillan, who as housing minister in the early 1950s vowed to build 300,000 homes a year. He made it far easier for developers to put up bricks and mortar, on the grounds that 'in a property-owning democracy, the more people who own their homes the better'.[5] The second, of course, was Margaret Thatcher, whose Housing Act of 1980 gave people the right to buy their council homes at a discount. It should be noted, however, that even in the 1970s many thousands of tenants, especially in the new towns, had bought their properties from their local council. But Thatcher blasted oxygen into the flickering fire and caused an eruption in home ownership. Between 1980 and 1987, the percentage of home owners went from 52 per cent to 66 per cent, with the vast majority of this increase coming from right-to-buy.[6] As someone brought up above a grocer's shop in Grantham, Thatcher understood very clearly the importance of property ownership to the aspirant middle classes. Indeed, most people feel deeply that their home is their castle, even if it is a one-bed flat with a window-box rather than a 100-room abbey with a safari park.

Council houses, of course, were never designed to be owned. In the 1920s the Labour government was explicit about being the Party of the Working Home, which aimed to build 'houses to be let not sold', according to its manifesto. And after the Second World War, the need became far more pressing because of the sheer volume of properties that had been destroyed by bombs. In areas such as Stepney in London a third of all homes had been destroyed in the Blitz.[7] This wave of council houses that were built had a higher purpose too. Aneurin Bevan, one of the founding fathers of the Welfare State and housing minister, was keen they should be as mixed as possible. 'We should try to introduce what was always a lovely feature of English and Welsh villages, where the doctor, the grocer, the butcher and the farm labourer all lived in the same street.'[8] His vision was shared by many across the political spectrum, especially the developers of New Towns, who believed they were helping to usher in a new Albion. The chairman of the Stevenage Development Corporation said: 'We want to revive the social structure, which existed in the old English villages, where the rich lived next door to the not so rich and everybody knew each other.'[9]

It was a noble aim and one rooted in the belief that the Welfare State was not just a safety net, but an empowering force. There was a hope that council houses would not only supply people with warm, comfortable homes, with bathrooms and labour-saving devices, but that they could also be an agent of real social change. Ferdinand Zweig, the economist, in his 1952 survey 'British Worker', talked about how social distinctions were blurring for a number of reasons, including 'council houses [which] are getting rid of the class barriers which formerly existed between districts'.[10]

David Ritchie, a Scottish teacher, was one of the first wave of post-war workers to receive a council house in Glenrothes, Fife. 'It was fairyland, a new house, with a hedge round the front and a garden and fence round the back, it was marvellous. I had a miner on one side, a journalist on the other, workers and professional people lived cheek by jowl. It was very exciting and strengthened the community.'[11] But this utopia didn't always win approval, not least in the new towns which were built after the war, as part of a plan which intended to move 300,000 Londoners out of slums and overcrowding in the city to beyond the green belt: Stevenage, Hatfield, Hemel Hempstead, Bracknell, Crawley, Harlow, Basildon and the extending Welwyn Garden City.

Harlow, from the start, was a new town with middle-class aspirations,[12] and John Lewis considered opening a department store there. While the town was still being built, Sunvic, a heating and electrical controls company that still exists, decided to uproot the company from Covent Garden, in the heart of London, to Harlow. It took all the workers on a coach trip to the new town to see if it appealed to them. Two-thirds voted in favour, some enthusiastically embracing the better-quality housing, some reluctantly agreeing in order to continue working for a good employer. One worker interviewed after the trip said the town was 'the sort of thing the planning boys dream up, but which doesn't work out. Social classes all mixed up, for example: nobody likes that, you know, people like to keep to their own class, in practice. Then, there's no privacy – think of it, front gardens in common.'[13]

Many of the new towns failed to achieve the aim of creating a mixed, classless community. Some were selective about whom they housed, siphoning off the skilled workers and their families. In none of them was there a genuine cross-section of society, and those that did have a broad range of classes rarely saw much mixing between professional classes and the working classes. Those that could afford higher rents colonised the better areas. As more and more tower blocks were built, the social divisions widened, with few if any of the professional classes willing to live 17 storeys up. By the end of the 1960s about 1.5 million people were living in these high-rise experiments,[14] many of them poorly constructed.

And, for many, council homes brought with them a sense of shame. Instead of being the bulldozer of social change, they were a barrier in its path. Ruth Bale, as a young girl, had been brought up on the Quarry Hill council estate, in Leeds. At the time it was the largest social housing complex in Britain, a brutal, concrete high-rise that for all its mod cons, electricity and solid fuel ranges was hated by most of the inhabitants. The planners' dream of large communal gardens, as with so many high-rises, backfired spectacularly. Parents wanted to see their children play outside, even if it was kicking a ball on the street, but were fearful of letting them play seven storeys beneath them, on a patch of grass far away, so the children were inevitably trapped inside.

Ruth's family then moved down to London in the mid-1950s – thanks to a council house swap, common at the time – in the hope that her father, a 'workshy' salesman cum bookie cum tailor, would find better employment. They moved to the 'rough' Boxtree estate in Harrow Weald, a huge London County Council development. Though they were no longer in a high-rise, they lived in fairly cramped quarters in a terraced, two-up, two-down house; she shared a room with her sister. 'My mother hated it, she thought the area was poor working class. And she saw herself as a notch above. Of course my father wasn't even working class because he didn't often go to work, but she had aspirations.'

The key aspiration was owning their own home. 'My mother would call those homes "private". My aunties and uncles weren't rich but they all owned their homes. There was a sense we were falling behind. We didn't fit in at big family gatherings, and my mother felt it. She was quite ladylike in some ways. She'd say things like "Oh, no finesse". She didn't like us playing out a lot at the front.'

Ruth is now a reluctant member of the Middleton classes, a regular at the local Women's Institute and a Radio 4 listener, and has enjoyed over the last 40 years comfort and security that her parents could barely dream of. The Middleton classes are the golden generation of, mostly, grammar-school children who didn't just jump but pole-vaulted up the classes. They started out in council homes and through luck, marriage or hard work and a canny knack of assimilation ensured they did not end up in one. They are now, wealthy or not (and plenty of them have fairly modest incomes), fully paid-up members of the consumer society – shopping at Marks & Spencer, trips up to London to take in a show, booking a cruise. They have ended up considerably more comfortable and confident than their own parents, and the springboard for this leap has been property ownership.

When right-to-buy was introduced, Ruth – by then a university-educated civil servant working as a probation officer, married and owning her own home – was determined she would help her mother to buy. She may have already become a home owner herself, but she was keen to wipe away the stain of council house ownership from the family, something she had fretted about as a girl. 'I don't know why it bothered me so much. I had a friend, at grammar school, called Brenda who lived in north Harrow. When you went round for tea you just knew they owned their own home. It wasn't, by today's standards, very big, but you could immediately tell. It was a symbol of respectability and comfort, and all the things we didn't have.'

By 1987 more than 1 million council houses in Britain had been sold to their tenants. The most recent figures suggest that 1.9 million former council homes are now owned.[15] A huge number of people were able to get on the housing ladder, at a discount, and surf the enormous property wave, many of them becoming very rich in the process. The trips to Benidorm, the overcoats from Jaeger, the conservatories and loft extensions were all funded by this enormous social project. It was not just the Middleton classes who took advantage, it was also the class who defined themselves then – and to a certain extent still do – as working class. Many now look unchanged from 30 years ago, with the same jobs, same clothes, same accents and drinking habits. In this respect they are radically different from the Middleton classes. But these are the Sun Skittlers – loyal readers of the *Sun*, regardless of their political affiliations. They are also frequenters of their local working men's club, where skittles is still played as a serious game, not some antiquated tourist attraction in a pub, serving 'hand cut chips', Pinot Grigio and Molton Brown liquid soap in the gents. The Sun Skittlers represent a wonder generation, who, despite never rising above foreman level in their factory, now face retirement with decent pensions in a home they own outright with no mortgage bill. Unlike the Middleton classes (many of them started out life in a very similar position) they have no desire whatsoever to assimilate into the class above. Indeed they would be horrified to have the slightest affiliation with Carole Middleton, pleated skirts from M&S and Taste the Difference ready meals from Sainsbury's. In terms of consumption they are very different groups of people, but in terms of assets and attitudes they are remarkably similar.

Steve, who is 58, is a classic Sun Skittler: a painter and decorator from Northampton, who enjoys Strongbow cider at his local working men's club. He's never had any aspirations to diversify into a more skilled trade such as plastering, let alone work in an office. He has been a home owner since the mid-1980s, and was able like many of his friends to buy a house when he was in his early 20s. By the time he took advantage of right-to-buy he was in fact on to his second property: 'I got divorced, moved back with my dad, who was living in a council house. We'd lived there since it was built after the war. I was born there. I didn't want to be like my dad. I loved and respected him and he worked hard, and we were never short. But I wanted to better myself. When my dad was younger, renting was what he did. That's all they knew back then.'

It was 1986, and Thatcher's right-to-buy was in full swing. Steve was offered 60 per cent off the market price by the local council. 'I bought it for £19,500 [about £46,000 in today's money]. It was three-bed, end of terrace with a massive garden. We had a front room, big kitchen diner, a bathroom downstairs, and three upstairs bedrooms.

'It was important to me. I always wanted to own my own property.' He only recently sold it, booked a £100,000 profit and moved in with his partner. 'We're now mortgage free. We can now enjoy life and can relax. It feels good, I have manually worked all my life, now I can chill out.'

But it was not a success for everyone. For starters, it was inevitable that the best-quality homes were bought first, the semis, the terraced houses, ones with gardens. This left local councils with an ever-diminishing pile of properties to offer residents, often poor-quality flats in high rises. The money never got ploughed back into building good-quality new council homes.

Those few that are left in council housing, just one in ten – against the 30 per cent of a generation ago – are frequently condemned. The very fact they live in council accommodation is itself a failure, in the eyes of many. Paying subsidised rent to a council house association has become reason for condemnation, but paying a subsidised purchase price to buy the place outright is reason for congratulation. At its worst this disapproval at the 'poverty of aspiration' spills into outright vitriol. Richard Littlejohn, the *Daily Mail*'s provocateur-in-chief, speaks for many when he calls them 'scum'. Struggling to label a family he once saw walking down the seafront at Blackpool, eating fish and chips at breakfast time and wearing tracksuits, he said it was possible they were Waitrose shoppers, but he thought it unlikely. 'I'm going with scum. Sorry, but there's no other word for it. For all I know, those children could have grown up to become brain surgeons.

'My guess, though, is that they're both living on benefits in some scruffy council garret, halfway up a burned-out tower block, surrounded by raggedy children who look pretty much like they used to on their jolly outing to Blackpool. We're now on to second- and third-generation scum, sustained by a patronising and non-judgemental welfare juggernaut. We've always had what sociologists prefer to call an underclass. But not on this scale and never so visible.'[16] It's the visibility bit that causes such consternation.

This fear of council house tenants has filtered beyond the pages of a (knowingly goading) tabloid into public policy. Plans of Wandsworth Council to provide new homes only to those who have a job or those who are in training were leaked to the press. A source at the council told the newspaper: 'We want to tackle the Jeremy Kyle generation of people who can't be bothered to get off the sofa. Having a council house should be a privilege not a right.'[17] Iain Duncan Smith, the Conservative Secretary of State for Work, and responsible for some of the Coalition's most radical policies, sums up the view of many that council estates are beyond the pale. 'Over the years, our housing system has ghettoised poverty, creating broken estates where worklessness, dependency, family breakdown and addiction are endemic.'[18] He is as evangelical about the benefit of property ownership as Aneurin Bevan was about council housing. For Duncan Smith ownership, rather than better-quality council housing, is the solution: 'Those who own are more likely to protect their assets, to protect their position of ownership and to engage in constructive behaviours that enable their assets to be protected and enlarged: behaviours that benefit themselves, their families and the community at large. Relieving asset poverty is tantamount to offering hope.'

It is unsurprising that many of those who are left in council homes feel dispirited, as if they have failed. The sense of shame that Ruth felt in the 1950s is just as strong today. Hayleigh Pain, a nanny in north London, was brought up in a council-owned home, a beautiful five-bedroom house in a Victorian terrace in Islington. When she was a child her family were, justifiably, proud of their property, and it never crossed their mind to own it. But by the early 2000s her mother had moved to a smaller place after her father died, and Hayleigh had become another Richard Littlejohn *bête noir*: a teenage, gymslip mum. She was forced to leave sixth-form college and she, her baby and her partner were given a council flat.

A decade on, and with three children, she lives in the same flat. Her attitude towards living in a council property now is radically different from when she was a child. 'It's awful. It's in a tower block. It was a big shock to go from a beautiful five-bedroom street property council house to a flat in a tower block. You have to get in a lift to go upstairs. My three children all sleep in one room. It's just not a nice place to live.' But it is not the quality of housing *per se* that makes her so unhappy, it is the fact that she rents it off the council. 'I wouldn't advertise the fact that I lived in a council flat. I don't want people to know. There is that view that if you live in a council flat, it's because you can't be bothered to do anything, that you've got no aspirations, that you are living off the state.'

She has no wish to be rehoused into a bigger place – even if there was one available that hadn't been sold off. She wants to buy. 'It's down to us to get our own place. We both work. The reason that we are still there now is that we can't afford anything in London because of the prices.'

Hayleigh is a classic Asda Mum – prudent, hard-working and aspirational, but continually hampered by limited income. Both she and her partner work; both are desperate to own their own property and ensure that their children's prospects are better than theirs. She has adopted many of the consumption habits of the modern middle classes – Wagamama, iPads, school tutoring, trips to Disneyworld, supermarket treats. But the key one, property ownership, remains firmly beyond her grasp, and it infects so much else. Levels of unemployment, long-term disability and poverty on council estates have increased markedly since the 1980s, with the proportion of tenants working in full-time jobs falling by a half in that period. One could argue that is because the best-quality homes, and with them the most aspirational tenants, transferred to the private sector. It was always optimistic that dockers would live cheek by jowl with doctors, but right-to-buy surely made it impossible.

It is not just on the council estates of Britain where social mobility has stalled. Across the country home ownership levels have started to fall. Not just fractionally, but substantially. This is the first time since the First World War that the number of home owners has fallen. It hit a peak in 2003, with 71 per cent of people owning their own home, but started to drift downwards as astronomically high prices made it impossible for young people to get on the housing ladder. The financial crash, and the subsequent refusal of banks and building societies to lend to all but the most creditworthy consumers, caused the percentage to fall to 67. We are nearly back to where we were after the right-to-buy revolution. If over the last century the rise of the middle class has been synonymous with the growth of property ownership, this immediately prompts the question whether the property crash has caused a decline in the middle classes. The number of owner-occupied households has dropped by 265,000 since 2005.[19] The then housing minister, Grant Shapps, instinctively realising that the fall in home ownership was linked to a stalling in social mobility, declared optimistically: 'The Age of Aspiration is back!', ushering in various schemes to encourage banks and construction companies to get young people on the housing ladder. It is too soon to know if they will be successful.

Many Sun Skittlers know that their children and grandchildren will never be able to own their own homes in their 20s as they did. The average age of today's first-time buyer, without financial help from parents, is 33. And the average deposit being handed over is £37,375 – one and a half times the national average annual wage. It is no surprise that the great majority of those who have bought under the age of 30 have received help from their parents.

With ownership comes pride and a desire to improve. It's what has made B&Q as big a company as Sainsbury's or Marks & Spencer and worth £5 billion. Portland Privateers all the way down to Sun Skittlers have spent considerable sums doing up their houses, ensuring their bricks and mortar keep on earning. Walk around certain postcodes in London, particularly Battersea, Barnes or Hampstead, and you will see the distinctive excavation chutes that come with a basement conversion project. The entire front of the house is sealed off, while a covered conveyor belt runs from below the front of the door, above the pavement, and into a skip on the street. The scaffolding contraption creates a sort of triumphal arch for pedestrians to pass under, immediately signalling that they are within just a few feet of a family whose children were born in a private hospital, who shop at Ocado and have a Miller Harris smelly candle burning in their Farrow & Ball painted hall. The further down you dig, the higher up you are. The space created will be used for a wine cellar or a swimming pool, possibly a gym and games room for the children. A subterranean panic room away from the real world.

The Wood Burning Stovers, with smaller budgets and a fear of digging ten feet under their foundations, choose the 'side return'. This building work involves adding about 30 square feet extra to the kitchens of terraced houses – not much, but the project tends to suggest that the owners drink coffee from a Moka pot and have logs stacked up neatly in the sitting room ready to burn their status brightly. Thousands of hours of dinner party conversations over Nigella's chocolate pots and intense conferral at NCT breast-feeding classes centre around 'doing the side return'. The best layout, the best builder, the transformational wonder of this precious extra space – it is a consuming passion for the WBS brigade. The mania for home improvement reaches down to the Sun Skittlers, even those who never converted their lofts or tacked on a conservatory. On estates there are often clear indicators of which homes are council and which are privately owned – the front doors. On many estates if you are a tenant your front door only comes in a particular design. Owners have often stamped their mark with stained-glass panels, brass door furniture and a little front porch that juts out and proudly boasts: here be owners.

One of the defining features of city life in Britain from the 1960s onwards has been how some areas have become gentrified, as home owners increasingly spent money upgrading their properties. Stockbridge in Edinburgh, Notting Hill in London,

Castlefield and Chorlton in Manchester – all have been transformed from working-class neighbourhoods into increasingly middle-class ones, and in some cases enclaves for the Portland Privateers. Out go the boarded-up flats with rattling windows, tatty newsagents and grimy workshops, in come the basement conversions and cafés selling flat whites and almond croissants. From slums to silos for the super-rich within a generation.

Just over a mile down the road from where I live in north London is Barnsbury, which has become not just gentrified, but 'super-gentrified', according to some academics.[20] It is now one of the most exclusive areas of Islington, indeed Britain, made up of handsome late Georgian terraced houses, where wistaria creeps up over the windows and Victorian villas are guarded by stucco sphinxes. The famous photo of Cherie Blair, in dressing gown and with dishevelled hair, accepting a bunch of congratulatory flowers on the morning after the 1997 Labour victory, was snapped in the heart of Barnsbury. It was the last property that Tony and she lived in before moving to Downing Street. Properties on that road now fetch £3.75 million and come with wine cellars, walk-in wardrobes, Zoffany wallpaper in the bedrooms and a wooden bicycle without pedals in the hall for Milo. But during the 1950s the same properties were slums, split into bedsits. It had been abandoned by the professional classes, many of whom had left to live in the New Towns, determined to find cleaner air away from the railway tracks and grime around Pentonville Prison (which abuts the area). In a 1960s survey of one Barnsbury street, out of 160 households interviewed 127 had no access to a bath, 138 shared a loo, 15 had no kitchen sink and 25 were living in overcrowded conditions. The architecture may have once been impressive, but it was under severe threat of being knocked down as slums.

A government scheme in the late 1960s, however, gave substantial grants to householders who rehabilitated old properties, as long as the owners matched the grant with their own money. This invariably meant that only those with funds were encouraged to do up large but run-down properties, and Barnsbury was acknowledged, at the time, to be the first area in Britain that took advantage of this change in the law. The first wave of gentrification saw secondary-school teachers, social workers, journalists and architects move into the area – the intelligentsia as it was then called. It cemented Islington as a north London outpost for the Labour party – they used to fly the red flag at every council meeting at the town hall. The UPVC windows that were favoured in the new-build houses of the time were shunned, and a Barnsbury Association policed all developments with a conservationist rod of iron. The Victorian cornicing was restored and the Georgian skirting boards returned. They set about transforming the run-down, bombed-out streets to their own tastes and managed to ensure the neighbourhood was designated as a conservation area. This involved changing the flow of traffic, turning many streets into quiet, access-only thoroughfares and pushing all the cars down the streets which were predominantly working class. Unsurprisingly, the residents on those streets were not impressed. Landlords, scenting the fortunes to be made from rising house prices, put enormous pressure on the remaining working-class residents, many of them immigrants living in bedsits on the gentrified streets, to quit. The entire character of the place had been changed in the space of 20 years.

But by the early 1990s, the time Tony and Cherie moved in, the squillions being made in the City following Big Bang meant that a new wave of even richer Portland Privateers moved into the area, investment bankers and high-flying corporate lawyers. The original working-class tenants are hardly anywhere to be seen. In recent years, with all houses costing well over £1 million, the best over £3 million, even those in the top 1 per cent, earning over £150,000, would struggle to afford to move to the area. Those that have done so have continued with the building work, adding cellars or basement flats for the live-in nannies, constructing glass boxes at the back, 'landscaping' their gardens, 'knocking through' to create vast kitchen-diners.

Barnsbury is an extreme example of how gentrification has changed many little pockets of Britain and in doing so caused great class resentment. The original Barnsbury gentrifiers were interviewed by the academics studying the area. They all expressed bitterness towards the red Porsches, expensive building work and lack of community atmosphere that came with the new wave of super-gentrifiers. They are, of course, expressing the same resentment that the working classes of the area felt when they themselves, the original 'pioneer gentrifiers', arrived 40 years previously. The new cohort, unlike those journalists, civil servants, authors, academics and social workers, has tended not to send its children to the local schools, favouring private education. Islington is far from being the best educational authority in the country, and if you have the money to dig out the basement of a £3 million property you probably have the money to pay for school fees. This has further changed the character of the area, well beyond the influx of fashion boutiques and over-priced cappuccinos.

Barnsbury is now a class ghetto. While most of the Portland Privateers like to think of themselves as community minded, their actions fail to deliver. Their community is, in fact, unrelated to their geography – it is connected to what they have and continue to consume. They feel connected to their neighbours because over a third went to Oxbridge, an astonishingly high percentage. They drive the same cars, their children attend the same private schools (outside the borough), they visit the same top-end restaurants, bars, hotels and beaches – all far from their postcode. They meet their neighbours often, but rarely in their own street. They are more likely to bump into each other in the BA check-in queue to Oman, or at a Wimbledon corporate hospitality suite.

These class ghettos have always existed to a certain extent. More than a century ago Charles Booth, who worked in the leather trade by day, spent his spare time mapping London by colour coding every single street by social class. Yellow was upper class and upper-middle class, those with servants – all the way down to dark blue, which was 'very poor, chronic want', and black, the bottom class, defined as 'vicious, semi-criminal'. The street you lived in determined your social standing.

A century on, and Booth's crude classification and colouring pen has been replaced by the science of geodemographics. This uses official data, be it from the census, the Land Registry or crime records, to classify and categorise every single postcode in the country. There are 1.9 million postcodes in the United Kingdom, so this is a laborious and complex process. Long roads in Glasgow or Liverpool will be split into four or even six postcodes. Even Barnsbury is made up of well over 20 postcodes. On average there are just 14 or so households in each postcode. The census doesn't get published at postcode level – in order to preserve the anonymity of people under data protection rules. But it does get published by 'an output area' of nine or ten postcodes added together. This is about 125 households. Names will be erased from all data released, but it's possible to work out the proportion of five-bedroom houses or Polish au pairs living in these larger areas.

What the geodemographers do is put all the census information into their database and start to cross-reference it with other commercially available data. In the era of the internet, most of us every single day leave a footprint of where we have been, what we have consumed. Even those of us who are scrupulous about ticking the correct data protection boxes can be caught out. If you have ever registered an electrical gadget for a warranty, if you have purchased a dress or garlic crusher, bought a cinema ticket, it has all been logged. And your postcode is the key. Every piece of information is attached to a postcode, from your debit card to your delivery address for the product that John Lewis sends to you. On top of all of this detective work, the geodemographer's job is made easier by about 8 million – or a third – of UK households regularly and willingly filling in surveys or small forms about their favourite cat food or white wine, all of which is fed into spreadsheets. Those innocent competitions in *Grazia* or the *Radio Times*, or little pop-up surveys on websites, are all a ruse to gather more data, and all of them will require you to fill in your postcode or email address.

It starts, usually, when you are just a day or two old. A company called Bounty has a long-standing contract with the NHS to come around maternity wards and hand out child benefit forms and free nappy rash cream. In return, they ask usually sleep-deprived and emotional parents about the name of their new child, the date of the baby's and the parents' birth, their favourite brand of nappies, their supermarket of choice, their email address and telephone numbers – and their postcodes. Little Archie or Kayleigh is logged into a database before they have even met any siblings or started their life in their new home. Their information, the purchasing habits of their parents, are already being sold to marketing companies and geodemographers before their birth has been registered at the local town hall or announced in the *Daily Telegraph*. When our latest child was born I had to tetchily tell the Bounty saleswoman that I did not want any of my data sold on to a third party. My suspicion is that the option would not have been offered unless I had forced the issue.

All of this data ends up being crunched by two main companies, which are funded by thousands of different organisations to do so – from a local council to consumer companies, who spend a lot of money buying these databases. These shops, marketing companies and nappy manufacturers then feed in some of their own information about their customers to help give as accurate a picture as possible about who spends money with them.

One of the companies is called Acorn, and the other is called Mosaic, and they are both able to split the country's 1.9 million postcodes into endless different social categories. There are 57 different Acorn classifications, 61 different Mosaic groupings. All of these categories are given names, some of which are innocuous, such as 'summer playgrounds' or 'sprawling subtopia'. Others are a fairly candid assessment about the status of those that live in these areas: 'burdened optimists', 'white van culture', 'multi-ethnic crowded flats', 'wealthy mature professionals, large houses', 'low horizons' or 'single parent, high-rise estate'. The key thing is that all the postcodes in Britain, and the households within them, are given a social class. It is a different way of looking at the world than that of the old-fashioned Office for National Statistics, which bases it all on the job of the head of the household. Acorn and Mosaic are therefore less male-orientated and more consumer-driven.

The location of your property, rather than the employment of its residents, is probably a more important factor in deciding where you send your child to school or the type of house you live in. The quality of housing stock is often a key factor in the types of people who live in a certain areas. Good state schools drive up property prices and change the nature of particular neighbourhoods – that is proven. What is surprising is how a postcode has become a driving factor behind the choice of wine you drink, the type of mobile phone you use, the make-up you put on your face, your favourite clothes brands, the television shows you watch.

It sounds absurd that where you live should have such an influence on your consumption patterns when we live in such a mobile world. But your postcode has been proven to have an uncanny ability to spot your propensity for certain products and shops. John Rae, at CACI, the company behind Acorn, explains the classifications are 'not describing you, they're describing your immediate neighbours. The basic principle is that, within certain limits, similar people tend to group together … So when I describe your Acorn type and describe the characteristics, 99 times out of 100 you will say yes, I recognise that of my neighbours; you may not recognise it of yourself, but you will accept it is a good description of your street.'

What makes these different social categories interesting is that – like Charles Booth's colour-coded maps of London – they are not based on stark income. The one piece of information the census does not collect is your salary; it doesn't shy away from asking who you share your bed with or to whom you pray, but it is squeamish about asking how much money ends up in your pay packet. It's all terribly British. The categories are clearly a measure of affluence, but it is a more subtle thing than income; it is the brands of perfume, coat, supermarket; the size of house, the length of car, the width of television. It's not how much money you have, but how you spend it.

There is a large element of chicken and egg, of course. Does a Portland Privateer drink a certain type of white Burgundy, drive a Volvo XC90, holiday at a Featherdown Farm because they live in Barnsbury? Or do they live in Barnsbury because they are fond of Chablis, seven-seater cars and glamping? It's a bit of both.

There is an increasing fear among certain academics that lifestyle by postcode is becoming calcified. Because it is now so easy to classify social groups, and because more and more companies that provide us with goods and services are doing just that, Britain is become more physically ghettoised. At a basic level, it means that John Lewis, Marks & Spencer or Sainsbury's just won't open in a certain area because their analysis has shown that there are not enough of their key demographic in that postcode. This means the vacant Woolworths will not be turned into a Waitrose, as happened down the road from Barnsbury, but rather a Poundland or Wilkinsons. The pattern of store openings, based on social classes and catchment areas, reinforces the character of certain places, condemning some run-down areas to be blighted by pound shops, pawnbrokers and bookies, while others bask in White Company shops, vintage crockery retailers and Joules outlets.

Many people are terrified of the surveillance society, of CCTV cameras tracking their movements. This is not what paranoid people should be concerned about – the biggest proponents of the surveillance society are the fashion chains, the washing-up liquid manufacturers, the department stores which every day are collecting data and categorising their customers, those that they want and those that they don't. You don't need a CCTV camera to spy. All of it is completely legal and much of it is harmless stuff, just used for marketing. It ensures people who might be prone to buying Brora cashmere gloves, or cut-price loo paper, are sent the right discount vouchers or promotional emails. However, the concern among some academics is that this seemingly innocent activity further ghettoises people. Most people would understandably argue that they are free individuals, able to make their own purchasing decisions, completely independently of where they live. But consumer companies indulge in a huge amount of what Sir Terence Conran called 'choice editing', from where they open shops to what they stock in those shops, and whom they target online. Why are only 'corporate chieftains' and 'golden empty nesters' thought worthy of Barbour jackets, and why does Iceland supermarket only send its discount leaflets to 'families on benefits' and 'rustbelt resilience'? If you think each Sainsbury's is a bland, corporate box selling identikit products across the country, think again. The company grades all of its shops according to its own sophisticated profile of its customers in the area and then tailors what they sell. More frozen food, fewer Taste the Difference ready meals will be stocked in their Birkenhead supermarket because there are lots of 'struggling families' in this area, more Puy lentils and vine tomatoes in the Cromwell Road, west London, store because a high proportion of 'flourishing families' live nearby. The social category you fall into and your geographic location, whether you are aware of it or not, determines what you are able to buy, thus further confirming your social status. At the start of 2012 Tesco went further, not just altering the products on sale but varying the promotions on offer depending on the social class surrounding the supermarket. Those shops surrounded by customers on benefits would offer a greater number of buy-one-get-one-free or special £1 deals.

We think that the march of the giant company – be it Tesco, Sainsbury's, Starbucks or Costa – makes us all uniformly bland, and creates identikit inoffensive high streets. Far from it: those big companies have spent a long time categorising us and choosing which of us are worthy of their special munificence, and which ones are not. And in the era of the internet they are able to make it even more targeted, ensuring that only specific people are singled out when they are testing a new promotion or trialling a new concept.

The postcode calcification goes deeper than just the shops, gyms, bars and restaurants that choose to open there. Because each area can now be searched, by postcode, thanks to the internet, it is just a matter of seconds before confirming whether Yeovil or Preston is either a 'craptown' or a 'chav-town' (both these websites exist). Potential home owners can immediately check if the area has a good school or a crime problem. Gross inequalities by postcode can be found all over Britain. Take the Wirral area of Liverpool. As a local authority it has the dubious honour of having some of the most deprived wards in the country, with 47.4 per cent of all adults of working age in Birkenhead, for instance, being in receipt of out-of-work benefits. But it also contains Hoylake and Heswall, home to golf courses and wood burning stove showrooms. It's not just consumer companies, but consumers too, who choose to boycott or champion certain areas.

Most of us realise the importance of location instinctively. 'Is it a nice area?' is one of those simple, but oh so loaded, questions we ask friends when they move to a new home. We don't really want to know whether the roads have pot-holes or whether the local church is a fine example of Victorian gothic; we are far more interested in the people: whether JD Looters hang out on the street corner, or whether the residents are wearing Boden skirts. I know a couple who hired a private detective to stake out the area before they decided to move. It was one of those classic neighbourhoods, found in London especially, where one side of the street contains £1.5 million houses, and the other a council estate with a reputation for drug problems – one of those areas that makes classification by postcode a very inexact science. Only after the PI had spend a couple of nights in his car verifying that the crack den was a respectable one (they exist) were they happy handing over their enormous cheque to the estate agent.

Paranoid behaviour? Possibly. But they were merely conducting the same level of geodemographic research that the companies perform on us.

* * *

Property, then, is a key factor in determining your class – whether you own it or not, whether you rent off the council or not, and where it is. But is it more than just a key to a better cup of coffee? Do the owners of Britain's assets still run the country? In the early 1880s Lord Derby urged a parliamentary survey to refute 'wild and reckless exaggerations' that most of Britain was owned by a small number of people. Bateman's 'New Domesday Survey' duly established that no less than 75 per cent of the country was owned by 7,000 people, with a quarter of England and Wales in the hands of just 710 people. Half the Scottish Highlands were owned by 15 lairds, with the Dukedom of Sutherland holding an unfathomably large 1.25 million acres. By the time that the 13th Duke of Bedford was attempting to rescue Woburn Abbey, this massive control of the property of Britain in a handful of aristocratic hands looked like a thing of the past. However, for all the destruction of country houses, a relatively small number of people still own an awful lot of Britain's Monopoly board. In 1982, Heather Clemenson, a Canadian scholar, went back to the Victorian research and found that 259 of the 500 or so great landowning families of the 1880s still owned some of the land. And the biggest casualty had been the minor gentry, the shabbistocrats, not the über-aristos. Nearly half the families owning 10,000 acres or more in the late 19th century still held all or most of their estates.

In 2010, *Country Life*, the magazine where you go to browse the classified ads for £7 million homes in Wiltshire and gawp at the 'girl in pearls', its rarefied version of the page three girl, did a good job of updating the survey. The one major change had been the growth of corporate ownership, with charities, government bodies and even supermarkets sitting on – if not huge acreage – at least very valuable land. The Crown Estate, the Forestry Commission, the bird charity the RSPB and City pension funds were the biggest landowners, and in turn they play a large part in determining the environmental and tax policies of the country. Meanwhile, Waitrose owns a 4,000-acre estate in Hampshire, which it runs as a farm, and Tesco's 2,979 stores alone take up 770 acres. In city centres the biggest landlords are usually professional property companies who own all the shopping centres and high streets.

Country Life found surprisingly little movement. A group of 36,000 individuals – only 0.6 per cent of the population – own 50 per cent of rural land while a staggering 24 million families live on the 3 million acres of the nation's 'urban plot', according to Kevin Cahill, who undertook the research. Let's not write off the old über-aristos. The Sutherland family may be down to a paltry 82,000 acres, but the Duke of Buccleuch owns nearly a quarter of a million acres, worth about £1 billion, and the Duke of Westminster owns about £6 billion of property, thanks to his large tracts of central London including Belgravia and Pimlico.

The Wallop family were never in the premier league of landowners. But like a surprising number of the aristocracy it survived the traumas of the 1950s, the Welfare State, the march of the high-rises and Bovis homes, super-gentrification and right-to-buy. For years the family farms were leased and the house was taken over by a small but upmarket Catholic prep school, while my grandfather exiled himself to Africa to grow tea and coffee. By the 1970s the lease was coming up for renewal and my cousin, the current Earl of Portsmouth, was determined to bring the property back into family hands – believing, as the Bedfords did with Woburn, that the house was inherently connected to the family. It was a seven-year battle to kick the school out, but he eventually did so and set about transforming the school chapel back into the family dining room, returning the dormitories to bedrooms and knocking down the Portakabin classrooms. He was helped in his mission to return the property to its former glory by taking advantage of an immensely lucrative compulsory purchase order that extended the M3 motorway through the estate. Thanks to wise investments and a resurgence in the value of farmland it is likely there will be Wallops living on those 4,000 acres of Hampshire well beyond the current Elizabethan era.

The Portland Privateers are the *de facto* elite in Britain, funding the super-brands, clothes and restaurants that set them apart. The old aristocrats, in contrast, are almost invisible as consumers, and can be some of the least snobbish and least insecure about the shops they visit and the food they eat. I know for a fact that the current Duchess of Bedford is a card-carrying member of Costco, the cash and carry chain, though when she whips out her membership card the cashier, when seeing the name 'Duchess of Bedford', has been known to mistake her for the local pub landlady. And my aunt, known to some of the villagers as 'my Lady', does her weekly shop at Asda. If we judge people on what they spend, the old über-aristos are almost beyond the modern class system. Added to which, aristocratic titles are fading in relevance to almost nothing, especially following the partial expulsion of hereditary peers from the House of Lords in 1999. Most people don't understand what all these handles mean, and how Lord John Russell is different from Lord (John) Russell, whether a Baronet trumps a Baron and why one is a Lord and one a Sir. Many newspapers and certainly the BBC seem incapable of grasping these complex rules. The current Duke of Devonshire has threatened to give up his title and be referred to as Mr Cavendish. My cousin, the Earl of Portsmouth, told me he too had thought about ditching it: 'I have been tempted, because I get fed up with the endless misuse of it. But on the other hand there are an awful lot of people in Hampshire, particularly on the estate, who like it. And it would disappoint people if you chucked it all in. And as it is a hereditary title, I feel it's not really mine to give away. And when it comes to raising money for charity, it does have a useful door-opening function.'

The titles count for less and less, but land and property still matter. Crucially, for the handful of aristos who still have estates, be it the Devonshires, Bedfords or more modest Portsmouths, the property roots them in the community. The old House of Lords claimed that the connection to the land gave them an inalienable right to rule. This was always a bit of a stretch; but their link to particular counties, towns or villages, generation after generation, was something many in those communities understood and even admired. And it is this aspect which links them to nearly all the modern consumer classes, notably the Sun Skittlers and Middleton classes – under pressure financially as never before and whose levels of home ownership are on the slide. They all understand that being a Marquess is all well and good, but owning your own maisonette is what really matters.

The one group that does not share this almost religious adherence to property ownership is the modern elite of Britain, the Portland Privateers. They are entirely divorced from their neighbourhood. Their ties of kinship are unrelated to geography and where their property lies. Yes, most are substantial property owners, but many are just as happy renting in Berne as owning in Beaconsfield, and are as much at home in Barbados as in Barnsbury. And Britain is the poorer for it. The old hereditary aristocracy was a faintly absurd concept, but most of them were in it for the long term – their land and bricks and mortar ensured that was the case. The new elite are in it to pay the private school bills.

CHAPTER 4

HOME

Farrow & Ball or B&Q? Habitat or Brighthouse? Gadgets, white goods, downstairs loos – why does the width of your television give so much away? Here we meet the Wood Burning Stovers.

One of its very first hits was the garlic press – a plain, heavy-duty, metal garlic press, which cost a couple of shillings, and became the implement of choice for any young student or singleton cooking in their bedsitter trying to rustle up a Katharine Whitehorn recipe for Balkan spaghetti.

And the only place you could buy it was Habitat, opened in 1964 by a young designer named Terence Conran. The garlic press, in some ways, made Habitat and the fortunes of Conran, who with his shops and range of products came to define what would later be known as 'middle-class taste'. For the generation of 1960s aspirational consumers, possibly born into the working class but perhaps the first to have gone to university, and with dreams of making a name for themselves, Habitat was the place to shop. Conran himself, now over 80, admits: 'I suppose Habitat was a middle-class organisation started by a middle-class lad.'

The shop was opened to sell his latest range of furniture, which had failed to be taken up by the department stores, but it was the knick-knacks, the accoutrements of daily life that drew the crowds and kept cash dripping into the tills. Conran claims that before Habitat there were no garlic presses. 'You couldn't buy garlic, so there was no point in a garlic press,' he says. There were also no duvets or woks, no globe-shaped Japanese-style paper lampshades for pendant lights, no flat-pack furniture, no Allen keys, no Le Creuset casserole dishes. As the satirist Craig Brown wryly put it, before Conran 'there were no chairs and no France'.

Most of the Habitat shops went bust in 2011, a good decade after he sold his business; the only two that survive are run by the DIY chain Homebase. An era has ended, killed off by the recession and poor management. Conran was left, he told me, 'absolutely heartbroken'. Now that it's gone it is easy to mock the middle-class love affair with Habitat. But its influence on British homes has been enormous, even on those homes where no one has ever bought a garlic press, let alone a chicken brick.

Habitat came about because Sir Terence had designed a collection of furniture called Summa, in an attempt to offer something stylish and cheap to young people setting up home. 'Young people had a bit of money at that time and they wanted to leave home. There was work for the young. It was a mini-boom time. Everyone was looking for flats. They were buying cars or Vespas.' The key thing was that it was flatpack. A quarter of a century before the first UK Ikea store opened in Warrington, Conran introduced to Britain the idea of furniture you assembled yourself. 'I thought flatpack had a great deal of potential. It was space saving and damage preventing.' At the time 80 per cent of furniture was delivered to people's homes damaged, and much of it was delayed. The standard wait between ordering a sideboard or bookshelf and its arrival was about 12 weeks. With flatpack the damage was at least going to be caused by the frustrated homeowner jabbing his own Philips screwdriver into the table leg, rather than by the shop or delivery driver.

Conran hoped Summa would knock G-Plan off its perch. This was the pre-eminent furniture range for an up-and-coming young couple setting up home: bright colours for its sofas, smooth lines for its coffee tables. But Conran thought it was out of keeping with the winds of change. 'G-Plan was fairly flashy stuff. The look was certainly not to my taste. It was what I would call show-off furniture. It was ...' – he takes a big suck on his cigar while he searches for the right word – '... *moderne.*' He drawls out the word. 'They were trying to say, "We are the successful, younger people because we have this *moderne* G-Plan furniture."' Flatpack wasn't *moderne*. It was modern. But after a few months Conran couldn't work out why the Summa range wasn't selling well. He went on a tour of the department stores and furniture shops that were selling the tables and chairs – and his heart fell. 'Shops selling them were deserted, depressing places. Some of the retailers selling them hadn't bothered to even take them out of the box. They were just sitting there dustily. There was no love of furniture.'

And then he realised that the only solution was to sell the products himself. 'The more I thought about it, the more I thought I'd really like to do a shop that sells furniture that has a philosophy and a point of view and where the sales staff really want to buy what they are selling.' Conran's ambition is often seen as pretentious. But his 'philosophy' was what he had picked up on his first-ever foreign holiday, a road trip through France in 1953 – namely, that well-made, utilitarian things designed for rural working-class communities, products that

one saw stacked up in provincial *quincailleries*, French iron-
mongers, had an intrinsic beauty: zinc buckets, paring knives,
colanders and – yes – garlic presses. So alongside the beds,
wardrobes and dining tables were sold smaller items, all
artfully displayed in over-filled bowls, or stacked up casually
on the black slate floors and against the whitewashed brick
walls.

Who were the customers they were aiming at? 'I remember
being asked that at the time. And I said: teachers. Someone on
the bad end of the pay scale for teachers. Interested in education and seeing the future.' This was not a shop for established
lawyers or bank managers furnishing their suburban villas in
Dorking. This was for the new breed of lower middle classes
– through education or aspiration they had left their parents'
working-class background behind – who were setting up home
in bedsits and flats, with a little bit of disposable income, and
were keen to display their cooking skills and continental tastes.
The first wave of the Middleton classes.

Habitat was an immediate hit. It opened in the same week
in 1964 that the 'imbecile goings-on' of the working-class
Rockers and slightly less working-class Mods saw a number
jailed for skirmishes at Margate; Cilla Black and Dionne
Warwick had a bust-up over whose version of 'Anyone Who
Had a Heart' was best; and the cost of living hit an all-time
high, with rump steak at ten shillings a pound. The Beatles
were soon spotted in the shop, and Kingsley Amis courted
fellow novelist Elizabeth Jane Howard in the basement. A
review of the new shop in the *Daily Mirror* that week raved
about the 29s 9d French porcelain coffee pot and the 3s 3d
birch twig egg and sauce whisk. 'Browsing around Habitat,
London's latest household shop which opened last week,

convinced me that once people are exposed to the tremendous excitement of the kind of goods it stocks, they will reject the second-rate,' the newspaper boldly said. The often scruffy objects that Conran had assembled were, the review continued, 'as much in the mood of the moment as a sleeveless shift dress ... Perhaps it's because of the new feeling for good design that is sweeping through the country that this beautiful, useful and often inexpensive kitchen equipment of the past makes such a strong appeal today.' The fact that this 'philosophy' of Conran – well-designed, utilitarian products refashioned for a newly rich, newly arrived middle class – caught the mood of the age was no accident. He decided to ask his friend Mary Quant (she of the mini-skirt revolution) to design the staff uniforms, and all his shop workers enjoyed a discount from Vidal Sassoon's nearby hair salon.

The shop supplied, he claimed, democratic furnishings for a democratic age. It promised to usher in an era in which you could walk into someone's home and have no idea what class they came from, merely whether they had taste or not. But four decades on, and with Habitat on the wane, Conran's democratising dream remains unfulfilled: the very fabric of people's homes is still woven with status symbols; the paint on your walls can never cover up the cracks between the classes.

* * *

Furnishing a home for the wealthy was never a great chore – they inherited most of it. The silver, the wardrobes, the bureaux, pictures, shelves of books were all handed down. My parents' wedding present from my grandfather was a chunk of the family library, which he gave partly in a bid to avoid inheritance tax, calculating that the taxman would never be able to value something invaluable. Even the linen was passed from generation to generation. As an undergraduate I went to college with sheets that had once been used on the servants' beds in the family house in Hampshire – I knew this because the corner of each sheet was carefully embroidered with the name of the house, a code and the date. They were from 1911, the famously hot year when everyone's starch collars melted, and they were worn thin and beautifully soft from decades of washing. Sadly, they eventually disintegrated before I could pass them on to one more generation. Conran himself, son of a successful businessman, had grown up in a house where most of the furniture had been inherited, with striking portraits of his ancestors lining the walls, some of which were sold off to pay the bills and send him to public school.

The very act of choosing your own household objects – rather than inheriting them – was mischievously identified as the epitome of being middle class by the castle-owning MP Alan Clark, who said of rival minister Michael Heseltine, 'The trouble with Michael is that he had to buy his own furniture.' My father quite recently remarked, when I said I rather fancied buying a portrait of an unknown but rather striking 19th-century gentleman from a local auction, 'But why do you want a portrait of someone who isn't an ancestor?' It was a genuine question. Many of the wall decorations he'd grown up with were pictures of fearsome countesses and dishonourable viscounts – relations one and all – and he couldn't comprehend why I would want a stranger on my wall.

How one furnishes one's home has always been one of the most important designators of status. Between 1954 and today, homes have become steadily more decorated, more furnished, more equipped, more comfortable. A car is likely to be parked outside, while inside electricity courses under floors and above ceilings. Fridges, televisions and an indoor loo are now so prevalent that the Office for National Statistics no longer counts them, whereas back in the 1950s they were studiously measured and audited as items of special luxury. And yet for all the progress and comfort, homes are still revelatory, possibly more so than ever. What do you see when you walk into someone's home, and what does the householder choose to display? As a contemporary newspaper review of Habitat said, the shop supplied 'kitchen props'[1] – objects to dress the stage that one's home had become. Not just the thickness of the carpets or the width of the television but the particular shade of grey on the walls (is it Farrow & Ball or Dulux?) and the brand of toaster (is it Dualit or Argos?) can immediately hint at your class.

Even the garlic press. These should ideally come from a holiday visit – akin to the one Conran took in the early 1950s – to a proper French *quincaillerie*. Failing that, this is the order of ranking for garlic press retailers: At the top is Divertimenti, the most aristocratic of all kitchen shops. Crucially, despite or maybe because of its Marylebone postcode and clientele sporting real fur, the products are resolutely utilitarian (they sell the world's best potato peeler for just £1). They are against gimmicks and brands – the two key facets of commercial life that many Rockabillies abhor, despite most of them being voracious consumers. Next in ranking is John Lewis, of course, supplier of choice for all household objects for the great swathe of the modern middle classes, especially the Middleton classes.

Then Lakeland, which is adored by the Rockabillies with an almost fetishistic fervour. Kirstie Allsopp, their pin-up girl, calls it a 'porn shop for anyone who has domestic goddess tendencies'. But though it sells a huge range of wonderful and unique products (both its clingfilm and sandwich boxes are second to none), there is always the suspicion that it is just a bit too gimmicky, a bit too Godalming to really pass the grade. Banana guards and poach pods are all well and good, but a proper cook knows how to poach eggs without the need of a piece of shaped silicone. And who, apart from juniors in accounts, takes a banana to work in its own little, aerated plastic case?

Next up is Ikea, which has taken on some of Habitat's democratising mantle. There are a mere 18 Ikea shops in the UK, but most homes have some item from there, be it an inexpensive chest of drawers or a set of children's plastic cups. The products are nearly always very cheap, and frequently quite stylish, with much thought having gone into the design. But the famously soul-destroying shopping experience, with the retailer insisting that bickering couples meander Theseus-like through the labyrinth of showrooms, before dragging heavy items off the warehouse shelves, means it is a brand that will always be low down the scale. The modern working class may have gained hours of leisure time compared with their grandparents, but much of it is now spent constructing flatpack furniture. It's social progress, but only in a limited way. The Davey lamp has been replaced by the Allen key.

At the bottom of the pile, as is often the case, is Argos. Poor old Argos, which started life as the Green Shield Stamp showroom, is unloved by both its customers and its shareholders. It offers an amazing array of products, many of them excellent. It is Britain's biggest toy and furniture retailer and a purveyor of no end of cheap domestic appliances, as well as high-end Dyson vacuum cleaners, iPads, video games, drying racks, lightbulbs and printer ink. A modern *quincaillerie* – but, and this is the crucial thing, with no 'choice editing', the key Conran philosophy, to make its range distinctive. Retailers have become one of the main drivers of social change in Britain because they carefully select what their shoppers can buy – helping to categorise their customers into different classes the moment they walk through the door. But at Argos, next to a fairly stylish cheap standard lamp sits the most trashy jewellery – diamante Justin Bieber bracelets and a £12.99 silver knuckle-duster ring that spells out 'Nan' in gold. 'A lovely gift for a special Nan', the catalogue says. More than this, the shoppers are treated as if they are the long-term unemployed queuing either for their Jobseeker's Allowance or the results of the 3.45 at Wincanton; forced to wait on plastic chairs nailed to the ground. Even McDonald's now trusts their customers to adjust their own seats. Argos does sell a perfectly decent garlic press, of the same price and quality as those sold in either John Lewis or Divertimenti, but it will always remain a defiantly downmarket brand.

Of course a garlic press usually remains tucked away in the kitchen drawer for most of the time. There is one object, however, that provides a far more public display of status once you step into the home – an item of utility refashioned for the descendants of the Conran classes: the wood-burning stove, which has been embraced by this group just as fervently as were the duvet, the wooden pepper grinder and an Elizabeth David cookbook in the 1960s. The stove, which gives off about the same amount of heat as a radiator, is bulky and often dirty and it is of course utterly unnecessary for the 96 per cent of households that now have central heating – up from just 30 per cent in 1970.[2] But this item of furnishing,

once a working-class object of necessity, has become transformed into both a symbol of conspicuous consumption (they
can cost well in excess of £1,000) and, at the same time, a
recession-busting eco warrior. The retailers claim the object
will save consumers money on their heating bills while reducing the need for gas-fired power stations into the bargain. It's
a potent combination for the biggest fans of these things: the
Wood Burning Stovers.

The stove serves as a point of focus in their sitting rooms – a
conspicuous alternative to the television. It says: 'Hey, we may
watch television occasionally, though if you catch us viewing
Downton Abbey we are doing so purely in an ironic way. There
is an M&S orchid on the hall table, a Roberts radio in the
kitchen playing *Women's Hour*, a half-finished *Guardian*
crossword on the sofa, and an Ottolenghi shallot and goat's
cheese tatin in the oven.' They are a curious beast, the Wood
Burning Stovers. Most would claim to be 'progressive', but
their outlook, and certainly their furnishings, are often nostalgic; they are suspicious of consumerism, and yet they are seekers of status and will travel far to track down the right
vegetable, side-table or primary school. They in some ways
closely resemble the Rockabillies, whom we will meet properly
in the travel chapter. Both groups look 'middle class', but Wood
Burning Stovers are Birkenstocks not flip-flops, Siena not
Suffolk, Toast not Boden.

The stoves themselves have gone from being a niche, and
expensive, luxury found in lifestyle magazines to a fully-fledged
badge of honour. They have even joined the great pantheon of
'things that give you cancer, according to the *Daily Mail*',
along with candle-lit dinners, bubble baths, talcum powder,
Wi-Fi and breast-feeding. Wood burning stoves have been

found to emit particles that 'can lead to fatal heart disease and cancer, toxicology experts warn'.[3]

Our houses are full of these stage props, from the cutlery drawer to the sitting room. We need to do a quick whistle-stop tour to show how different brands, patterns and even colours have become laden with class as never before. However, before we start that tour we need to untie the knotty problem of language, and what different classes call the same thing.

Nancy Mitford, the author, famously penned a (partly tongue-in-cheek) essay about language and class in 1955, spelling out the terms used by the upper class, or 'U', and those the rest, or 'non-U', used. Some, even at the time, were quite old-fashioned terms that were already falling from favour across all classes, such as 'ice' rather than 'ice cream'. But she cleverly crystallised what everyone knew – namely, that different classes spoke differently. It wasn't just accent, it was also vocabulary that marked out the elite and the middle classes, particularly the rising lower middle classes, just below them. Sixty years on, most of these have faded into the mists of time, though they were still very much alive in our family when I was growing up. I was always corrected by my mother if I used the word 'perfume', a word it was made clear to me that ladies never used unless they were ladies of the night. The correct term, as Nancy Mitford knew, was 'scent'. 'Pardon?' was equally unforgivable. The far sharper, earthier 'What?', preferably barked, was the term the upper class always used. 'Pudding' was always used over either 'sweet' (Nancy Mitford's non-U designation), or 'dessert', the term – thanks to the rise of the restaurant industry – that became its replacement. It didn't matter if the dish in question was a weighty suet number or a delicate sorbet – it was always 'pudding'. A further generation on and hardly anyone, save for a handful of proper aristocrats, really observes these terms. My children say 'Pardon', and I shrug my shoulders.

But one thing that has not faded is the strict vocabulary used for rooms in the house. It is the sitting room, never the lounge. Airports and hotels have lounges, homes do not. Occasionally, in large houses there is a separate drawing room, a word that has slight pretensions to grandeur but is used liberally by smarter Rockabillies and proper aristos. But the strictest of all rules is what you call the smallest room in the house. And, of course, using such a twee term as 'smallest room in the house' immediately marks you out as *déclassé*, desperate to hide your working-class background – someone who probably uses a loo-roll cover and has a novelty doorbell chime. The Middleton classes may, in their newspaper, department store and supermarket of choice look exactly like the old upper classes, but scatological terminology is the key stumbling block. It is never the toilet, nor the lavatory. It is the loo. Like 'What?', this is plain, simple, direct. A hallmark of those with the confidence of knowing they were born to be in charge and that they are always understood. Interestingly, Nancy Mitford said U people used either 'loo' or 'lavatory'. But I am assured – by those that know – that the Queen uses 'loo'. According to my father, the only person to use 'lavatory' in his house when he was growing up was the nanny, a sign that it was a 'genteel' word to be avoided.

As an aside, the *Telegraph* style guide insists on lavatory. But this document, which sits on the desk of every staff writer at the newspaper, banning the use of certain words and offering guidance, is the last bastion of old-fashioned form. Gays, for instance, are always 'homosexuals' and couples have 'sexual intercourse' not 'sex'. Every time I have to type the word lavatory in copy for the newspaper (it happens surprisingly often), I slightly shudder and fear that readers will think I have actively chosen this word.*

But, let's be clear: how you decorate the downstairs loo is now more important than what you call it. Back in 1954, of course, the very concept of an inside loo was a middle-class one. In 1950 half the homes had no bathroom, let alone an indoor loo. By the mid-1960s there were still 1.5 million homes in Britain without a bathroom. The 1951 Women's Institute House at the Ideal Home Exhibition, which was the most popular attraction at the annual event, did feature an indoor loo on the first floor, but more people cooed over the outside loo with its own washbasin.[4] Katharine Whitehorn recalls that when she worked on *Women's Own* magazine in the late 1950s they were not allowed to run features on bathrooms because not enough people had them and any article would promote envy.[5]

Now that everyone has an inside loo, the middle classes have taken to using the room as a gallery to their success. The Victorian middle classes had cabinets of curiosities to display their rich and varied hinterland. Their modern equivalents have a downstairs loo. Those that don't have 10,000 acres and 36 bedrooms in Northumberland to their name have to satisfy themselves with a few square feet of space. Condensed into this cubicle must be the following items, all framed: a school

---

* *The Times*, which has lost its dominance when it comes to setting guidelines for English, has a far more liberal approach to the whole loo/lavatory/toilet debate. The *Times Style Guide* states: 'Lavatory can now be used interchangeably with toilet. Reserve the use of loo for informal contexts.'

or university sports team photo; a university matriculation or graduation photo (double points if it is of one of those we-are-all-wearing-loo-seats-as-necklaces-larking-about group shots of the Junior Common Room); any newspaper clipping in which you have appeared (triple points if it is an appearance in *Private Eye*); a photograph of you posing outside Buckingham Palace clutching your MBE; any awards (though a jokey 'Most catches dropped in a season' certificate is clearly preferable to a 'Legal 500 rising divorce lawyer' accolade); a photograph of the loo's owner posing with a celebrity, sports star or world leader (double points if it is signed with a personal message). Deduct points if it is a member of the Royal Family. If you really are well enough acquainted to receive a Christmas card signed Elizabeth and Philip you would know that it is vulgar beyond belief to frame such a thing. Instead, it is left casually but prominently atop the chimneypiece (Nancy Mitford says mantelpiece is non-U, though this distinction really has fallen from usage) or piano. The Queen, bless her, ensures that her card is enormous and invariably involves a photo of herself – so all your guests spot it the moment they enter the room.

My parents, having both hated much of their school careers and not having gone to university, never really entered into the spirit of the competitive downstairs loo. There was a newspaper clipping, and (a little showy this) a drawing of the family coat of arms. But they played the trump card: a framed Spy cartoon of a great-uncle. These were the fairly flattering caricature portraits done by Leslie Ward and published in *Vanity Fair* during the late Victorian and Edwardian periods. He worked his way through most of the aristocracy, so there are plenty of these prints to go around, and they now serve the purpose of showing that even if you have failed to achieve distinction yourself, you are descended from someone who did.

Jeffrey Archer's greatest social crime – far greater than infidelity or perjury – has been the almighty chip on his shoulder which manifests itself in his endless need to preen himself on his success. No more so than in the choice of how he decorates the guest loo of his penthouse flat in London. It contains a Renoir, a Courbet and a David Hockney self-portrait, hung on wood-panelled walls. In doing so, he completely fails to grasp the point of this room – it is, yes, a place to show off, but the cartoons, pictures, photographs and emblems must be artfully self-effacing.

The downstairs loo, for the Middleton classes or Rockabillies, is what the parlour was for the 1950s working classes: a public place that revealed your status. The parlour was the sitting room at the front of the house – where the aspidistra was kept flying and an occasional table really was occasional. High days and holidays were the only times anyone trod in these rooms, but the cushions were plumped, the grate was cleaned and the rug beaten just in case someone called. The room was not for living in, but for display – proof that the family was proud, respectable and clean.

And it was brutally hard work keeping the house clean. Not for nothing did William Beveridge name squalor as one of his five 'giants' that needed to be slain by the Welfare State. Dirty curtains, grimy windows and unwashed front steps were frequently cited by the working class as reasons to disapprove of their neighbours, and the most obvious signifiers to distinguish between the so-called 'rough' working class and 'respectable' working class. By 2013 squalor has mostly been slain along with disease. The jury is still out on idleness, want and ignorance. But this was achieved, after the war, not by the introduction of Beveridge's national insurance system, but by a revolution in people's own homes: the introduction of so-called 'white goods'.

So, let us return to the kitchen – or, in the case of Portland Privateers and some of the wealthier consumer classes, the separate utility room – and examine electrical appliances. If the garlic press and chicken brick were the emblems of a middle-class life of comfort in the 1960s, it was the washing machine in the 1950s. No other domestic appliance better encapsulates the post-war consumer revolution than this expensive, noisy and temperamental piece of kit. It can now be picked up for a mere £180 from Argos, the equivalent of just three days' work on the national minimum wage, but back in the late 1950s it was not unheard of for women to opt for a washing machine rather than an engagement ring, such was its allure, and expense. Then, it was possible to spend more than £100 on one – almost £2,000 in today's money.

My father-in-law reckons his family was one of the first to buy a washing machine in Workington, in 1952, though it was a pretty basic piece of kit that only saved some of the labour of wash days. 'It was a square tub, a top loader, with an agitator in the bottom. You filled it from the tap with a hose. It had a rubber wringer attached to the top – a mangle you operated by hand, though it was never called a mangle. The beauty of it was when you pulled an article of clothing out of the machine it was straight into the wringer; you wrung the water out of it and it ran back into the machine. There was no mess, no transfer of boiling water.' It still required plenty of elbow grease but it was a liberation nonetheless. 'The women were very pleased

with it. I had been involved [in the weekly wash day], as everyone in the house was, and believe me it was bloody hard work.
The whole place got steamed up to hell; you had this boiler
boiling away, you had the dolly tub full. When it came to sheets
and blankets, two men had to come in just to lift them out and
put them into the mangle.'

He was just one of many to hail the innovation, which was
for most people a serious investment. A 1956 study, undertaken by Mass Observation, found that the average housewife's working day was 15 hours long, at the start of this
labour-saving revolution. Of course, the benefits of this craze
for white goods were most felt by the middle class – the many
hundreds of thousands of households who before the war
would have employed one or two live-in servants, but now
could no longer afford to, or find willing applicants to fill the
attic rooms. The upper middle class still had staff, even if they
weren't necessarily live-in, to do their washing. Some of the
last people to invest in washing machines were those who
could best afford them – because they continued to pay humans
to do the labour.

The companies selling these machines promoted their products relentlessly as a cut-price cook or housemaid. Kenwood
used the catchphrase 'Your servant, Madam', while Mercury
vacuum cleaners' line was 'Drudgery's out!'. Colston Classic
dishwasher played on the housewife, who may not have been
the one handing over the cheque, but was undoubtedly the
one increasingly making the purchasing decisions: 'You may
be beautiful, but a Colston is in better shape to be a
dishwasher.'

At the time these appliances were thought by many to be
agents of great social change, with their valves and rotary

blades able to whizz away social divisions. The economic journalist Norman Macrae noted in 1963 that the 'solicitor's wife with three children and no mother's help in Wimbledon' and the 'steel worker's wife with the same size family in Middlesbrough' led very similar lives. 'Each has the same modern equipment in her kitchen and a vacuum cleaner cupboard.'[6] This was in part true, but as the decades progressed, and the gadgets piled up, the divisions became clearer than ever.

It is difficult to imagine, in an age of remote-controlled lights, Sky Plus boxes and in-car DVD players, quite how few appliances there were in the average house of the 1950s. Even at the end of that decade not enough homes had either central heating or a telephone for the Office for National Statistics to measure them, fewer than a quarter of homes had a car, and just one in eight had a refrigerator. The washing machine, though, was really starting to take off, with just over a third of homes having one, and ownership of these gadgets was particularly prevalent in the north of England. Televisions, too, had become the norm, with two-thirds of homes owning one within just seven years of the Coronation.

Of course, all of this was made possible by the advent of electricity – one of the great democratising forces of the 20th century. In 1966, the year the first electric train service ran in Britain, an advert appeared in magazines from the Electricity Board Showroom entitled 'Plug into Electric Living', which pictured a housewife wearing a house coat, gazing wistfully out of her modern, airport lounge style glass-fronted house, waiting for her husband – or is it the postman – to ring the doorbell. 'Electricity … why, you take it for granted! To the older woman, electricity means cleanliness, relief from all the work of fires and boilers, from being tied to household chores. Electricity means she can sit back and relax, just when she needs a break. The woman in her 20s or 30s can't imagine life without electricity. It gives her the soft light, sweet music, fresh food, hot water, warmth in the home, freedom from the drudgery her mother didn't enjoy.'

The implication was that now she was no longer on her hands and knees brushing the carpet, she had the time to day-dream about an affair with her next-door neighbour, but the advert also shows that it was still a relative novelty for many. Electricity was also significant in giving teenagers their own space – they could now retire to their bedrooms in the evening to do their homework, or read, or listen to the radio. Impossible in an age of gloom and darkness.

Now, the Wood Burning Stove kitchen has not just a washing machine and a dryer, but also a dishwasher. In addition the following gadgets are considered imperative: a toaster, an ice-cream maker, a bread maker, a food processor and an electric whisk. These are necessary because of the need felt by many of the WBS school to distinguish themselves as home cooks. The ultimate proof of having escaped the tyranny of the supermarkets is to make as much of one's own food as possible. This, of course, is hard work and time consuming. But the expensive, bulky bread maker is a short cut to achieving domestic goddess status. It may be an ugly machine, but it produces something so low-tech, so centuries-old and redolent of some peasant idyll, it is forgiven its place atop the kitchen work surface. On the same basis, the microwave is often absent from their kitchens, despised as an engine to process cellophane-wrapped ready meals and banished from the house entirely or at least hidden in a cupboard or utility room.

Wood Burning Stovers look down on most electrical appliances, except where they are strictly necessary, or where they are elegantly slim. Hence the iPad is considered perfectly acceptable, so too a retro Roberts radio, which looks as if it could be straight out of the 1950s, playing *Mrs Dale's Diary*. For them, a house full of gadgetry and wires is a sign of being low class, of being obsessed with material goods and of desiring an electrical bypass to happiness.

Those who most readily embrace gadgets are the Asda Mums and the Hyphen-Leighs. Juicers, popcorn makers, SodaStreams, electrical deep fat fryers, George Foreman grills and Gordon Ramsay waffle-makers can all be found in these households. In the same way that Asda Mums enjoy branded food, and Hyphen-Leighs like distinctive branded clothes, both groups take comfort in a well-known name on their kitchen gadgetry, especially if it is promoted by a TV cook, be it an Antony Worrall Thompson knife block, a Hairy Bikers tagine or a Gordon Ramsay electric searing griddle.

Rockabillies just adore Jamie Oliver and snap up any saucepan, spice grinder or barbecue tongs with his name on – a crucial bit of kit when grilling on the beach in Suffolk. The WBS gang, tutting as they walk past the Raymond Blanc two-burner gas barbecue in John Lewis, do make one celebrity chef exception: Nigella and her kitchenware. That's because she can get away with pretty much anything on account of her Establishment lineage, her beauty and the fact that her products are classy wooden salad servers, melamine bowls and stainless steel measuring spoons – not an electric plug in sight.

This explosion in gadgetry is a result of the astonishing deflation that has happened in the white goods industry in the last half-century. This has come about as technology improved exponentially and manufacturers outsourced labour to the Far East. Back in 1958 there were just three 'automatic toasters' on the market, with the Morphy-Richards Automatic Electric Toaster costing the equivalent of £120 in today's money. Now one can pick one up in Argos for £4.99.

But there were two other impetuses to the white goods revolution. The 1953 budget had cut various taxes, crucially purchase tax on luxuries such as washing machines, vacuum cleaners, refrigerators, televisions, radios and cars from 66 per cent to 50 per cent. This was one of the key measures that would allow Harold Macmillan to declare four years later, 'Most of our people have never had it so good.'

And the lubricant that greased this engine of social change was hire purchase. This form of borrowing had been in existence since the 19th century, but it took on a life of its own in the 1950s and 60s, as demand for expensive labour-saving devices rocketed in the jet age. And, as payday loans have become a source of angst for many now, so HP or buying stuff 'on tick' was often looked down upon half a century ago. But it was the only way the aspirant Middleton class families could afford to keep up with the consumer revolution.

The concept was simple. The consumer puts down a small deposit and can take away the goods. But – unlike with a credit card – the television or three-piece suite remains the property of the hire purchase company until the consumer has paid off all their instalments, usually over a few years. Of course, the instalments in total add up to much more than the original price of the goods. Alongside the lowering of purchase tax in the 1953 Budget, restrictions on HP had been lifted – putting yet more fuel into the jet engine. Its importance was highlighted by the fact that it was tackled as a subject in the second-ever edition of *Which?* magazine in the spring of 1958, published by the newly formed Consumers' Association.

Very few could have afforded to buy many of the domestic appliances outright, and credit cards were in their infancy. American Express did not arrive in Britain until 1963, and the first fully-fledged UK credit card, Barclaycard, did not arrive until three years later. So it was not surprising that even John Lewis – always the most financially conservative of department stores – was happy to ply hire purchase.

Which? reckoned from a survey of its members that the average family owed about £200 on hire purchase (about £3,500 in today's money). And its members were decidedly middle-class professionals, educated and politically aware. It boasted in 1959 that its original 5,000 members included 13 architects, 65 army officers, 203 doctors, 32 peers and other titled people, 17 teachers, 32 clergymen, 3 journalists, 29 RAF officers, 1 former cabinet minister, 1 bishop, 6 MPs and 5 magistrates.

My father-in-law happened to end up at the coal face of the HP revolution, in Workington, Cumbria. While he was setting up his first hotel after leaving the merchant navy, he found he had time on his hands in the mornings and took a part-time job from an acquaintance who ran a domestic appliance shop, R. McCulloch. It started off as a repair business, but soon branched into sales – offering west Cumbria's steel town the gleaming industrialised products that promised an end to drudgery. McCulloch needed someone to go around collecting bad debts, so my father-in-law, the most unlikely bailiff, took on the job of knocking on doors. 'They were renting televisions at 8s 6d a week, but by the time we got to them they were sometimes £15 in debt.'

As is so often the case, working-class consumers had calculated exactly how to, if not beat the system, at least take full advantage of its weakness. 'It was very common to go into someone's home and find two, or even three, televisions or washing machines.' If their machine broke down and they had not kept up with their payments (which entitled them to free mending), they just went along to the next company and hired another TV set or washing machine. Hire purchase had one huge advantage over other forms of credit – return the product and your bad debts were as likely as not to be cancelled. And with no national system of credit checking in the early 1960s, it was very easy to have three washing machines or televisions, and not have paid more than a few shillings for any of them. 'Workington people don't like paying and they are all capable of living above their income,' says my father-in-law disapprovingly of the town, which remains resolutely working class.

The use of credit or hire purchase was not in itself an indicator of class (even Harrods offered HP), but it was common for many middle-class commentators to sneer at the working class for using it. Nella Last, the diarist in Barrow, whose everyday chronicles were dramatised on television by Victoria Wood, said in 1956 of her cleaner: 'Mrs Salisbury often makes me gasp. She was paddling around in a nasty old pair of rubber-soled shoes. I said, "Oh, Mrs Salisbury, look, you are making marks all over the carpets. Haven't you brought your old slippers?" She said a bit mournfully, "No they have fallen to bits, these old booties are all I've got" – and yet she is paying for a £108 TV set and a "racing" bike for her schoolboy, though he owns one good enough to go to school on it!!'

Middle-class disapproval of working-class splashing out on household appliances is as strong now, if not more so. During one of Jamie Oliver's campaigns a columnist in *The Times* wrote: 'How come they've got no decent food in the fridge but they can afford a 50in plasma TV, commentators moan? Because of years of interest-free credit and "buy now, pay later" deals, that's why.'[7] Hire purchase hasn't disappeared; it has just renamed itself 'rent to buy' and one of the most successful retailers of the last couple of years has been Brighthouse, which sells a large range of leather dining chairs, Nintendo Wiis and Samsung mobile phones to people who pay weekly instalments until they have paid back enough (often as much as twice the retail price of the item) to own it outright.

But it is not so much the method of payment as the size of the television itself which garners most criticism. Let us move from the kitchen into the sitting room. This is now, in most homes, dominated by a large flat-screen television, especially the homes of Sun Skittlers. By 1974 four times as many of the very poorest households – earning under £12 a week – had a television as had central heating. The flickering light of *It Ain't Half Hot, Mum* was warm enough for most, it would seem. By the mid-1980s the Office for National Statistics stopped recording how many households owned a television, taking the view that any family that did not own one was a statistical anomaly. To this day the less than 1 per cent of consumers who don't own a television are not those at the very bottom of the socio-economic scale but a certain hard-core faction of Wood Burning Stovers, who refuse to let themselves or their children be corrupted by the small screen. Or rather the large screen.

For, while it is highly unusual to have no television at all, it is rare to find a WBS household with a screen above 40 inches – for at this grotesque size there is a fear the electronic monster will pose a threat to both the stove itself and the pictures, especially if the machine is mounted on the wall. 'Vulgar', a word rarely used by the WBS for fear of being seen as a snob, is reserved for anyone who attaches a large television above their mantelpiece. The average size of new televisions was 21 inches in the mid-1990s, but thanks to improvements in technology it leapt up to 37 inches before the end of the noughties and it is now fast approaching 50 inches. In the eyes of many who carry their home-made couscous to work in a Tupperware box, they are the ultimate symbol of rampant, electronic consumerism whose purpose is to drug the owners with a constant stream of talent shows and ITV celebrity programmes. They fail to see that a £1,000 stove that combusts bits of wood is at least as consumerist and environmentally unfriendly as an item of technology that both entertains and informs.

Part of the objection is that Wood Burning Stovers, being curiously old-fashioned, believe walls are for pictures. Even though they've spent a fortune on Farrow & Ball paint or Sanderson wallpaper, the walls of the sitting room have to be covered in pictures. The easiest way for this group to distinguish themselves from the great mass, from buyers of branded and processed goods, is to purchase a picture from the Affordable Air Fair or a car boot sale, or ideally something they find during their August trip to Umbria. Preferably it should be modern, bold, large and, that dread term, 'a conversation piece'.

Rockabillies go for framed family pictures – of weddings and holidays, and of their children prancing about, possibly taken by a professional photographer (a friend of a friend), inevitably in black and white. Even chocolate-smeared Ottilie or Rufus can look passable when captured in slow-shutter-speed black and white. The key look is to have a welter of photos hung as if it were the Royal Academy summer exhibition, in a jumble of artful disorder.

Bizarrely, while framed posters are completely acceptable, a shop-bought print is deemed *déclassé* by Rockabillies or the WBS class. Worst of all is a Jack Vettriano print – *The Singing Butler* being the nadir – or anything by Beryl Cook. This is not a matter of taste; it is a matter of class. Both are pilloried by the garlic crushers for the greatest sin of all: being popular. Vettriano is lambasted for his pictures being 'badly conceived soft porn', while Brian Sewell, the art critic, said only 'fools' could buy Cook's bestselling comic pictures of ordinary daily life, which had 'the intellectual honesty of an inn sign for the Pig and Whistle – a vulgar streak'. These two artists are enormously popular, which means they will be ever cast out into the wilderness to be enjoyed only by Asda Mums – a favour they are only too happy to return. When Cook died, one fan paid this tribute: 'She made people smile everywhere, her work was so special to normal working-class people. Brilliant.'

My father-in-law, like so many working-class children, grew up with prints of *The Boyhood of Raleigh* and '*And when did you last see your father?*' – improving, historical and narrative works that had been bought from the Co-op, like all of their furniture.

Let us leave the sitting room and pass through the hallway and up the stairs. As we do so, can you catch a hint of a certain scent? The delicate but unmistakable fragrance of magnolia and vanilla? If so, you are in an Asda Mum household. Nothing quite defines your class like your preponderance for air fresheners. Once upon a time air fresheners, which came in an aerosol can, were just a little common. Smart people, if their house smelt, opened the window. But in recent years the multi-billion-pound household goods industry has spawned a mass of different products, all of which promise the buyers quite literally the smell of success. Traditionally, the upper classes relied on freshly cut flowers – or hyacinth bulbs at Christmas time (a poinsettia was irretrievably blousy) – to scent their homes and prove to the outside world they could afford a gardener, or the leisure time to propagate plants themselves. Then along came scented candles. Functionally, there is no difference at all between a £38 Diptyque Heliotrope candle and a £4 Brazilian Mango candle from Glade. But in class terms one is a countess, the other a coal miner, though the dowager of all of these, Jo Malone, has completely lost its exclusive aristocratic image and become increasingly common – in both senses of the word. It was the scent that Jade Goody – the reality television star and archetype Hyphen-Leigh – chose to wear to her grave. Nonetheless, smelly candles remain a cut above and the default gift of choice for a Wood Burning Stover short of inspiration for a birthday present.

In the hierarchy of fragrance, scented wax is followed by those smelly sticks in a jar (pretentiously called 'scent diffusers'), which are a notch above pot-pourri (even Poundland now sells pot-pourri), which in turn trumps anything made by Ambi Pur or Glade. Asda Mums, mostly, are responsible for the astonishing success of 'plug-ins'. An Ambi Pur 3volution Oriental Spice is the smell of an Asda Mum household distilled. The scent of bamboo and star anise, combined with the electronic gadgetry, make this the ultimate symbol of a home that still has a 1954 front parlour mentality. This is a proud home where money has been spent making it right.

Nostrils clear, we enter the bedroom. Here, in the most private of sanctuaries, matters of taste and class collide and it is difficult to disentangle one from the other. Is it modern or *moderne*? Is it a brass bedstead or just brassy? One person's comfortable is another person's outrageous oligarch's oil-spill of *luxe*. Portland Privateers often hanker after the crushingly boring good taste espoused by the property developers, the Candy Brothers, in their temples to 'luxury' – the chief of which is One Hyde Park in London, a block of flats that boast of being the most expensive square footage on sale in Britain. It carefully steps back from Iraqi dictator chic (you won't find any gold taps in the bathroom), but manages to be vulgar all the same. The padded leather walls, the suede banquettes, the lights that dim at the flick of a wrist waved in front of a control panel, the vast oversized fur throws that pile up on the bed: all of these are signs that the owner is just too busy to do it themselves. An interior designer is hired to strip the house back to a white cube, as if it were a modernist art gallery, before the escutcheons of success are pinned to the wall and nailed to the floor. It's not the supersized cost of these furnishings; it's the international five-star hotel look of the place. Too much Abu Dhabi, not enough Abingdon.

The Wood Burning Stovers, as they have done for decades, hanker after something more traditional, a little bit of country house. This love of the old is not new. In the 1970s Conran himself recommended the farmhouse style as 'a manifestation of the wave of nostalgia which is sweeping through every developed part of the world'.[8] An Aga was the perfect welcome 'for a farmer returning from his fields – or a fugitive from the city rat race'. The 1980s, an era famed for its revival of chintz, championed by the design company Colefax & Fowler, saw the Sunday supplements become stuffed with adverts for sets of china, silverware, decanters. The rural, pre-industrial idyll enraptured the *Good Life* middle classes just as much as the Victorian middle classes had embraced the Arts and Crafts movement. Suits of armour, sherry decanters and ironwork gates were promoted as 'future heirlooms'.[9] In the 1980s my parents-in-law bought a brass barometer they'd seen advertised on the back of the *Sunday Times* magazine. This object, naff nostalgia bought in the hundreds of thousands, could almost be a more accurate symbol of the aspirant middle classes than the bought council house.

Even more ubiquitous than the barometer, as the Thatcher era gave over to Major and Blair, was slapping liquid history on the walls, via Farrow & Ball paint. The shades all came with laughable names such as Radiccio, Elephant's Breadth, Mouse's Back, Dimity and Brassica (I really haven't made these up), but it was the promise of heritage, of a bit of National Trust authenticity, that made the extremely expensive paint so popular with the *Homes & Gardens* crowd: Print Room Yellow and Picture Gallery Red for the Rockabillies who can only dream of living in houses with print rooms and picture galleries as their grandparents might have done; and for the Middleton classes there is Cook's Cream or Larder Blue from Fired Earth to remind them of how far they have travelled since their grandparents were in the servants' hall and scullery.

But for the Wood Burning Stovers the hunt is always on for something that is unequivocally authentic, as part of their relentless quest to escape all that is deemed synthetic and manufactured. And when it comes to décor that means 'vintage'. They shun most things bought out of a catalogue (unless it is from the likes of Cabbages & Roses), or the porcelain frogs and comedy draught excluders from Lakeland that the Middleton classes might fall for. Vintage is a word that has become a catchphrase for many of the modern consumer classes. It neatly sums up not just a look, but a whole philosophy in the way that Terence Conran envisaged back in the 1960s. Ironically, for all the dreams of country house living, the real cornerstone of the vintage vibe is the adoption of working-class products and materials. In the same way that Conran stocked Habitat with pre-war brown teapots and wooden clothes pegs, nothing pleases the modern WBS decorator more than wooden church chairs with prayer book slots in the back, tin mugs to store toothbrushes, jam jars for 'wild' flowers, metal light pendants that once hung on factory floors, Bakelite wall clocks, quilts that look as if they have been made by your grandmother. Of course much of this stuff is fabricated or artificially distressed and sold with an enormous mark-up.

Aspiring to the look is not the sole preserve of WBS consumers; the large, popular retailers have got in on the act. An impressively large array of Farrow & Ball paints can now be found at Homebase (though not its slightly more downmarket, but far more successful, rival B&Q), while both Tesco and even B&M, a discount store that took over many of the vacant Woolworths shops, have co-opted the word 'vintage' to sell slightly more upmarket furnishings and sugar bowls. These products are invariably made in China. Meanwhile the recession has only served to accentuate the craze for old, broken furnishings in the belief that second-hand, hand-crafted objects are symbols of sensible thrift. This is in most cases a myth perpetuated by the WBS classes, who just can't bring themselves to buy something at half the price from a 99p Store or ScS.

Kirstie Allsopp is the vintage vibe's girl guide. Having perfectly tapped into the middle class's obsession with property, the television presenter moved on to imploring her followers to hand-blow their own Christmas baubles, visit car boot sales, rummage around skips and crochet their own napkins in order to save precious pennies in the recession. The key message is that even on a budget your house can look like a cover spread for *Homes & Gardens*. This is technically correct and it's hard not to admire Allsopp (and her ilk's) ingenuity, but these crafty, home-making activities require phenomenal amounts of spare time, the sort of luxury that only comes with a Rockabilly house stuffed full of 'help', be it a nanny or cleaner.

Cath Kidston, the designer who epitomises the middle-class rage for nostalgia, admits that there is only a thin line, if one at all, between 'junk' and 'vintage', the only difference being the price and whether it has passed through the correct hands – be it After Noah in London or one of those little antique shops you find in Wiltshire. Buying a £40 'Bevelled Vintage Mirror, with distressed Cream Effect' from B&Q just won't do. You get a better quality of distressing in the Cotswolds or the Yorkshire Dales. As one particularly smart shop in Winchcombe, just outside Cheltenham, boasts, 'Perhaps you own a rustic country home and need a faded or distressed pine table. We can help!' Even better, as hundreds of Kidston kids discovered, was the 2010 Chatsworth attic sale, when the Duke and Duchess of Devonshire sold off hundreds of surplus mantelpieces (or should that be 'chimneypieces', as we are talking about Nancy Mitford's nephew), statues, chairs and door knobs, raising an eye-watering £6.5 million. You couldn't get more authentic. Kidston herself recalled an early success in a radio interview: 'I can remember buying a pair of antique leather armchairs from a car boot sale in Gloucester. And I put them on the back of the truck and drove up to London and sold them on the Monday morning. I think I paid £50 for them. I sold them for £1,000. I can remember thinking – that's just unbelievable.'[10]

She has created an empire that makes £15 million in profit every year on the strength of this insatiable demand for products that most working-class consumers of the 1950s and 60s would have gladly swapped for a new formica table and metal sink. She is self-aware enough to admit that her look is despised by many. Her taste is perilously close to that espoused by the WBS gang, but they are suspicious of her Cotswold-tweeness, and many *Guardian* readers think Kidston's fabrics sum up all the smugness of the smelly candle brigade. She herself has said her look provokes a '*Marmite reaction*' – 'People either love it and want a little bit of it very much, or want to stab us.' She is, incidentally, a cousin of Allsopp, who also divides opinion just as sharply. Another *Guardian* reader described her as a 'smug, useless toff'.

It is the commercialisation, the branding of what is meant to be an artless, car-boot look that arouses such a sneer from the purest of the Wood Burning Stovers. They are resentful of how effortlessly Kidston and Allsopp co-opted their look and style and packaged it up, popularised it and sold it on to Debenhams and B&Q, where Allsopp acts as a design expert. Conran wanted his good, simple designs to be democratic, something that a newly qualified teacher could enjoy. His heirs want to keep the look to themselves.

* * *

Back in 1958 Raymond Williams wrote in his ground-breaking work about the British working class, *Culture and Society*, that many people thought 'the working class is becoming more bourgeois because it is dressing like the middle class, living in semi-detached houses, acquiring cars and washing machines'. But he went on: 'It is not "bourgeois" to possess objects of utility, nor to enjoy a high material standard of living ... the worker's envy of the middle classes is not a desire to be that man, but to have the same kind of possessions.'

Now, in 2013, there is nothing more bourgeois than to desire the objects of utility – though not the standard of living – of the working class of the 1950s. We have come full circle. When luxury was a bucketful of coal and an inside loo, one moved up the social ladder by acquisitions – fridges, televisions, washing machines, three-piece suites. The microchip, the valve and cheap labour, first in Taiwan, then in China, meant that even families on modest incomes could enjoy fabulous comfort and entertainment without leaving home. Even if it was bought on tick. Now we all have this comfort, the ultimate luxury is furnishing your home with a 'look'; a look that ideally involves few plugs, and with all the technology hidden behind a Farrow & Ball painted cupboard under the stairs. We have all become set designers, dressing our private homes as if they were public stages.

CHAPTER 5

CLOTHES

In an era of 'democratic' fashion and bland, uniform high streets, how do we end up despising some garments and hankering after others? Here we meet the Hyphen-Leighs.

In November 2002, Danniella Westbrook, a former *EastEnders* actress more famous for her cocaine habit than her skill on screen, was pictured in head-to-toe Burberry, the fashion label. Not just her, but also her handbag and her daughter, clutching a buggy lined in the distinctive Burberry beige, red and black check. It was as if she had rubbed herself with glue and rolled in the pattern. The tabloids called it a 'fashion crime'. Burberry had trouble on its hands.

The picture was splashed across the tabloids and the newly emerged celebrity magazines of the time, especially *Heat*, which had honed an irreverent mocking tone towards actors and singers. The reaction seemed to hint that Burberry's trademark check, which had been embraced by many celebrities, was becoming a bit of an embarrassing rash. It was the undoing of a lot of good work by Burberry, which in the previous few years had skilfully reinvented itself. The company, part of the Great Universal Store empire, which owned Argos as well as various downmarket clothing catalogues (including a line of Ramsay Street shell suits, inspired by the Australian soap opera *Neighbours*), was a dull raincoat manufacturer. But it had an illustrious history, supplying everyone from Humphrey Bogart in *Casablanca* to Roald Amundsen on his trip to the South Pole, and held two Royal Warrants. The new management successfully traded on that heritage and widened the appeal of the company while taking it upmarket onto the catwalks. Kate Moss was hired as a model, Mario Testino as a photographer, a range of not-outrageously-priced accessories such as sunglasses and bikinis were offered, as well as ultra-expensive luxury garments. The company was spun off from its Argos parent. All appeared to be going well. 'Doing a Burberry' became shorthand for successfully re-launching a tired old brand.

The Westbrook incident was not a one-off blip, however. Over the following year, Nick Griffin, the leader of the far-right British National Party, was pictured arriving at a local council election count in Oldham flanked by two minders wearing Burberry baseball caps. Burberry was spotted on the backs of a number of football hooligans during a particularly troublesome England vs Turkey match. And then pubs and clubs started banning any clientele who were wearing the scarves or hats. Alan Bannerman, owner of the Phoenix bar in Dundee city centre, said: 'If a young man walks in with a shaved head and a Burberry cap and shirt, I wouldn't think twice about whether he was trouble. I believe I speak for at least 90 per cent of pub owners in Dundee. Burberry has become the badge of thuggery.' The company, and its ability to survive as a high-end catwalk brand untarnished, was being questioned not just in the tabloids, but increasingly by the serious fashion press and marketing magazines.

It got worse, because then along came the chavs. Back in 2002, when Westbrook was smothering herself with the Burberry lotion, this term had hardly any traction, and was used only by a handful of people in pockets of the country. The etymology of the word is fascinatingly opaque, but by 2004 it was on everyone's lips. Indeed, it was *The Oxford English Dictionary*'s 'word of the year' (this is often a class-based word; in 2011 it was 'squeezed middle'). It was used mostly in a derogatory, occasionally ironic way, frequently both, to describe a member of the lower working classes, especially a sub-segment that had a penchant for designer labels, heavy gold jewellery, tracksuit bottoms and white trainers. The term cleverly yoked together a fashion look with a social class. Pram-face, Croydon facelift, chav. And Burberry was the brand more than any other associated with this class. The *Sun* ran a whole series of articles that supposedly stuck up for the chavs as they were being vilified left, right and centre – and all the pieces were printed on pages edged in the Burberry check. In the run-up to the Euro 2004 football championships both Posh Spice and Coleen McCloughlin, then girlfriend of Wayne Rooney, were spotted wearing Burberry bikinis. Then Goldie Lookin Chain, a comedy rap group, spray-painted a Vauxhall Cavalier car in the distinctive Burberry check. They called it the 'Chavalier'. At this point Burberry's headquarters, which had remained aloof from the whole hoo-ha, intervened and ordered the car to be destroyed for breach of copyright.

Christopher Bailey, the head designer, tried to be diplomatic. 'I think it's easy to be cynical. We allow individuality in England, and I think that's why, certainly in the design world, we're respected – because we allow that expression.' He claimed many fashion houses had made themselves too exclusive and Burberry's success had been precisely because it had not been snobby about widening its appeal. 'It doesn't need to be about this small clique of people who are the only ones who understand it. This is a democratic industry and I love that.'

But that was the problem. A luxury goods brand, by definition, can't be democratic. Its allure rests in being exclusive, not inclusive. It has to be out of reach of the mass market, not just in its prices, but also in how and where it distributes its products. Rita Clifton, the chairman of the consultancy Interbrand, explains the secret of a high-end, elite brand: 'At core you've got to get a great product. Retail experience is critically important. Where you buy it, how you buy it, whether the staff are knowledgeable and well presented, this all matters. But the one thing you can't control is who buys and wears the brand. You can have the wrong sort of customers.' Burberry had the wrong sort of customers.

In many ways, the Burberry chav movement was no different from the Teddy Boy movement of the 1950s or the Casual subculture of football fans in the 1980s. They should be seen as attempts by a small section of the working class to assert their individuality from the drab, mass-market look of the time by appropriating a bit of high-class fashion. For the chavs it was top-end Bond Street designer labels; for the Casuals it was the chic tennis brands they'd spotted on the Continent when watching their football teams play in Europe; for the Teddy Boys it was the New Edwardian (hence the name) look that was being marketed on Savile Row for those with aristocratic wallets.

One of the buyers of Burberry was Hayleigh, who now looks – and consumes – as if she is a fully paid-up member of the Asda Mums or even Wood Burning Stovers: dressed in Next, sipping cappuccinos. But in the year Westbrook was pictured overdosed on Burberry she was 17 and had just had her first baby. For her, Burberry was something more than just a simple badge of status; it and the other chav brands such as Dior and Ralph Lauren offered hope and security. 'When my son was born he had a Burberry sleeping bag thing, like a little blanket that had poppers at the bottom. One side was the check pattern and the other was blank with the Burberry logo. It cost £200. And I took lots of pictures of him in it. And he had some little Burberry slippers, which he never really wore. And those Burberry trousers which you rolled up at the bottom so you could see the check on the inside. Ralph Lauren T-shirts, a Timberland coat – I'd spend £400 on kids' designer clothes.' She wasn't working, and her partner worked as a cook in a pub. How did you afford it? 'I saved up the money. On reflection I would never do that now. For me it was showing to everybody else that I was not just another teen mum. And I was young. A lot of this spending, I think, was because when we were growing up we never had brands; shoes were given as Christmas presents and a coat as a birthday present. And even now, though I'd never dream of putting the kids in Ralph Lauren T-shirts – that's chavvy to me – it is very important that my children look nice.'

The official line from the company was that the UK was a very small part of its global empire and it was suffering from no more than a little local difficulty. Behind the scenes it was working frantically hard to take control of the situation. It started aggressively to crack down on fakes, and also to take control of its supply chain. Many, indeed most of the accessories covered in the red, black and beige pattern, were made by licence holders, who paid Burberry a fee. The fashion company fought to take these licences back. The manufacturing of baseball caps was stopped, so too little whisky bottles covered in the check. Moss, the girl from Croydon, was replaced by Rosie Huntington-Whiteley and the Old Etonian Eddie Redmayne. At one point a third of Burberry products had the check pattern on them; this was drastically reduced to less than 10 per cent.

A decade later, the company has been enormously successful at repositioning itself once again. The company is now worth over £4 billion; its catwalk shows are the highlight of London Fashion Week; it makes beautiful, elegant clothes for beautiful, elegant people. Westbrook is but a dim memory. So too the Chavalier. But the scorn that many showed towards Burberry-clad chavs has not faded. It came about not only because of deep-seated class prejudices among many Britons, but also from a fear of anti-social behaviour that was whipped up by both the media and the Government, at a time when the crime rate in Britain had just passed its peak. Most of the anti-Burberry sentiment was, of course, directed at the wearers of the brown-and-red check, not the brand itself. But the clothes and the wearer became intertwined. In the new millennium, it seemed, what you wore was still very much part of the fabric of your social class.

*   *   *

There is a famous photo from the Hulton Archive entitled 'Toffs and Toughs', taken in 1937, which shows two young Harrow schoolboys, clutching silk top hats, with carnations in their buttonholes, leaning imperiously on their canes, outside Lord's Cricket Ground. They are dressed in morning coats, with the distinctive 'sponge-bag' striped trousers, waistcoats, bow-ties and detachable round collars. Meanwhile, three scruffy-looking, slightly younger working-class boys, in open-necked shirts and scuffed shoes, one of them wearing shorts, grin with great amusement and some derision at their 'superiors'.[1] The Harrovians appear oblivious to the sniggering going on just two feet away. It brilliantly, in one shutter-frame, encapsulates the gulf in dress and attitude between the top end and bottom end of pre-war society. But here we were, more than 70 years after that famous photo, just as obsessed by the tiny details of decoration: of how a beige and red plaid, or the back-to-back woman and man logo on a Kappa tracksuit, or the weight and cut of an Argos bracelet immediately signified a social class. And more than that – derision of that class.

At the other end, the morning coat, the uniform of the Rockabilly or Middleton for any wedding or a trip to Buckingham Palace to pick up your OBE, is so potent as a symbol of privilege that it sends a shiver of fear through many. David Cameron, a former public relations man who is obsessed – possibly more so even than Tony Blair – with how the public view his background, turned up to his sister's wedding in a standard lounge suit. This was remarkable because he was an usher at this wedding and all the other ushers were wearing morning suits. Cameron himself is a fully paid up member of the Ocado-shopping Rockabillies, for whom a country church wedding automatically entails checking one's waistcoat, morning coat and sponge-bag trousers haven't been attacked too viciously by the clothes moths. Not to wear one was perverse in the extreme and done purely for the benefit of the cameras. He did not want to be cast as that boy outside the cricket ground. Absurdly, what Cameron would or would not wear to the Royal Wedding became the subject of a heated debate in the week before the big day in 2011, with one tabloid screaming: 'You're a toff, just get over it.' For the record, he eventually did the right thing and put on a morning coat.

In the last 60 years there has been a great democratisation of fashion. Anyone can wear anything. Plummeting prices and mechanised, offshore garment production have meant that the majority of consumers can afford a merino wool cardigan, wool suit or silk skirt, in the same way they can afford a 40-inch flat-screen television. Tesco sold 10,000 £25 cashmere jumpers in the space of two weeks during Christmas 2001, popped into shoppers' trolleys alongside the pint of milk and mince pies. And following a radical reappraisal of what is or isn't acceptable to wear out in public, more or less anything goes. Apart from at weddings, a Duke is just as likely to wear a pair of jeans as a dustman, and a Lady will lounge in a tracksuit as regularly as a ladette.

Fashion is meant to be society's great leveller. But this utopia has never been fully realised. Where once it was the decorations, the fabrics of the garments themselves – tweed caps, flat caps, ladies' gloves, buttonholes, tie pins, nylon stockings, cufflinks, silk – that divided society, now it is mostly the brands. Everyone from a JD Looter up to the Duke of Cambridge wears a hoodie – the key issue is: Where is it from? Which company made it? More than ever, certain labels stick out as brightly as high-visibility jackets alerting oncoming traffic to the class of the wearer. In one camp, Boden swimming trunks, Jack Wills low-slung trackie bums, a Joules tweed jacket edged in pink ribbon all scream: 'Yaah, watch out you don't get trampled by my polo pony.' Meanwhile, Golddigga purple studded fur boots, a Juicy Couture baby pushchair in brown and pink stripes emblazoned with 'Juicy Princess', a Marc B handbag and a pair of leopard print denim shorts from Henleys all flash:

'Steer clear, I'm council house chav.' Or at least, that's how it can often seem.

Even more complex are the brands that once upon a time started off as elite, such as Burberry, but have been hijacked and are now suffering from 'prole drift', to borrow the rather marvellous phrase of Paul Fussell, the American academic, who noticed the adoption of high-end fashions and habits by the American proletariat, and despaired at the 'class sinking' of society.[2] Ralph Lauren and Hackett have been hit by this phenomenon in the past. Ugg boots most certainly have fallen into this camp, and Barbour quilted jackets and Hunter wellington boots have crept in recently. So too salted caramels, Phuket and Molton Brown.

How class has seeped into the very fabric of brands and garments is a strange turn of events. And it is one not entirely of our own making. It has come about because, alongside the great democratising influence of fashion in the last 60 years, there has been a competing tension – the increasing need felt by consumers to strike out, to distinguish themselves from the mass market. This tension has been well understood by the high street companies that have supplied the great majority of clothes sold and worn in Britain. And they, in turn, have done an excellent job at both fuelling those anxieties through clever marketing and targeting very specific and different customers. We like to think, most of us, that in an age of endless choice our decisions – not least what we wear when we get up in the morning – are governed by free will. But the brands that ended up in your wardrobe chose you, just as much as you chose them.

To get to the bottom of this, we need to wind the clock back to a time when choice was not just limited, but almost non-existent for great swathes of the population. In the run-up to

the Second World War, and in the years immediately after-
wards, it was hardly conceivable that a working-class man,
even in his Sunday best, could be mistaken for a City stockbroker. The upper classes and the working classes – and all the
gradations in between – dressed differently from each other. It
was mostly a question of money, but it was also a question of
availability. Lola Smith, an East End girl, who left school at the
age of 15 to work in an upholstery factory in the mid-1950s,
was a member of the first generation ever to be described as
teenagers. Years later she became a Sun Skittler, using her
burgeoning income to take holidays abroad. She dreamed of
dressing differently from her parents, though her options were
limited. 'When we were 15 we'd have our clothes made by a
dressmaker if it was something different. We'd get *Vogue*
magazine and cut a skirt out of that page, and a jacket out of
that, and go down to what we called the lane – Spitalfields –
buy the material and go to a dressmaker and get it made up. It
wasn't expensive. Two pounds or so.'

Do-it-yourself seamstressing was also an abiding childhood
memory for George Davies, a working-class Liverpool lad who
went on to create three of the biggest clothing brands Britain
has ever known – Next, George at Asda and Per Una at Marks
& Spencer. 'My mother was a snob. She was a very proud
woman. In those days she thought all clothing shops in
Liverpool were so rubbish, the quality was not good. But she
was an amazing seamstress. I can remember the whole family
in the farmhouse sitting down and cutting patterns and sewing.'
When he won a place at grammar school, he was sent off in a
blazer with customised silver buttons.

If you wanted to stand out from the crowd, and money was
tight (as it was for most people), your only real option was to

make it yourself. Otherwise, your choice was limited to just a handful of shops, whose main purpose was to attempt to help their customers fit in, rather than stand out. Two of the leading companies of the time enabled the aspiring working class, and lower middle class, to dress in a cut-price version of what their superiors wore, even if they possessed little or no skill with a thread and needle. They were Marks & Spencer, especially for the women of Britain, and Burton for their husbands.

Of course, I am biased. Montague Burton, as I've said, was my great-grandfather. Originally known as Meshe Burton, he was one of hundreds of thousands of Jews who escaped the Pale of Russia in search of a better life, and in 1900 he arrived in Hull at the age of 15 speaking only Yiddish and a little Russian. He had hoped to reach New York, but either he was, like many, tricked into thinking Hull was the gateway to the land of the free, or he just ran out of money and never left Yorkshire. He started his career in England as an unlicensed pedlar, selling shoe and boot laces from a basket, hawking them around door to door among the poorer back streets of Leeds. He ended it having become Britain's sixth biggest employer, producing 13.5 million uniforms during the Second World War, and clothing one in three of all demobbed soldiers, having landed one of the key Government contracts to provide a three-piece suit to all men leaving service – the 'full monty', as legend has it (though there are other explanations as to how this expression was coined). Burton, at the time, boasted of being the biggest tailoring company ever seen, with its enormous manufacturing facilities in Leeds turning out 1.5 million buttons a week. The Hudson Road factory boasted its own savings bank, an opera society and 13 billiards tables for workers' recreation, while its staff sports club could turn out two football teams, five cricket elevens and a ladies' cricket team.[3] Most impressively of all, it contained the biggest canteen anywhere in the world, able to serve 8,000 cups of tea in five minutes.

Perhaps his greatest achievement, in his eyes, was the way he helped working-class people climb up the social ladder. He himself had gone from penniless Jew to a knighthood in one generation, and he was keen that others should better themselves. To a tailor, that meant dressing as smartly as possible, of being able – through the judicious purchase of some clothes – to quite literally disguise your background. Some of his adverts at the end of the 1920s make this desire clear: 'Montague Burton clothes will assist your upward endeavour.'[4] The annual report in 1933 boasts about improving the style of working-class men: 'We are justly proud in having made a considerable contribution towards making Britain the best dressed country in the world, so far as men are concerned.'[5] In most countries, he believed, two-thirds of the working men 'wear garments that fit no better than overalls and are made of material very little superior to dungarees.' He later wrote: 'The caste in dress, which used to separate class from class, can be said to have disappeared in my own business lifetime.'[6]

He actively sought out working-class customers and even used to have shop workers parading outside the entrances to football grounds on a Saturday afternoon with sandwich boards around their shoulders, to catch the eye of any working man looking for a 25-shilling vicuna suit.

By the 1950s there was a hope that the big chains of clothing stores could play their part in ushering in a classless society. Laurence Thompson wrote in the *News Chronicle* at the time: 'Before the Welfare State there were broadly two classes of consumers, the middle classes who had the money and the working classes who hadn't. Now there is only one class and I am told that many a débutante wears a Marks & Spencer nylon slip beneath her Dior dress as if she were just a Gateshead factory girl.'[7] This remained one of the abiding characteristics of the big chains even up to the 1980s, when Next was described breathlessly as the first chain that allowed secretaries to dress so elegantly that they could be mistaken for their female boss. And for many, the ability to assimilate and match the look – if not the accent or swagger – of those in the class above has been the overriding concern in their choice of clothes.

My father-in-law, who had made it to grammar school, would, as an older teenager, meet his fellow scholarship boys at the Tognarelli espresso bar in Workington, which exists to this day. On a separate table were the 'town toffs', boys who'd all left the grammar school at the age of 13 to go off to public schools – the sons of doctors, owners of successful shops, managers of the steel works. You could tell, from their accents and confidence, and their motor cars parked outside, that they were a class above. But by the mid-1950s, with money coming in, the working class could at least start to match them sartorially.

'Pre-war I would have had a flat cap, a pair of trousers and jacket of indeterminate origin and a very down-at-heel pair of shoes. That's how a lad of my age and class would have dressed. But as it was, in the early 50s I had a Harris tweed jacket with dark brown trousers from the Co-op and brown brogues from Saxone. No one looked better, in my opinion.' But though both groups of young men looked smart, there was still a division in where they shopped. 'The toffs would never have stepped inside the Co-op, they went to Burt Curwen, the gentleman's outfitter, but we didn't think much of his outfits.'

Burton would have been the natural choice for an aspiring working-class lad wanting to make a good impression, and there was a branch in Workington. But Burton didn't offer credit, nor a dividend as the Co-op did, a crucial draw for many. 'My grandfather was on the Co-op committee – we were obliged to shop there, partly because of the divi and the credit and savings clubs which were available. Co-op shoes, drapery, hardware, grocery, tailoring were all very good quality, slightly dearer than Burton, but the divi took care of that. As a result, we bought nothing at Burton and bought nearly everything at the Co-op.' But despite the appeal and quality of products on offer to the working classes shopping at the Co-op, style was fairly low down on its agenda. 'I can remember going to Carlisle [30 miles away] for a pair of Saxone Wegians, after longing for them. A very nice pair of shoes. They were 63 shillings (about £70 in today's money). The sort of shoes Gene Kelly wore. Really lovely. The Co-op never had anything like that.' But though he shopped in different stores, and fancied himself as a snappier dresser than the town toffs, he had no particular desire to stand out and certainly no interest in celebrating his working-class roots. He was already on the way towards the Middleton classes.

The Teddy Boys revolted against all of that. They burst onto the scene just before Bill Hayley started rocking around the clock – in that seismic year of 1954. At first they were a south London working-class phenomenon, and the term Teddy Boy was a derogatory reference to the fact these teens had hijacked the clothes and style of Savile Row, which at the time was attempting to recreate the look of the Edwardian dandy for young aristocratic men about town. But it wasn't because they wanted to look like toffs; they wanted to steal elements of their style and fashion, parody them, make them their own, and create a whole new look.

Remembered fondly now as a movement that ushered in quiffs and 'brothel creeper' shoes, Teddy Boys, despite being few in number, were widely feared, especially after a boy on Clapham Common was murdered by a Ted, who had been taunted with the words 'flash cunt'. A common practice among Teds was to place fish hooks behind the lapels so anyone grabbing their beloved long jackets in a fight would get their fingers trapped in rather nasty fashion.[8] There was a real fear that Teddy Boys, like chavs two generations later, were downright degenerate and that their influence was spreading. One middle-class Mass Observation interviewee, in 1957, said: 'Death penalty should be kept. I don't think they should have done away with the cat [o' nine tails]. It might have curbed these Teddy boys.' But what the chavs, Casuals and Teds all have in common is a desire to celebrate their working-class status. They don't want to be like the drab, dull, pencil-pushing middle classes or the upwardly mobile Middleton classes in their Harris tweed jackets from the Co-op. They have no desire to assimilate, they want their own style. And if that upsets the mainstream, so be it. This was very similar to the case of the JD Looters.

During the London riots of 2011, JD Sports, a chain of leisurewear shops selling trainers, tracksuits and a few items of casualwear, appeared to be the clothing retailer of choice for the looters to steal from. One of the rare moments of comedy was when pictures were published of a looter on the pavement outside a JD insouciantly trying on a pair of trainers, to make sure they were the right size, before putting them under her arm and walking off with the booty. This episode turned out to be the tip of the iceberg. Some looters queued up in smashed-up stores to use the machine that takes off security tags, before casually popping their stolen goods into a JD Sports draw-string carrier bag, which swung from their shoulders like a class tag, just as a canvas Whole Foods tote helps label the Wood Burning Stovers.

Peter Cowgill, chairman of JD, explained to me at the height of the troubles how his company had become a magnet for the disaffected – and indeed criminal – underclass. 'We are the premier branded sport and leisurewear company in these areas. And I know it sounds like a plug, but we are the destination of choice for aspirational young people.' Even for rioters? 'You'd be surprised – the harder hit the area, the more significant branding and design of the garment becomes. These people don't have mortgages, or cars. Their clothes are the strongest status symbol they have. We provide the best collection of brands available to these people.'

What is the appeal of these brands sold by JD, and indeed the shop itself? One was the price. For less than £60 consumers can buy a heavily branded pair of Diadora trainers, an Adidas top or Nike hoodie. These are not dirt cheap by any stretch of the imagination, but they are affordable to the majority of young people. And for that price the consumer is getting a very clearly branded piece of clothing that is associated with a number of edgier sports and music celebrities that these manu-facturers have assiduously cultivated. Though it is right to scorn the looters' wholesale plundering of these products, their desire to own them is understandable. It is the same desire for status, bred from insecurity, as drives sales of Mulberry ostrich handbags in hot fuschia, with a £3,500 price tag, Alexander McQueen skull T-shirts at £400 a pop, Diane Von Furstenberg wrap dresses which cost at least £320. These are some of the branded items that the Portland Privateers wear with as much zest and pride as the JD Looters wear their apparel – they just happen to cost 10 to 100 times as much. There is plenty of high-end, ultra-expensive fashion to be had in Bond Street, Selfridges or on business trips abroad, but the items that end up in the shopping bags of Portland Privateers are those that shout about their provenance just a little too loudly. The Bond Street brethren may claim that their desire for these products is based on a discerning appreciation of the craftsmanship and design, but that's not the itch that is being scratched. Why else do McQueen's skull scarves do so well? Or Louboutin red soles? Or Tiffany key pendants? Or a belted, multi-pocketed Belstaff jacket? They are no more subtle than a Nike swoosh or a leaping Puma.

The Portland Privateers justify their extravagances by pointing out that they work ludicrous hours and pay their taxes, but both they and the JD Looters share a sense of entitlement. And both choose to demonstrate that entitlement through the very public display of fashion badges.

The other appeal of JD, as Cowgill pointed out, was location and assortment. What makes you shop at a certain place? At the most basic level, the answer is that you can get there easily and you like what they sell. Retailers site their shops in areas where they think there are enough potential customers to justify the expense of opening an outlet. This may seem an obvious point, and when so many high streets appear to be the same it may also seem an irrelevant one. But not all towns have a JD Sports, JJB or Claire's Accessories, and equally most don't have a Mulberry, John Lewis or Hobbs outlet. One of the few places you can buy Paul's Boutique fashion in London is at the Gallions Reach Shopping Centre, situated in the bleak hinterland between the Beckton gas works and the sewerage plant at the easternmost end of the Docklands Light Railway, where the only food outlets are McDonald's and Subway and the two grocery stores are a Tesco Extra and a 99p Store. And among the few places you can buy Louboutin are Harvey Nichols, in Manchester or London, and a boutique just off Bond Street.

Retailers decide where to open up by using sophisticated modelling techniques and data scraping, which ensures that there are plenty of 'the right sort' of shoppers in the postcodes within the catchment area. They pick those existing and potential shoppers by using Acorn, Mosaic or their own internal customer loyalty databases. As previously mentioned, these metrics don't just measure the income of customers, they measure whether they are home owners, if they have a second bathroom, and their propensity to buy wine over the internet, read the *Daily Mail* or the *Sun*, to holiday abroad on cruises or at home at Center Parcs; they split out the horsey types who like Ariat from the hoodies who favour Asics.

The clearest illustration of how carefully retailers choose their store locations is Jack Wills. This is a brand only a decade old, but one that has built up a loyal and very clearly defined clientele: public school (and those who aren't but wish they were), floppy-haired, rugby-playing, green-welly, university types. In short, the Rockabillies. The children of parents too grand to queue at 5 a.m. for a Ryanair flight to their summer holidays; instead they own or rent a holiday home in Burnham Market, Salcombe or Rock – all towns where there is a branch of Jack Wills. This is not a coincidence. The brand is inextricably linked to these wealthy, *Telegraph*-reading, second-home-owning, *Downton Abbey*-watching, Waitrose-shopping towns. Which other brand would avoid opening outlets in Cardiff, Newcastle and Sheffield in favour of having branches in Aldeburgh, Eton and Durham? It is unsurprising that none of the Asda Mums or Hyphen-Leighs, even the most brand-aware, had come across Jack Wills when I quizzed them. They just don't hang out in Chichester. However, Asda Mums do know all about Hollister – a brand that produces almost identically priced and similar-looking hoodies, thick-waisted and low-slung trackie bums, pink polo shirts, sleeveless puffa jackets aimed at wealthy college kids. It's not just that one is English and one is American. It's that one is in the yachty towns and one is in all the big shopping centres. The brand, therefore, reinforces – as many other shops do – the character of some towns, the money spent on those high streets, the class of the people doing that spending, the desire of those customers for a certain type of coffee shop, for the new range of Cath Kidston ironing board covers. Like attracts like, so in Burnham Market, Padstow, Aldeburgh and Salcombe you will also find a branch of Joules, a slightly more countrified version of Jack Wills, more Cotswold point-to-point than Cowes Week, possibly aimed slightly at the mothers of Jack Wills wearers but very similar nonetheless. The hoodies come with thick canvas drawstrings, often in pink, finished with a little brass aglet. The blazers are edged with ribbon, the wellies have a flower pattern lining, the children's shoes look like little kittens with a button sewn on for the nose and little cat's whiskers ('Martha just adores them'), the caps are tweed, the dog blankets are twee. The chance of spotting a Juicy Couture 'Juicy Princess' children's buggy in these towns is close to zero.

Stand outside a branch of JD Sports in Beckton, as I have done, and you will spot one every 45 minutes. In this way, postcodes calcify. And the wheels of consumer mobility start to rust.

The founder of Jack Wills, Peter Williams, has gone further in his ruthless pursuit of a certain type of customer. He has never advertised on television – a trick that many brands adopt, including Poundland and John Lewis (until five years ago), helping to build up loyalty among their customers by word of mouth. But Williams has spent plenty promoting the brand. His first ploy was to send one of the signature Jack Wills hoodies to the head girl and boy of every public school in the country. Since then, the company has sponsored the Eton vs Harrow polo match (don't ask) and yacht club balls, and designed T-shirts for the Eton rugby tour. Its emblem is a pheasant in top hat and tails. Its changing rooms are fitted out like public school dormitories – all poster-covered walls, and the floorboards of the shops are reclaimed oak. And the company hires what it calls 'seasonaires', attractive brand ambassadors who are paid to wear the clothes and host parties in various 'correct' locations around the world from the Méribel ski resort to beaches in Cornwall. They give out branded neon 'party pants' – unavailable from any shop.

He has also adopted, as Boden did until recently, a refusal to hire celebrities as models for the brand; instead he just uses glorified customers – honey blondes who look as if they might have gone to boarding school in Wiltshire. There are differing views within the industry about the best approach, but all agree it is crucial who is the 'face' of your brand. Rita Clifton at Interbrand explains: 'You need to signal through all your controlled and managed communications who you expect to buy your brand. Be that Rosie Huntington-Whiteley or Eddie

Redmayne. Who is seen to be using and loving your brand is critically important. Be it on the catwalk or the red carpet. That's what builds premium into the brand.' Boden is a hugely successful brand that started off as pure Rockabilly but has edged into Wood Burning Stove territory (though the militant end of the WBS can't stand its David Cameron toff connections). Founded by Johnnie Boden (Eton, Oxford, stockbroker), its first models were originally Johnnie's friends, who were captioned in the catalogue with twee descriptions 'Susie prefers puddings to starters', 'Edda's favourite English word is Fantastic'. Buy a bit of Boden and you too could adore scuba diving and be scared of spiders.

The alternative approach is to pick a celebrity who most embodies the aspirations of your customers. For Littlewoods, which has never strayed too far from its origins as a catalogue retailer for the working class of Liverpool, it is Coleen Rooney, wife of Wayne, who is a shining example of how you can – just through the power of consumption and expensive hairdressing – transform yourself from chav to *Vogue* cover girl in less than a decade. Celebrities, especially in our judgemental age, are invariably divisive. For every girl who thinks Coleen is a style icon, there will be one who can't stand her. Brands know this and gladly accept the trade-off – loyalty among a certain section of shoppers is preferable to indifference among everyone.

The big retailers too adopt this ruthless approach to postcodes, celebrities, brand affiliations and where they will and won't go hunting for new customers. Per Una was a brand started by George Davies for Marks & Spencer, aimed at a slightly younger, more fashionable, sequin-embossed section of customers than the grand old dame of the high street had previously catered for. He was meticulous about which branches of M&S would and would not get the brand. But he went further. Once he decided which branch got a Per Una section, he then specified which particular items of Per Una clothing that branch would have. Each store was different, depending on the class of customer in the catchment area. 'What I did, I divided up stores into bands. But I never called them classes, or numbered them. I called them Roma, Prato, Firenze; I named them after Italian towns. I knew, but nobody in the stores knew, which one was higher than others. The bands were done by how people lived. Clothing doesn't start first. Life starts first.

'I would then match up towns that then had a similarity. It could have been that Shrewsbury and Perth were in the same category.' So the reason your local branch of M&S doesn't have the nice, sparkly dress that Twiggy wears in the advert is that someone has decided that your local town doesn't have enough customers in that particular category to buy that particular class of fashion.

This quest for the right location, and in turn the right customer, is something that has always obsessed retailers. Back in the 1950s John Lewis employed someone called Patrick McAnally, who went on to become one of its most senior 'partners', running its research department. He would now be called 'head of customer insight' or some such tosh, but back then most of his job involved scouring weekly sales figures to see whether sales of nylons were beating those of 'modern foundation garments'; analysing reports from the Registrar General; standing with a clipboard outside various department stores, examining customers who came in and out, and noting whether or not they looked in the window; and visiting a town to see if it might make a good location for a new John Lewis or Waitrose shop. He was obsessed with ensuring that the company, then a rag-bag collection of different department stores all trading under their original names, attracted as many customers as possible, especially the upwardly mobile working woman, who was transforming the spending power of many families. He was also keen on ensuring that the wrong sort of customer stayed away. The company's current status as 'Britain's most middle-class brand' owes much to his work during the 1950s and up until the end of the 1970s when he retired.

In 1955 he examined Harlow, one of the New Towns, to see whether John Lewis should become one of the first of the big stores to open a shop there. Many of the working-class house-wives who moved to Harlow found that their new homes, full of labour-saving devices, left them with plenty of time on their hands and were keen on spending that new-found leisure time shopping. The town had potential, it would seem. But McAnally was not convinced. This he made clear in his report, which he had his secretary type and send to the chairman, as he always did. 'It is suggested by the Harlow Corporation that theirs is a particularly prosperous town, because a large proportion of the inhabitants belong to what the registrar general describes as social classes I and II.' He said that 19 per cent fell into this group. But he pointed out that the 19 per cent figure in the 'professional' and 'intermediate' categories (or what might then have been called upper and upper-middle classes) was not that spectacular when compared with Chelsea on 35 per cent and Harrogate on 28 per cent, and he was criti-cal of how the official statisticians classified certain occupa-tions, which put scientists in Class I. Once that was taken into account, 'Harlow might not look so high class. I should not think that scientists should be regarded as outstandingly promising customers for a department store.'[9]

He continued: 'The safest base for trading would be the working classes, not the 19 per cent of the population in social classes I and II. This seems to imply reducing the assortments and making sales more pointed.' In other words, John Lewis would have to cut back on some of its better-quality haberdashery and ladies' fashion to win over enough working-class shoppers to justify a new outlet, and that was not something he was prepared to recommend.

Throughout his decades at the company he fired off regular memos to the chairman, most of them in dry, concise fashion revealing the latest trends in business: time and motion studies, colour-coded charts, 'the technique of brain storming'. There are thousands of these memos – many of them the result of McAnally spending hours counting cars, people and fur coats with his clipboard. They unashamedly make clear that John Lewis's success rested on 'high-class shoppers', and that the company would wither if it failed to supply them with the increasingly sophisticated goods they required. Doncaster was eyed up as a potential location, despite its apparently small number of Class I and II shoppers. 'It's not just another slummy northern town. Quantities of respectable, boring council houses, many with space for garages,' he wrote. 'Middle-class cohesion or snobbery is more developed than in Barnsley or Rotherham, which are both three years behind Doncaster in car registrations. Other symptoms – Lucille's fashion parade, music at Danum Hotel on Sunday evenings, out of 13 cars parked outside Odeon, 2 were Jaguars, 1 a Rover, 1 a Zephyr.'[10] A John Lewis customer was one with a decent car, a desire to move on in the world, to do up their council house with some nice furnishings and perhaps dress up before going out to listen to some live music at the local hotel. For McAnally, 'snobbery' was not a negative term. Rather, it indicated a purposeful state of ambition and 'cohesion'. And it was for that very reason that Swansea was dismissed. 'The area does seem rather lacking in the constituents of gracious living. There is no Rolls Royce or Bentley agent ... Swansea does not have exactly the character that is now considered suitable for a Partnership store. It is rather too small and low class.'

A running sore for the company was the poor performance of the John Barnes department store in Hampstead, which John Lewis had taken over in 1940. In January of 1958 McAnally went to investigate. 'The customers one sees in John Barnes are not much to look at, and many of the surrounding buildings are 19th century houses from which the glory has departed.' He rattled off his analysis of the catchment area, which on paper looked very wealthy, with more Class I residents than in Chelsea. But on the ground, he could tell, it wasn't up to scratch: 'Kilburn: working class and unsatisfactory intellectuals, many coloured people. Hampstead old town: wealthy professionals and artistic. Priory: to the south west of John Barnes; terraced houses, much converted; middle middle class; many intelligent families.'[11]

Unsatisfactory intellectuals – the Wood Burning Stovers of their day, who would go on to make such a fuss about the proposed McDonald's in their neighbourhood in the 1980s – were clearly to be disregarded along with scientists; indeed, McAnally goes on to call them 'outré types'. He was also concerned that 'young Jewesses with plenty of money' were not being catered for. There was not a single evening dress on display the day he went to visit. He interviewed local residents about why they didn't shop there and he summed up one of the responses. 'The dresses all looked alike, "frightfully provincial", and they scorned the idea of making John Barnes a fashionable shop, mainly because it was unlikely to offer sufficient snob appeal.'

The shop eventually closed down in the early 1980s, before the McDonald's arrived, unable to compete with Brent Cross, the country's first out-of-town shopping centre, which had opened (with a John Lewis) a few years previously.

Snob appeal, then, was the key to John Lewis's success. As it is to this day. Craig Inglis is the company's marketing director and the man responsible for the tears thousands of women shed at the 'red dress' television advert that seemed to sum up the wholesome, comforting security of the department store – with you from birth to old age. He refuses to use the term 'middle class' to describe his customers, knowing that they come from a number of different categories, rather than from one large mass in the middle. The company, like many retailers, uses the Acorn classifications. 'The top 5 per cent of our customers represent 36 per cent of our revenues – within that top band, wealthy executives are massively over-represented,' Inglis says. He acknowledges the power of the postcode in driving customer loyalty. 'The value set you have is driven by affluence. It's not where you live that determines it. But where you live ends up being a subset of who you are and how affluent you are. In reality, we do congregate. Inevitably where you live sums up your affluence and what you aspire to.'

A son of a lorry driver and school secretary from Levan, 'a pretty grim mining community' in Fife, he admits that the department store cannot and should not be all things to all people, and that may mean actively ignoring those lower down the Acorn scale – the sort of family he grew up in – to keep its core customers happy. 'The Board had a long, active conversation. Should we broaden our base, should we extend downwards into that [Acorn] table? And we reached the very firm conclusion: no, we shouldn't. The impact of that would be not just in our marketing but in our whole proposition. We would have to make changes. Inevitably, there is a real risk that you would alienate the group here [he points to the top of the table] who would think that we were selling cheap and nasty products. We'd dilute our core proposition.' Diluting it would mean losing the snob appeal.

Of course, most John Lewis customers would be appalled at being labelled as snobs, indeed many would profess to neither know nor care about the brands they are buying in their local branch, whether it's in Cribbs Causeway or Edinburgh. The hardcore are the Rockabillies – a class whose roots are loosely in the old British country elite, but which has swelled far beyond its upper-class and upper-middle-class origins. At heart they are county rather than city, Labrador rather than Louboutin. They have just a fraction of the income of the Portland Privateers, though equally they don't have the outgoings. To an Asda Mum, both groups are 'middle class' or 'posh'. But while the PPs are a minority group based in a few postcodes in the Manchester suburbs, Surrey and London, the Rockabillies are a far larger but less visible group spread far across Britain, particularly rural Britain from Caithness to Cornwall. Crucially, the Rockabillies have a radically different attitude towards consumption. The older ones shun brands – or so they think – alleging that a lustful pursuit of a £6,000 handbag or £600 pair of shoes is immoral. They hate any jacket, handbag or hoodie (yes, even this lot wear hoodies) with a visible logo, deeming branding to be vulgar. Their criteria for fashion are comfort, fit, quality and price, with an abhorrence of paying too much and a distaste for big, flashy labels. For them, Marks & Spencer will do just fine (though they miss that lovely Stuart Rose); so too will House of Fraser, Fenwick, Gap or Phase Eight. They might even consider buying a pair of those comfy-looking shoes they saw in the back of *Telegraph Magazine*; and a trip to Poundland isn't out of the question for some party balloons or cut-price mint imperials. But John Lewis is their favourite. Why do they shop there? Because, as Rita Clifton of Interbrand says: 'The staff look clean, tidy and nice. You feel as if your son or daughter could work there. You know that none of the mothers will be smacking their children inside the stores.'

The younger Rockabillies are more brand aware and behind the success of Jack Wills, Boden, Johnnie B, Joules, Whistles, Reiss, TM Lewin and Thomas Pink. They have far fewer qualms about their polo shirts, hoodies, wellies or jackets carrying a logo. But what really drives their fashion choices is the look – all beach-kissed, boarding school, snazzy, polka-dotted brightness.

There are two items of clothing that make up the male Rockabillies, both old and young: a jacket and a pair of trousers. The jacket is a heavy, oversized, waterproof tweed number used for walking the dog, trips to Sainsbury's on a Saturday morning, out ferreting or shooting (the pockets are especially designed so the flaps can be buttoned open, for ease of access to one's cartridges). It comes in shades of lichen green, loden green or moss green. But mostly just green. Possibly with a faint check. It is not to be confused with a traditional gentleman's tweed jacket. This is a defiantly bulky, outdoor piece of clothing designed for cold Northumberland Novembers and biting Dartmoor Decembers and is supplied by only one or two companies, namely, Musto, the ridin', shootin', yachtin' brand promoted by Zara Phillips, or Schoffel, the German company, whose 'Ptarmigan' £500 jacket remains the key look for any Rockabilly man over the age of, say, 26. Obviously, at this price it is only worn by the wealthier members of the class, but those lower down the income scale are still prepared to splash out on a cheaper version, knowing they will keep it for years. But though the jackets are distinctive you won't see any brand anywhere on the garment.

When they are out shooting it is twinned with plus-fours, a tie with a pheasant motif (though why you would wish to decorate yourself with the image of an animal you about to kill in large numbers is a mystery), and a pair of Le Chameau wellington boots (they have their doubts about Hunter wellies ever since the company started to make bright pink ones and brought out a Jimmy Choo welly; also, the Duchess of Cambridge wears the more understated French brand). On a trip to Sainsbury's or Majestic Wine ('absolutely cracking value') it is fashioned with the second key item of this uniform: a pair of red trousers. Not bright pillar-box red, but a peculiar shade of deep pinky-burgundy, which is then faded. Boden call the shade 'raspberry', Lands' End call it 'vintage brick'. There is even a blog dedicated to this one item of clothing: 'Look at my fucking red trousers!' and very amusing it is too. The younger Rockabillies' penchant is for the brighter, pinker versions, especially the short versions from Jack Wills – perfect for an afternoon of banter over Mojitos on a sunny day outside the Holy Drinker on Northcote Road, Battersea.

Rockabillies are also fans of Barbour jackets, but they have started to have suspicions about this quintessentially Sloane brand. These waxed, dark green outdoor jackets were for decades the country uniform, worn by beaters and barons alike. They were seen in large numbers on the Countryside Alliance marches of 1998 and 2002, when nearly half a million protested in Westminster, ostensibly against the fox-hunting ban, but in truth more against what they saw as an irretrievably metropolitan elite who had failed to grasp the basic needs and aspirations of rural Britain, and their core constituency, the Rockabillies. The fact that many lived in Fulham was neither here nor there.

There is still much residual fondness for Barbour among this group, but the company's push to attract a younger crowd with the revitalisation of its Barbour International sub-brand has started to raise a few eyebrows. These International jackets, which look like belted biker jackets, with their brash branding stitched onto the breast pocket, along with the cheaper padded garments which come in pink, purple or even gold, have been adopted by a customer base a world away from beaters and loaders, whippers-in and whippets. The company has assiduously cultivated this urban clientele, selling its jackets on websites such as Asos.com, known for its young, fashionable customer base. One Asda Mum in particular that I met aspired to buying a Barbour jacket for her nine-month-old child. 'I don't have one, but I really like them. I would dress my baby in a Barbour coat. I like the little name on the pocket. It's quite posh.' The managing director of Barbour told me that he believed the company had suffered for many years from being seen as solely a supplier of 'country garments for toffs'. But how do you win over a new class of consumers without alienating the customers that give you your heritage? Simple – you segment them.

In the same way that McAnally meticulously categorised the correct postcodes for John Lewis shops, now brands group customers into different little boxes. It's like at a wedding, where you desperately try to ensure that Great Aunt Lucinda never meets the pole-dancing girlfriend of the best man. Hours of preparation, seating plans and stress go into ensuring everyone enjoys the same family event, while all experiencing a faintly different day. Barbour has various sub-brands, Heritage, International, Classic Country and Sporting. The Sporting stuff (big oversized green jackets, shooting, fleece gilets) is distributed to a handful of huntin', shootin', fishin' shops and websites, and these retail outlets are not allowed to sell any of the edgier International brand. Equally, Asos.com is not given any of the Classic Country or Sporting stuff to sell, and concentrates on the more urban ranges, including International and Heritage.

Barbour's approach is just a more transparent version of what most retailers do – from supermarkets refusing to stock various gourmet products in some postcodes, to Jack Wills preferring to open a branch in a tiny, second-home-owning, Bananagrams-playing seaside town rather than a vast Sheffield shopping centre. Everyone is at it. Even the mass retailers of middle Britain. In fact, especially them.

Of course, you might have thought the age of internet shopping would see an end to these class ghettos. If you can go trawling down the great virtual shopping mall online, does it really matter which shops are on your actual high street? Well, just £1 in £10 is spent on the internet, despite the proliferation of iPads among the Wood Burning Stovers and Asda Mums alike, and the percentage of what is bought online is lower when it comes to clothes. This is, of course, likely to creep up over time, but it is easy to overstate the internet's impact.

And there is another reason why web retailers make the class divide in fashion if anything more distinct rather than less. Just when Burberry's chav problems came to a head, a report was published by a think-tank called the New Economics Foundation, entitled 'Clone Town Britain'. It neatly encapsulated the anxieties of many consumers and was an astute analysis of how retailers had become ever larger, partly in a bid to negotiate better rents from powerful landlords. The landlords had become more conservative, keen to ensure they received large and reliable payments from their tenants, so they tended to favour substantial, well-known chains with national coverage. The winners were the supermarket chains, large fashion brands and coffee shops; the losers were butchers, independent boutiques and the traditional British tea room. As the writer Nick Foulkes said at the time: 'The homogenisation of our high streets is a crime against our culture. The smart ones get the international clones – Ralph Lauren, DKNY, Starbucks and Gap; while those lower down the socio-economic hierarchy end up with Nando's, McDonald's, Blockbuster and Ladbrokes.'[12]

The report overestimated the sameness of each town, and failed to take into account the scale of customer categorisation that went on within certain chains, ensuring that the M&S in Hackney in fact stocked a very different selection of clothes from the M&S in Hereford. But it was true that many of the independents were being squeezed out, and this was being made worse by the rise of so-called 'fast fashion', pioneered by Zara, Topshop, Primark and H&M, able to get cut-price versions of catwalk looks onto the high street in a matter of weeks, ensuring that many high streets not only had the same shops, but also the same fashions on offer within those shops. But with every movement there is a reaction, and the internet was perfectly poised to offer consumers freedom from this encroaching homogenisation. A number of little brands, which had started as catalogue retailers targeted at a few niche post-codes, successfully exploited the internet, able to offer discounts and promotions aimed at particular email addresses. Though some of the high street retailers, notably Next, have enjoyed success online, those that have made the most of the potential of the web have been brands without any real chain of shops and aimed at very particular demographics: Boden, Asos, Toast, Loaf, White Company, though this temple of all things pristine and perfect now has quite a few outlets.

And since then a number of other brands have come to prominence, without the aid of any high street chain or even national advertising. But they have used two of the main forces driving modern Britain – celebrity and the internet – to build an incredibly loyal following among one social class in particular: the Hyphen-Leighs. Adept at spotting status possibly more than anyone else, especially among clothing brands, these consumers tend to be young, in part because when you are a teen the desperate need to belong to an identifiable tribe – while rejecting any major mass group – is at its height. They tend to have lower incomes than average and know that purchasing a distinctive handbag or pair of trackie bums is an inexpensive method of asserting their rank. Double-barrelling their children's names is an even more public way to highjack a once grand practice and make it their own. But what really distinguishes them is their enthusiastic embrace

of the look espoused by modern reality television celebrities –
a strange hybrid of slummy mummy, with its slouchy, pyjama-
and-slipper look and Bond Street bling. In fashion terms, they
look up to Cheryl Cole, Coleen Rooney, Abbey Clancy, Amy
Childs and Beyoncé. Most of these role models have achieved
their fame through being a WAG or appearing on reality
television, and what they wear is what continues to keep them
in the public eye. The outfit modelled on every trip to the local
corner shop by one of these Made-in-Chelsea-Essex-Big-
Brother-Come-Walk-My-Celebrity-Dog-With-Me is snapped
and posted online, analysed, critiqued and available to
purchase within minutes. The Hyphen-Leighs may aspire to
some of the couture brands, but they enjoy the high street
versions, especially now money is tighter than ever. Plus, they
are brighter, shinier and more fun than the real thing – fast-
food equivalents of leather accessories and patterned blouses
to come out of Milan *ateliers*. They are Disneyfied versions of
high-end fashion for an infantile age.

Paul's Boutique, Lipsy (so successful that Next snapped up
the business), Henley's, Golddigga and Superdry are the key
suppliers to this class. All of these brands, to varying degrees,
have played the reality TV card, either by rapidly copying the
look that some of these personalities have worn, supplying
celebrities with free product to show off, or signing the stars
up to 'design' their own range. Lipsy has an Amy Childs (from
The Only Way Is Essex) range of clothes, as well as a collection
called Little Mistress by Lauren Pope, a page three girl,
'entrepreneur and music producer', and another to come out
of the TOWIE stable. On its website it also has a large 'As seen
on Celeb' logo stuck on top of any item of clothing spotted on
Little Mix, The Saturdays or Tulisa.

Paul's Boutique originally started as a Portobello Road market stall, and then graduated into a trendy niche brand available in Selfridges, before it became the epitome of Hyphen-Leigh style. Its 'handwriting', as the fashion press say, is to take a look and, in ice-cream terms, sprinkle it with hundreds and thousands, pour on some raspberry sauce and shove in a flake. More is more. Its handbags are oversized, padded and studded, many of them made from bright pink or white leather, and they usually have dangly charms or colourful ribbons hanging off the handle; its quilted jackets are embroidered with big bold labels, especially the 'I ♥ PB' logo; its tops are sequined, trashy and graffiti-inspired; its pink furry booties look like Uggs, but as the website says: 'It wouldn't be the same without gold-stitched PB branding and rear logo.' The company doesn't have its own retail outlets, but the clothes are mostly sold in Bank, a chain owned by the same parent company as JD Sports and which stocks Paul's Boutique, Lipsy, Ribbon and Red or Dead. The shops can be found in retail parks next door to the JD and are a world away from the achingly tasteful home of the founder, Paul Slade, where antlers are mounted on walls painted Farrow & Ball lichen shades and where the kitchen table is made from wood reclaimed from a Blackpool ballroom.[13]

Jodie, 28, a mother of four from east London, is a fan of the brand. She twins her bag, covered in skulls, over-sized roses, and logos with a Juicy Couture denim jacket studded with gold and pink sequins, picking out the name of the brand across the back. Her shoes are very distinctive Converse high-top trainers, which lace up the ankle, but which also happen to be toeless. Part sandal, part boot, Converse call them a Hi CT thong. 'I like glitzy stuff. I like Paul's Boutique. It's girly and a lot prettier than a lot of stuff.' I ask her what she would buy if she won the lottery and had to spend it on clothes. Zara, or anything in Selfridges, she says. But she has no interest in any of the Bond Street brands. 'Burberry and Mulberry are all a bit boring. Everyone looks alike. I'd just never wear that catwalk stuff. I like to look different; I like it when people check me out.' Even if that risks people judging her? 'I don't mind. I was brought up around here and if people want to call me a chav, fine. I suppose I am a bit of a one. I'd say that my style has a bit of a swagger. I like to look different.' She's not a chav, in the fashion sense. Yes, she embodies that original Teddy Boy spirit of refusing to fit in, of desiring to strike out from the drab mainstream. But she doesn't want to do it by purloining Bond Street labels. That is one of the defining attributes of this group of consumers: an enviable confidence about who they are and what they want, often mistaken by a fearful mainstream as a swaggering arrogance. Another fan of Paul's Boutique, Natasha, who owns five of their handbags, says: 'I love how bright and different they are. A Mulberry handbag is boring and ugly, but these are the trendiest stuff, really well designed and unusual.' Chavs aspire to big, bold, ultra-expensive brands. Hyphen-Leighs have already got there by buying the cheaper, exaggerated version. Colour, studs, gold, trinkets, pattern, logo, it's all there – sometimes a McDonald's can be more fun than Michel Roux.

* * *

Clothing creates social tribes more clearly than any other consumer product, because it is such a public statement. Of course not all sartorial cliques are related to class; some are mostly an age thing; many proclaim the wearer's music allegiances or sexuality. But a great deal are rooted in social anxieties and social confidence, whether the members of that tribe realise it or not. I refuse to buy a pair of 'fucking red trousers', however much I like the colour, because I am terrified that I will slip back into the Rockabilly class from which I escaped. But when I don some Boden swimming trunks to play cricket on a beach in Dorset, I realise that I have failed and am semaphoring my class in a way that makes me eminently punchable. So too, by wearing a Lipsy playsuit twinned with a Paul's Boutique Kimberley handbag, the consumer is proclaiming herself a member of the Hyphen-Leighs and inviting judgement. That is what class does. It segments us and differentiates us. It encourages us to think warmly about the group we are already a member of or aspire to be, and to look down on the groups to which we believe we are superior or from which we have escaped. Occasionally, it makes us despise ourselves. Nothing makes this judgement easier than brands – appropriately derived from the word for the exterior markings on cattle, seared into the skin, which allowed cowboys to herd them into different pens.

We too have been herded. How I ended up in Boden swimming trunks, and not in ones from JD Sports, is a process I did not have full control over. The catalogues that land on my doormat are determined by the postcode I live in, and the different databases on which I have ended up; my local high street and retail park have a collection of shops that more closely matches my lifestyle than I care to think about; while the adverts that I see on my computer, when I am reading a newspaper's website on the internet, are related to the online shops I have previously visited or products I have searched for. They go by the cute name 'cookies', but they are just a sophisticated, highly electronic version of McAnally's clipboard. Hey, Johnnie Boden emails me on a more regular basis than my own mother – is it any wonder I end up handing money over to him rather than JD?

Sixty years ago, it was perfectly acceptable soon after first meeting someone to ask what school they went to and what their parents did for a living, and to then draw conclusions about what sort of person they were. Now we don't even have to ask such intrusive questions. We merely look them up and down, clock the 'I ♥ PB' logo on the handbag, the Jack Wills branding on the rugby shirt, the camel logo on their green wellingtons, the particular shade of pink toggle used by Joules on their hoodies, or the large, cartridge-bearing pockets on the Musto green coat. Clothing is no longer our class disguise, it is our calling card.

CHAPTER 6

EDUCATION

Class war in the classroom. Can Britain ever be a classless society with a two-tier education system? We meet the Asda Mums again.

There are few Oxford colleges more elegant than Magdalen, which exudes an effortless, aristocratic superiority. It has its own deer park; a stunning bell tower from which its choir sings at daybreak on May Day morning; Edward VIII, Oscar Wilde, Lawrence of Arabia and C.S. Lewis are all alumni; the college can boast a greater number of Nobel Laureates than Ireland; it has won University Challenge more often than any other institution. It has never been the grandest of the colleges but there was always a sense that it was a cut above. It was a beautiful college for beautiful people.

So, there was an added spice when it emerged in the spring of 2000 that an application from an extremely bright, 17-year-old comprehensive school pupil from North Tyneside to read medicine at the college had been rejected. Her name was Laura Spence. And over the following months she was used by politicians and academics in an ill-tempered battle over elitism, Oxbridge and the standards of education. It was, and acknowledged to be so, outright class war. Toffs in their mortar boards and old school ties, sipping sherry, were ranged on one side, with ragged-trousered comp kids, waving the Communist Manifesto, on the other. Or so it seemed, so antagonistic were the arguments. It was not edifying, and came just three years after Tony Blair's government had come to power with the key election manifesto 'education, education, education' and a promise that class divisions were well and truly over. But the Laura Spence affair, which had started off with just a small story in the local paper, underlined how the British education system could never be divorced from the question of class.

At first glance, it didn't look good. Magdalen, which then had cocaine-snorting Lord Freddie Windsor as an undergraduate, had turned down Spence, who went to a comprehensive in Whitley Bay, a slightly down-at-heel coastal resort near Newcastle. Oxford's undergraduate intake was made up of 47 per cent private school pupils, despite private schools only educating 7 per cent of schoolchildren. Spence was applying for medicine and appeared an ideal candidate to help redress the balance. She had already gained 10 A-starred GCSEs and was predicted to achieve straight As at A-level. She had, off her own bat, taken an Open University maths course to boost her chances. But it wasn't to be, after she failed to shine in her interview, a notoriously tough exercise that favours, in the words of one Oxford academic, 'middle-class bullshitters'.[1] The rejection from Magdalen had come five months previously, but her headmaster, an American, persuaded her to feature in a local newspaper story after she had been offered a place and a £65,000 scholarship to Harvard following her A-levels. If America's elite educational establishment could see her potential, why couldn't Oxford? Her headmaster saw the case as simple, outright prejudice. 'As an American who was active in the civil rights movement, I see this as an issue not about admission, but about discrimination in a selection process. Many of the arguments mirrored those used to defend racism in employment back in the 1960s in the United States.'[2]

It was picked up by the national press and the letters pages hummed with indignation, with readers blaming the 'blatantly inequitable Oxbridge entry system', and its bias against women, its bias against the north east and most particularly its bias against bright, working-class pupils. Tony Parsons, author and professional working-class champion, raged: 'The elitist, pea-brained snobs of Oxford's Magdalen College have turned away Laura because she did not "show enough potential" at her interview. What they mean is that she did not have the right accent for Oxford. That she didn't go to the right school for Oxford. That she comes from the wrong part of the country for Oxford. We should all be getting mad as hell, not least because Oxford and Cambridge receive millions from our pockets. These final bastions of privilege and snobbery do not deserve one lousy penny from public funds until they understand that in this day and age the old school tie is only good for one thing: hanging some chinless old snob from an Oxford lamppost.'[3]

If this was a bit of harmless red-top rabble-rousing, Magdalen was in for a shock, because the story was about to go nuclear. Anthony Smith, the urbane President of the college, was given a tip-off. A former colleague who was now Gordon Brown's speechwriter telephoned Smith to tell him that Brown, then the Chancellor of the Exchequer, was about to give a speech but that Magdalen shouldn't make 'too much of a fuss'.

Standing in front of a Trades Union Congress gathering, Brown stated: 'It is scandalous that someone from North

Tyneside, Laura Spence, with the best qualifications and who wants to be a doctor, should be turned down by Oxford University using an interview system more reminiscent of the old school network and the old school tie than justice. It is about time for an end to that old Britain where what matters more are the privileges you are born with, rather than the potential you actually have.'

Smith, who saw his mission at the college to improve social justice, decided that, in fact, he would make a bit of a fuss. A former television producer (and one of the founding fathers of Channel 4), he had run the nightly news show *Twenty Four Hours* during the Wilson years, and 'bullying politicians' were 'meat and drink to me'. He and the college fought back, and pointed out that every one of the 23 candidates interviewed for the five medicine places at the college had the same grade predictions as she had. Of the five that had been offered places, three were women, three were from ethnic minorities and two were from comprehensives. It was unfortunate for the college that Spence's interview assessment – these are always sent to the applicant's school – fell into the public domain. The notes accepted that she would make a brilliant doctor, but she was, 'as with other comprehensive-school pupils, low in confidence and difficult to draw out of herself, despite being able to manifestly think on her feet'.[4]

Critics of the college saw the release of the notes as dirty tactics, and as an admission that it recognised that comprehensive school pupils were at a disadvantage but failed to do anything about it. It was the smoking gun which proved what so many people expected – that the system was rigged. The mud-slinging went on for weeks, with David Willetts, the Tory Education spokesman at the time, neatly summing up the quality of the debate: 'Behind the painted mask of New Labour's false modernity, lurks the dogmatic and ignorant prejudices of old Labour. Under pressure, the government reverts to type, invoking the ugly and outdated slogans of the class war.'[5]

And more than a decade later the class war continues to rage in the classroom. If anything it has got more intense, not helped by a Coalition government stuffed full of public school pupils and Oxbridge graduates and ones that look as if they have stepped out of the pages of *Brideshead Revisited* at that. They present, to their opponents, a particularly tempting punchbag, a collection of smug, expensively educated millionaires, who allegedly call public servants 'plebs' and perfectly sum up all that is wrong with the British education system. Two-thirds of the ministers in the Coalition are privately educated and indeed five of the 23 cabinet posts in the initial 2010 cabinet were Magdalen alumni. The two most senior positions in the land, the residents of numbers 10 and 11 Downing Street, were members of the Bullingdon Club at Oxford, notorious for its landed gentry membership and its champagne-swilling, plant-pot-throwing, plate-smashing, drug-taking antics.

It is easy to allow such excesses, eagerly reported in the tabloids, to colour our judgement of the education system. Rather than be grateful that our political leaders have enjoyed some of the best education in the world, we hold it against them. The idea of the man in charge of our economy being educated at an elite institution is somehow abhorrent. There may be a thousand and one reasons to despise George Osborne, but I don't believe that his degree from Magdalen is one of them. But then the education system in Britain has always been indivisible from the question of class, which seeps into every aspect of learning, from the French ballet lessons little Freya is taken to at the age of three, to the private tutorials given to Mungo, the postcode juggling to squeeze into the good local school, the row over inner-city children sent to Eton ... all the way up to the senior common rooms of Oxbridge. And along the way the arguments become very confused.

Most of the wailing centres on two separate issues. The first is whether you can buy your way to a better education. And secondly, if you have gone to an elite university (regardless of where or what you have done before the age of 18), do you stand a better chance of landing a top job? These are not difficult questions to answer. The answer to both is 'yes'. But conflating the two issues, as many people do, in a rage about the lack of social mobility in Britain, misses the point.

And it fails to help people such as Laura Spence. But then she probably didn't need any help. A decade on, after Harvard and then a stint as a postgraduate at Cambridge, she is now a successful doctor back in her home town of Newcastle.

*　　*　　*

It should never have ended up like this. The educationalists of 1954 would have despaired at the mess, and at the bickering that now colours the debate on education. Back then, the year when so much seemed possible, the Countess of Mountbatten, last Vicereine of India, opened the country's first purpose-built comprehensive school: Kidbrooke. Built on the site of a former RAF aerodrome on the outskirts of south-east London, it was designed by London County Council to be for 'the children of the heroes of the Second World War'. Those that ran it, including Roy Hattersley's wife who was the deputy head, hoped it was the presage of a new dawn, where the divisive 11-plus would be banished for good.[6]

The grammar schools of the 1950s and 60s were rightly lauded for offering millions of working-class children a golden opportunity to start climbing an educational ladder, a ladder which ended with university, a professional job and just a little bit of swagger. It was for many the catalyst, freeing them from a life of manual work and low expectations.

Terence Stamp, the actor who came to symbolise the excitement and the breaking down of class barriers in the Swinging Sixties, was one of many to put his success down to having passed the 11-plus. 'It changed my life,' he said in a radio interview, explaining that his parents had put huge pressure on him to pass. 'They were all hoping this next generation would not be galley slaves like they had been.' The son of a merchant seaman, based in the docks of east London, he knew the importance of passing it and getting into Plaistow Grammar School. 'I didn't want to be one of the hapless ones that went off to work for Ford's at Dagenham or drove a lorry for Tate & Lyle's at Silvertown.'7

Ruth Bale was another of the same generation, who saw it as an escape route – not necessarily to a career, but to a richer life, away from the tabloid-reading, ITV-watching world that her parents inhabited in their council house. 'It changed everything: the books I read, the culture I consumed, my aspirations. My German teacher took us to see *Der Rosenkavalier*, and I suddenly realised there was a world beyond *Double Your Money*.'

But for every child that passed the 11-plus, there were three that didn't. That was the nature of the tripartite system that came into being after the war. The top quarter of children who passed the 11-plus went off to grammar school, the rest either went to secondary moderns or technical colleges. Your social class was already being cemented at this young age. The exam designated millions as failures, whose only prospects were a few more years at school, before quitting at 15 to spend their lives at a factory conveyor belt or as a back office clerk. Anthony Smith, the man at the centre of the Laura Spence affair, was himself the son of a minor clerical civil servant, whom he describes as upper working class. 'When you passed the 11-plus, you just left those primary school friends who hadn't passed. And when you went to university you left behind those grammar school friends who hadn't gone. And you never saw them again.' The education system provided the foundations for the British class system – before children had a chance to make a mark in the world, they were segregated, segmented and judged.

Comprehensives would end this dramatic parting of the ways which split up so many childhood friendships, or even families. Kidbrooke was a controversial endeavour from day one. A right-wing magazine, *Time and Tide*, went so far as to suggest that the school's motto should be: 'All Equal and All Stupid'.[8] Questions were asked in Parliament by MPs worried about its likely impact. The theory was that comprehensives, while not demanding any entrance qualifications, would combine the best of grammar school teaching with the vocational lessons offered by secondary moderns and technical schools, which many believed to be doing little but making permanent the low social status of their pupils. An article in 1955 in the *News Chronicle*, written by John Laird, a New Zealander who had spent the previous two years teaching at various secondary moderns, attacked the lack of discipline, the lack of parental support and the absence of reading except for comics (the Playstations of their day – seen as ruinous to the moral well-being of children).

He concluded: 'We are still turning out from our State schools a very large number of children who in speech and writing recognisably belong to a "lower order".'[9]

There was also a concern that grammar schools, though in theory accessible to anyone bright enough to pass the 11-plus, were in fact the preserve of the middle classes. A survey of four central London grammar schools found that just 52 per cent of places were taken by working-class children – a figure well below its 70 per cent share of the population. And a report in 1954, 'Early Leaving', found that once at grammar school, a third of the children of unskilled or semi-skilled parents did not stay on for the sixth form.[10] My father-in-law was one such pupil. He grew up in a poor, working-class household, but nonetheless a bookish one – his grandfather who brought him up knew, as many solid union men did, that education and self-improvement offered a route out of the pit or, in his case, the steel works. But despite his passing the 11-plus and winning a scholarship to grammar school, the cost of a university education loomed large. 'As I got to know the sixth form and the routes out of it and the routes to university and all of the rest of it, I realised it could well be a problem. For instance, friends of mine who had gone on to university, with scholar-ships – county majors – were still needing a couple or three quid a week sent to them. They needed financial support. If I don't get a scholarship, I thought, we are in the clag.'

So he left at 17 to start as an apprentice engineer at the steel works – a job which within a few years paid enough for him to have 'a girlfriend, a car, and a regular smoke'.

Despite the early misgivings, politicians of all parties embraced the comprehensive system, not least Margaret Thatcher when she was Education Secretary. Kidbrooke, which was perpetually in the spotlight when it opened – with visits from the Queen Mother, Princess Margaret and most politicians – was deemed a success thanks to its disciplinarian headmistress. Comprehensives were to be 'grammar schools for all'. Leading sociologists, such as A.H. Halsley, strongly supported the idea, saying comprehensives would enhance social mobility and help bring about a more egalitarian society.[11] The final nail in the coffin for grammars was in 1975, when the Wilson government announced it would withdraw all financial support from direct-grant grammar schools – prompting the grammars with the highest reputation for academic excellence such as King Edward VI School, Birmingham, to choose independence and leave the state sector. The state system became more equitable, but the gulf between state and private became ever wider.

By 1975 there were 3,069 comprehensives with 2.46 million pupils, far more than all other state schools combined.

And by the time I went to school they were very much the norm – not that I would really have known it. From the age of two, when I was sent off to the Ladybird nursery in west London, till the age of 18, I was educated privately. And not just any old private schools, but some of the most exclusive in the country, whose fives courts, Greek handwriting competitions, rugby tours to South Africa and manicured lawns oozed superiority and separateness. This was not a two-fingered salute to the state sector on the part of my parents; they simply believed that if you could afford something you should pay for it (including healthcare and holidays). Plus, it was just what every single one of their contemporaries did.

Of the schools I went to, the most distinguished was the boarding school I attended between the ages of eight and 13. It was called Summer Fields, and it was blessed with a perpetual golden glow thanks to its location among the lush meadows of north Oxford, running down to the Isis, and the clientele. Old Boys included a former Prime Minister (the patrician Harold Macmillan) and an England cricket captain (the gentlemanly Gubby Allen); the school was smart rather than flash. Cricket and Latin were its twin religions, corporal punishment just about still existed (I can remember us all gathering round in the changing rooms to examine the cane marks on Charles Money's bottom), and war films were shown on the projector screen in the gym on a Sunday afternoon. The school's claim to fame, and its great attraction for a smart crowd of parents, was that it was one of the main 'feeders' to Eton. The parents were a curious mixture of old aristocracy and proto-Portland Privateers, people who were starting to make serious money in stockbroking and insurance, and a third bunch made up of Rockabillies, Barbour-wearing, ruddy-faced army types, who'd stand by the side of the 'rugger' pitch and shout encouragement on Saturday afternoons and drink tea out of a flask in the days before Starbucks made it to north Oxford.

We were informed by one history master that discussing money, politics or religion was forbidden at dinner parties. Only a crashing snob could have diverted our lessons about the Armada into tutorials in etiquette. But it was always crystal clear, among us pupils, who had money and whether it was new or old. When the school was raising funds to build an indoor swimming pool (it already had a perfectly good outdoor one), to celebrate its 125th anniversary, it became known that the entire bill, well in excess of £1 million, had been met by just five sets of parents. They included a Royal Duke, a Saudi Arabian arms broker, the owner of one of Hong Kong's great mercantile dynasties, and I forget the other two.

In my class there was a Russell (now brother to the Duke of Bedford), a Baring (of banking fame, before Nick Leeson destroyed the great institution) and a Parker Bowles; there was also at the school Stonor, Hon. R.W.R.T., heir to one of the most beautiful Tudor houses in England; Ulster, Earl of, the next HRH Duke of Gloucester; Guadalmina, Marques de; Hardwicke, Earl of, the youngest member of the House of Lords and one of a number of Old Summerfieldians who would go on to be caught by the *News of the World* offering cocaine to the tabloid's fake sheik.

For most of the time the large discrepancies in wealth and status between us group of privileged north Oxford school-boys was not apparent. But as time went on, one soon learnt to read the signals, and not just from the size of the Caran d'Ache pencil sets or the thickness of cricket pads.

At the end of each summer term there would be Sports Day, an event greatly looked forward to by the non-sporty types such as myself because of the picnic provided by one's parents. Mine, confirming their aristo/Rockabilly class, would always provide a game pie from Fortnum & Mason and some quails' eggs (the salted caramel of their day back in 1984), along with cherries from Sainsbury's and chocolate fingers or Club biscuits. Scotch eggs were most definitely frowned upon, but so too was anything so vulgar as knives, let alone tables and chairs. It was all devoured on a tartan picnic rug, eaten with one's fingers (or possibly a fork), spread out alongside the Ford Granada as one fought to stop the golden retriever knocking over the celery salt.

However, for the Portland Privateer parents, Sports Day became a picnic arms race. It was not just the flashiness of their Range Rovers that would catch the eye, it was the barbecues, the bowls of fruit, the cushions on the grass, the napkin rings. One year a parent brought along a horse box, in which a full-blown kitchen appeared to have been set up, complete with apron-wearing chef, serving burgers for any passing child. In due course the parents of the Prince Wenzeslaus of Liechtenstein arrived with not just chef, but butler too, to serve guests at their cloth-covered table. Finally the headmaster felt compelled to write a letter to remind parents that Sports Day was meant to be about the athletics, not the amuse-bouches.

We were endlessly lectured about the importance of good manners – I was hauled up to the deputy headmaster's study after I failed, at the age of 13, to talk to the lady on my left at a prefects' dinner party – but respect towards others didn't stretch much beyond the school gates. On the other side of the athletics track was the Cherwell School, one of the very best comprehensive schools in the country with 35 Oxbridge places won over the last three years. It is where many Oxford dons send their children, and it was about as Wood Burning Stove as it was possible to get in the state sector back then. Many of the pupils would walk down a public path that bisected our playing fields on the way home or to school. We, whose only knowledge of the comprehensive school system was gleaned from *Grange Hill* or *Adrian Mole*, would refer to them as 'yobbos', before going back to double Classics and being told how we were the cream of England. In truth, we were scared of them, and the cans of Vimto they would lob over the fence onto the eighth green of our golf course. Not just because they were five years older than us, but because they came from a world we did not know.

Private schools have two defining features. One is that they foster an air of exclusivity in all senses of the word. The public schools, in particular, come with their own languages and customs, which engender a sense that the world is made up of outsiders and insiders. Even within the schools there are usually a myriad of different houses, clubs and societies, all with their own hierarchies. I failed to get into Eton, which was something of a heroic achievement for a Summerfieldian (kids, top tip: make sure you always turn the exam paper over to see if there are any more questions). I ended up at Radley, a rather hearty public school also in Oxfordshire, where new boys were 'stigs', houses were 'socials', teachers were called 'dons', the rugby pitch, a place of worship more sacrosanct than the chapel, was called 'big side', and only prefects were allowed to walk across it. A byzantine system of ties, socks and caps denoted whether you had won your third-eleven colours for playing real tennis or your house colours for putting the shot. It was all rather silly. And it served to both bolster the arrogance of those who were insiders and exacerbate the adolescent insecurities of those who were not.

But it achieved the second defining feature: breeding academic success – particularly in getting pupils into Oxbridge, which it did as a matter of routine. Importantly, the school entered a good chunk of the sixth form into the exam, hoping that if they threw enough mud at the barn door, some of it would stick. Many presume I was guaranteed a place at Oxford because I went to public school, and therefore must have oozed confidence, shallow charm and superficial brilliance in my interview. The truth is the interview was a car crash. It's possible that the décor, the book-lined walls, the cosy battered armchair that I was ushered into, the overly hot gas fire on a mild winter's day were all things that I was comfortable with, things that immediately put me at an advantage. I don't know.

All I remember was the mounting, blind panic as I realised that I was catastrophically ignorant. It was the most terrifying 20 minutes of my life. My hours on the fives court, my ability to tip a gamekeeper and knowledge of how to address a Duchess? None of that mattered. Not one jot.

It didn't start well and it sort of went downhill. The mythical 'Why is Shakespeare better than *EastEnders*?' or 'Is it worse to be cruel to a fox or a flea?' questions weren't bothered with at most colleges. All that mattered was your enthusiasm and curiosity about the subject you wanted to study for the next three years. I was asked, as nearly all humanities students are, to choose a topic I'd like to talk about. I said Disraeli, whose life and times I thought I knew intimately. At one point, Leslie Mitchell, the history tutor who was leading the interview, becoming a little exasperated, asked in his distinctive drawl: 'So, what happened in 1870?' Silence. I remember the fire getting hotter as I racked my brain for any nugget. Nothing. 'Um, I'm sorry I can't remember what happened in 1870.' Honesty was the best policy, I thought. 'Well, a lot happened,' he answered. More silence. For the record, I think it was the Franco-Prussian War.

I did ask after the event, indeed a full three years later after I had sat my finals, and we were all treated to dinner in the senior common room, why on earth he had let me in. Apparently I had already won a place on the basis of the exams that you had to sit a month before the interview. So while the fabled public school cockiness counted for nothing, other less celebrated public school offerings – the hiring of the very best teachers, who were prepared to spend their lunchtime running history clubs, the access to a brilliant library and the expectation that you would use it, the honing of a slick, contrarian writing style that they knew impressed Oxbridge examiners – these things did give you an enormous advantage. Also important was the knowledge of which colleges were most suited for each applicant – and, of course, the very fact you were entered in the first place. The school, though not a massively academic one, at least had a respect for learning; class sizes were small, exam results were posted very publicly on the school notice board, and no glory was attached to failing. Captaining the cricket XI or rugby XV gave you god-like status in what was an undiluted Victorian institution. Play up and play the game. But if you were unsporty, didn't have a girlfriend you could meet in London, were too square to smoke on the school roof, hadn't passed your driving test, then getting into Oxbridge was accorded grudging respect. Private school got me into Oxford. I have no doubt about that. But it wasn't the interview.

And the statistics attest that public school gets an awfully large number of pupils into Oxbridge to this day. The most recent figures show that the proportion of Oxford undergraduates that have gone to independent school has fallen since Laura Spence's day, but only marginally, down from 47 per cent a decade ago to 43.3 per cent.

This has become the key yardstick, latched onto by academics and politicians alike, mostly because it is very easy to measure. Not until it hits 7 per cent, reflecting the education establishments of the country, will fairness have been reached. But of course private schools, while mostly filled with the children of Portland Privateers, Middletons and Rockabillies, are not exclusively so. Smith, at Magdalen, said: 'I once was looking through the list of undergraduates and saw that the only one that really came from a genuinely working-class background, whose parents were manual workers, was someone who'd been to Eton – because they had been on a scholarship.' About a quarter of all private school pupils are on some form of scholarship. One would expect those children particularly to do well when it comes to getting into Oxbridge. To crudely equate a rising number of comprehensive pupils at Oxbridge with rising social mobility is misleading. After all, most of the comprehensive pupils that have got in come from Wood Burning Stove families, where books line the walls and the *Today* programme is on at breakfast time. Laura Spence herself is a case in point – her father, Alexander, was a Northumbria police constable who worked in criminal intelligence. Her mother, Elizabeth, was a teacher.

Many of the Sun Skittlers, in contrast, have very little desire to do well at school, which they see as a stumbling block before they start their life, rather than the stepping stone to a better one. It is not just parents, but teachers too, who can dampen any educational aspiration. Considerably less than half of state school teachers would advise their brightest pupils to apply to Oxbridge, according to a recent survey.[12] Magdalen's Anthony Smith told me he'd long despaired at how few comprehensive teachers are prepared to enter their children for the top universities, even though his college was spending £250,000 a year trying to encourage more applicants. 'There is a militant anti aspiration among much of the working class,' he said. 'I heard a truly worrying tale: of a teacher at a comprehensive school who told a pupil's mother that she would never see her daughter if she got into Cambridge – she would no longer be good enough for her.'[13]

As far back as 1954 there was this odd belief that somehow the working class were betraying their roots if they showed any inclination to 'better themselves', and any sign of aspiration was essentially a middle-class phenomenon. Joan Woodward, the academic, wrote that year: 'During the last 10 or 15 years workers have begun to adopt the standards of the Middle Class way of life with the result that much that was good in the Working Class way of life has been lost.' She bemoaned that you used to be able to walk through the working-class district of Bermondsey and doors were left open – but no more. 'The competitive spirit has gone right through the whole class now until the dock worker eggs on his child to win a scholarship at the grammar school.'

But despite this 'competitive spirit' only a quarter of men admitted to English universities in 1955 were the sons of manual workers[14] in an age when nearly two-thirds of the workforce were manual workers. Exact equivalent figures for today are hard to come by, and slightly meaningless bearing in mind the collapse in manufacturing industries. But one thing is clear – the explosion in university students in recent years has not particularly benefited Asda Mum or Hyphen-Leigh families and all those others at the bottom of the socio-economic pile. The extra places have mostly gone to women, and to children of white-collar workers. Over the last two decades the increase in graduates among those whose parents were in managerial or professional jobs was 10 per cent, among those with parents in teaching, nursing or administration it was 11 per cent, but among those whose parents were manual workers the increase was just 5 per cent.[15] And at Oxbridge just one out of 100 of its undergraduates were entitled to free school meals, compared with one in five school pupils across the country.

Simply, not enough comprehensive pupils apply. Statistics show that those that do apply have only a slightly worse chance of gaining a place than those from private school. But without a volume of applicants to choose from, admissions tutors are left with little option.

Ironically, private schools themselves have become more elite because of rising standards and higher fees. The difference in A-level results between the private and the public sector has steadily become wider. It is unclear exactly why this should be so, but some of the worst private schools have gone bust, or merged, helping to raise standards at the remaining ones; and standards at comprehensives have slipped, maybe because of a refusal to embrace a competitive culture, an insistence that no one is a loser, when clearly – when it comes to exams – that can't be true. In 2010, A-level candidates at independent schools were three times more likely to get straight As than candidates at state schools – and that statistic flatters the state sector because it includes England's 164 remaining grammar schools. If you remove grammars from the equation, more children got three As at A-level in the country's tiny handful of fee-paying schools than in the entire population of children at comprehensives.[16]

Although the percentage of UK schoolchildren going private has remained remarkably constant at 7 per cent, it did dip when the recession started to bite hard. And that fall mostly came from British families dropping out and seeking refuge in the state sector; meanwhile the number of foreign pupils has risen sharply. The recession, in fact, merely exacerbated a long-running trend – private schools have become astronomically expensive.

This was not always the case. Radley, the public school I went on to, while markedly less golden than Summer Fields, was assuredly an upmarket establishment that based itself slavishly on the workings of an Oxford college. Many of the pupils were children of army officers, successful farmers, Harrogate accountants and Weymouth stockbrokers. There was a sprinkling of the mega wealthy, but there was not a single full-blown aristocrat and the great majority were Rockabillies, who'd cut back on foreign holidays to pay for the school fees – hence the disproportionate number of public school children who ended up smoking pot and groping each other on the beaches of Cornwall in the summer. I can remember feeling distinctly embarrassed when my father came to pick me up from school in a new Mercedes (he'd upgraded from the Ford Granada), as it gleamed ostentatiously amid the battered Volvos and Rovers that most parents owned.

Back in 1954 the termly fees at one of the country's top public schools, St Paul's, were £30, for tuition, plus £15 for extras such as lunches and books.[17] That is under £2,000 a year in today's money. Now they are £20,000 a year. And that's a day school. Boarding school fees now are often more than £30,000 a year and have risen by three times the rate of inflation since 1993. The days when a moderately successful dentist, surveyor or hotelier from Exeter or York could send children to private school without too much thought are long gone. Higher-rate taxpayers who want to educate four children privately from the age of 11 at boarding school need to build up a pot of £1.2m to do so. This is an astronomical sum of money, even for those that turn left when entering a plane and are entitled to a discount for the *Times* births column.

This trend has been made worse by the schools themselves treating the establishments as if they are private health clubs and splashing money on fish pedicure centres (I kid you not – at one Essex fee-paying school there really is one) and indoor fencing galleries, which push the fees up yet further. The £1m indoor swimming pool at Summer Fields set a trend across all prep schools in the area as they vied to build higher climbing walls, more acoustically perfect music centres and Olympic-quality fletching for the archery team. This has served to make more stark the differences between the state and the private sector. The only members of the consumer classes who can really afford to attend these establishments are the Portland Privateers and those on scholarships – the very rich and the fairly poor.

The preponderance of both of these groups explains why there is a slightly higher proportion of ethnic minority pupils in private schools than in state schools. Just over a quarter of pupils in private schools are from ethnic minorities. When boarding schools are excluded, this proportion rises to 28.5 per cent. The latest figures for state schools in England show that 24.5 per cent are from ethnic minorities.[18] Race was once entangled in class, but the modern consumer classes are mostly colour-blind, especially when it comes to education. A small but significant number of British Indians and British Chinese have made shedloads of money and chosen to spend it on their children – giving birth privately and sending their children to private school. They are also far more likely to pay for private tutors. Added to this are all the children of super-wealthy foreigners. You can see why private schools, despite their image as quintessentially white-middle-class establishments, are in fact cosmopolitan, Portland Privateer centres, with a small sprinkling of scholarship children from Asda Mum families, many of whom come from ethnic minority backgrounds. A leading private school headmaster lamented recently that plenty of children from poor Afro-Caribbean families were entered for scholarships, but no 'little skinheads with the St George's cross tattoos who come from families where maybe nobody has worked'.[19] It seems that in most ethnic minorities fewer people have qualms about the private system in the way that many wealthy Wood Burning Stovers do.

Many WBSs and Rockabillies themselves attended private school, but when it comes to educating their own children they are either relying on a stash of family money salted away, or – in most cases – using another route: relocating to an area with a good state school and employing a private tutor.

Tutors were once considered an unseemly extravagance for pushy, and wealthy, parents. They were used when Florence or Marcus just weren't very bright and needed that extra leg-up to pass common entrance or O-levels. But the tutor now is very much part of the fabric of the state sector, with the names of the best ones passed around furtively at coffee mornings like a dirty secret, as if you were divulging the mobile number of your local drug dealer. Nearly one in eight state school children across the country have received private tutoring during 2012, it was estimated.[20] Tutors are the salvation for Wood Burning Stovers who are appalled at the idea of private school (and for whom it is unaffordable) and yet deeply, desperately want their child to do academically well enough to make it into a good university. Tutors' waiting lists can stretch to as much as five years in particular London post-codes. How many comprehensive school pupils get into Oxbridge without even an hour's private tuition of some sort? Not that many.

But so endemic is tutoring that it has stretched down to Asda Mums, whose ability and willingness to spend money on their children, despite being on a tight budget, marks them out as a completely different breed from the Sun Skittlers. 'It's a crime to treat yourself, but I'll always look after my girl,' said one, Michelle, whom I met. And it's a mantra which neatly sums up Asda Mums. While they mostly buy their own clothes from Next, Primark, Debenhams or Asda itself, their children are treated to a variety of expensive brands, from Ralph Lauren, DKNY and Abercrombie to Organix, Chessington World of Adventures, and Shirley, the very good maths tutor at the end of the road. Swimming sessions, baby yoga, music lessons, football coaching, cubs, art classes, tutoring – each of these can add up to over £100 a month per child, sometimes more; essential spending for Asda Mums, determined that their children's education should surpass their own. This tutoring is not to get their children into a private school; that is not an option. It is to ensure they do well in their exams, and ultimately make it to some form of university.

For those that do have aspiration, the other, more expensive and more inconvenient route is by postcode hopping. For most this is a matter of selling up and moving to be near a good state school. By 2011, parents were paying premiums of £77,000 on average to buy homes near leading state schools. Property prices were 35 per cent higher than the UK norm, with an average asking price of £298,378, if you wanted to live in the catchment area of one of the country's top 50 schools based on their GCSE results.[21] This is essentially selection by mortgage.

Others go a more circuitous route. I know of one couple with impeccable leftist credentials who have taken 'playing the system' to extraordinary lengths, seemingly having dedicated most of their waking hours to the betterment of their child. Attendance at various different churches, of various different

creeds, membership of clubs, choirs and temperance movements – nothing has been ruled out in the bid to make sure the
child attends the best state school in London. The latest ruse
involves them letting their family home in the north of the
capital, and renting a smaller place in the centre of the city,
which happens to back onto the favoured educational establishment. To ensure that the school is not suspicious of the
sudden move, they undertook all this a year before the application forms had to be submitted. The cost to the family is
substantial, about £9,000 a year, because of the difference
between the rent they have to pay on the new place and what
they receive on their family home.

What makes these machinations so absurd is that the couple
will not countenance private schooling – on moral grounds. To
them, archetypal Wood Burning Stovers, the private system is
a blight on Britain's reputation for decency and fairness. And
yet they are prepared to allow a child from a council estate,
who has lived in their new borough since birth, to be denied a
place at the excellent state school in favour of their own child.
Somehow the fact they are spending £9,000 on this postcode
charade is more acceptable than paying £9,000 for school fees.
But when their darling son scrapes into Exeter University or
King's College London they can crack open the prosecco and
claim he didn't buy his way in.

And this is what it is all about. Getting into a good university. Because they believe, correctly, that three years at a good
university, ideally a Russell Group one, or even better Oxbridge,
is a significant leg-up in life; whereas being offered a place at
London South Bank University or the University of Bedfordshire
is, for a Wood Burning Stover, akin to being given £100 vouchers to spend at Brighthouse or Iceland supermarket. They

know a good university matters, not just for the cachet it brings, but for the doors it opens. The Sutton Trust, which does an excellent job of tracking social mobility data, has calculated that 82 per cent of barristers, 78 per cent of judges, 53 per cent of so-called 'magic circle' solicitors from the top law firms, 45 per cent of the top 100 journalists and 15 per cent of top medics went to Oxbridge. These percentages should be compared with the 1.2 per cent of the university undergraduates in the UK who currently attend these two elite universities.

There has always been a certain amount of snobbism about universities. Durham, Edinburgh and Exeter used to be the ultimate choices for Sloane Rangers in the 1980s, possibly only beaten by Prue Leith's cookery school and Lucie Clayton College, which taught flower arranging and secretarial skills. Now, thanks to Mr and Mrs Kate Middleton, that title belongs to St Andrew's. Before then, the really grand, the aristos and better-connected Rockabillies, mostly didn't bother with university. My parents certainly didn't, along with many of that generation of privately educated debs and debs' delights. David Mayhew, the chairman of Cazenove bank and regarded as the brightest star of his generation in the City, started his working life in the square mile straight out of Eton in 1961. A university education just wasn't a prerequisite to success in stockbroking or merchant banking. In fact, it was probably regarded as a sign of being a dangerous intellectual. But the snobbism about which tertiary education establishment you attend has intensified since the New Labour government set an ambitious target on taking office in 1997 that 50 per cent of school leavers should attend university. Back in the 1950s, fewer than 5 per cent of school leavers went to university, and it was just 15 per cent throughout most of the 1970s and 80s, but it is now 44 per cent, despite the introduction of punitive tuition fees. And many of the newer institutions offer degrees that make the works of Mickey Mouse look like those of Marcel Proust. The public and employers are not fools; they know a first in Tournament Golf from Duchy College in Camborne, Cornwall, or top honours in Waste Management and Dance from Northampton, will carry less weight than a third from Glasgow, Birmingham or Leeds.

But this seems to have come as a shock to some in charge. Alan Milburn, the former cabinet member who in 2012 was commissioned by the Coalition government to conduct a study into access into the professions, said: 'Education is the great mortar of social mobility,' mixing his metaphors (I think he meant engine oil, or lubricant, but we'll put that to one side). 'I find it startling that we have 115 universities in this country, but the top professional employers only recruit from 19 of those on average.' Well, of course they do. Deloitte, Unilever or the Ministry of Defence want their employees to have finished three years at university with a capacity for hard work and rigorous thinking – something that is unlikely to be the case if they spent their time doing modules in David Beckham studies. Milburn is the latest in a long line of senior figures to call for universities to fiddle their entrance criteria. He has suggested that the universities look at the large number of different socio-economic groups in Britain and pick equally from each group. 'The professions that are particularly serving the public – like medicine, like law – they need to be better acquainted with the public they serve.'[22]

This is an intriguing argument, but one that is surely flawed. When the 'anti-elitist' protester Trenton Oldfield disrupted the

2012 Oxford vs Cambridge Boat Race by swimming into the path of the oars, someone quipped that it was unlikely he'd carry on protesting if an Oxbridge-trained doctor offered to sew his head back on. Do we really want our law courts or operating theatres to 'represent' the full spectrum of Britain, a country that includes unintelligent as well as clever people? Or do we want those professions to be staffed by the brightest? The sort of individuals that flourish in the world of briefs and barbiturates are the type who are quite good at studying, passing exams and as a result more likely to have gone to Oxbridge.

Journalism is a trickier one. Although it does, in some areas, require a modest education, it should also reflect the world on which it reports. That is its purpose. Whether it can do so successfully when its staff have come from a very shallow pool of applicants is debatable. Can nation speak unto nation if it has never known a world outside of Beaconsfield, Barnsbury and the quads of Oxbridge? Of course the real problem is not that Oxbridge graduates hog a disproportionate number of the best jobs. They have received the best education available in Britain. It should not necessarily be a cause for scandal that a third of everyone with a listing in Who's Who attended one of these two universities. I want my elite to be well educated.

The risk is that Oxbridge itself draws from a fairly narrow pool and is far too reliant on the public schools of England and Scotland. As with sausages, you can only get out what you put in. That is the real worry. The number of Oxbridge graduates who dominate public life – one hopes with some justification – is nothing as compared with the number of public school people who do so. They are increasingly grabbing the best jobs. The Sutton Trust, in its analysis of 2,300 of the leading figures in academia, journalism, law, medicine, business and politics found that 70 per cent of judges had been privately educated, 68 per cent of barristers, 55 per cent of solicitors from the top firms, 54 per cent of the top 100 journalists and 51 per cent of top medics. So, in fact, there was a higher proportion of public school figures in most of these professions than Oxbridge graduates, especially when it came to medicine and journalism.

Michael Gove, the Education Secretary who won a scholarship to a private school, was right to highlight how some newspapers, particularly those that most champion social mobility, were hardly shining beacons themselves: 'It's not just the judiciary and around the Cabinet table, it is in music, in the new generation of actors and in sport. And of course one of the places you'll find the most public school boys is in the *Guardian* editorial conference,' he said.[23] The editor is a public school boy and so too are most of its leading columnists. The right-wing press have much fun baiting Polly Toynbee, who is the paper's leading rent-a-republican, but a woman who chose to send two of her children to private school.

In the professions and indeed nearly all walks of life, public school pupils appear to flourish disproportionately. Even sport, which traditionally was seen as the great passport to a brighter life for working-class heroes – be it boxing, football or cricket – is increasingly dominated by people whose education was paid for. Ed Smith, the former England cricketer, has pointed out that when England toured Pakistan in 1987–88, all but one of the 13 players selected were state educated. He compares that with the England Test team who beat India at Lord's in the summer of 2011. That squad included eight privately educated players and three state-educated ones. In rugby union, at the 1987 World Cup, 62 per cent of the players were state educated; by 2007 that had dropped to 36 per cent.[24] At the 2012 Olympics, 36 per cent of Britain's medallists went to private schools.[25] One of Team GB's athletics squad was Old Summerfieldian and Old Etonian Lawrence Clarke, heir to the Clarke baronetcy.

Eton has now managed to infiltrate areas that once would have once shunned its alumni as toffs. Douglas Hurd, Margaret Thatcher's Foreign Secretary, lamented in his memoir: 'If I had not gone to Eton I would have become Prime Minister in 1990.' Now, of course, a mere twenty years later, there is an Etonian in Downing Street, one at City Hall, and there's one on our screens almost every evening. Hugh Laurie, Dominic West, Damian Lewis, Tom Hiddleston and Eddie Redmayne: all old Etonians. The generation of Michael Caine and Terence Stamp, working-class lads who passed the 11-plus and came to define the era of class barriers being smashed down, seems a distant memory. As Michael Gove said, 'One almost feels sorry for Benedict Cumberbatch, a lowly Harrovian, and Dan Stevens, heir to *Downton Abbey* and old boy of Tonbridge, is practically a street urchin in comparison.'

To us at prep school the then Labour leader Michael Foot was a bogeyman, who would – it was threatened – come into our dormitories at night and slap VAT on school fees and send us all to the local comp. The Labour party (before it was New) wanted to abolish the private system by making it unaffordable. Thirty years later the debate is exactly the same: How do you make a two-tier system fairer? It's just that the solution being suggested by politicians is different. Instead of raising the ladder higher, by making the fees of private schools even more expensive, most politicians focus on lowering the ladder for university applicants. They concentrate their minds on university entrance (because they have more control over this aspect of the system) and they think the solution is to make exam grades less important than socio-economic classification. What each generation of politicians and their advisors have failed to grasp is that most pupils and their parents want to climb this ladder. Most of the modern consumer classes from Asda Mums to Portland Privateers want to trade up to the educational equivalent of Taste the Difference, and they resent anyone who insists their only option is the Basics range, or that the quality of premium range is diminished.

* * *

If we are defined by what we consume, the brands we buy, the shops we frequent, the food we eat – well, the school we went to shouldn't matter. But it does, it always has. And that's because, more than ever, education is, in fact, seen by parents as a consumer product – something to be bought, something to be acquired, even for the great majority that can't afford private school. There are still substantial costs involved – be it hiring a £40 an hour tutor or uprooting your family to a different postcode. And those shut out, refused entry tickets to this great race, understandably feel a certain level of resentment.

A good education – or rather an expensive one – is the surest way of guaranteeing a high-profile, status-giving job. In the days when just 5 per cent went to university, a degree was a ticket to success, and most people who secured a degree had been through the grammar school system. Grammar schools were far from perfect, but they produced every prime minister from Wilson to Major. Now that close to half of school leavers have a degree, university has lost its cachet. The opening up of higher education to millions of extra young people, while undoubtedly a good thing in principle, has only – as we will see later – added to the resentment of many graduates about the lack of 'graduate' jobs available. It has also served to increase the distinctiveness and status of private schools.

The snobbism over which individual school you went to has now more or less disappeared. Whether you wear a Bhs or Barbour jacket, rather than whether you went to Radley or Rugby, is the kind of distinction that exercises our consumerist minds. But though the different shade of a particular school tie may no longer be of paramount importance, whether your education was private or not plays a key part in your chances in life. These private schools, mostly, do a pretty good job – and the best do a superlative job – at educating their pupils and facilitating their entry to Oxbridge and Russell Group universities. But for as long as they exist in their current form the British class system will exist, as it did back in the 1950s and 60s with the divisive 11-plus. It is just not possible to split the nation's children at the age of 8, or 11, or 13, and put them in two separate systems, and not expect them to grow up into adults whose minds are naturally inclined towards separating the world around them. What is intriguing about the consumer age we live in is that this inclination now finds its outlet in separating out those who shop at Asda from those who shop at Aldi and those who holiday in Blackpool from those who travel to Bordeaux, but they separate the world all the same. And it is to holidays that we now turn.

CHAPTER 7

HOLIDAYS

*Club class or Ryanair? Did the great package holiday
revolution broaden our horizons? Here we meet
the Rockabillies properly.*

Benidorm, a sleepy and picturesque fishing village, south of
Valencia in Spain, had 2,726 inhabitants, three small hotels
and eight boarding houses in 1957. Surrounded by orange
groves, it had few amenities, was difficult to reach and had
only recently started to enjoy the luxury of running water. Two
years later it had 34 hotels, four cinemas and 30,000 visitors
each summer. And by the summer of 1977 it was welcoming
12 million tourists a season, a large number of whom were the
British working class. The town – though in truth it was now
a major conurbation – had become synonymous with the Brits
Abroad, a generation enjoying cheap continental lager, late-
night dancing, banana boats, garlic, sunburn and package holidays for the first time.

This revolution in travel, which allowed the working class
to travel not just out of their home towns and counties but to
straddle the globe in search of fun as only the aristocracy and
plutocracy had been able to do a century before, was in part
the brainchild of Vladimir Raitz. An enterprising journalist,

Raitz can lay claim to be the father of the package holiday industry. In doing so, he helped millions of families realise they had every bit as much right to enjoy themselves as their bosses, and in the same style. Leisure was once the ultimate symbol of being either upper class or upper-middle class – the freedom to relax, to play games, to idle. These are things that can only be done with a surfeit of income and time. But within 60 years of Raitz's brainwave of package holidays, many millions of families, from the humblest of homes and with the most basic of education or low wages, could expect to enjoy a week in the sun and see the world.

In 1949 Raitz was just 27 years old and working at Reuters, the newswire service, when he was invited by a colleague to visit Calvi, on the French island of Corsica, which before the war had hosted a water polo club, the Club Olympique. It was being revived. The object was to summer on the island, enjoy the clear Mediterranean waters by day, and dance and drink by night. 'To say the installations and living conditions were primitive would be putting it mildly. Then tents were furnished with camp beds: two, three or four to a tent, standing directly on the sand. You were expected to keep your gear in your suitcase throughout your stay,'[1] he recalled 50 years later. Washing was done in a *bloc sanitaire*. 'The bar, thankfully, functioned beautifully.'

Raitz had a ball, and when his colleague asked him whether he wanted to be in charge of rounding up some British travellers for the following summer he jumped at the chance. But he realised that the journey by coach from Britain to the island, many hours off the south coast of France, would be too arduous to contemplate. Flying was the only option.

Tracking down a plane in 1949 was easy – Britain was awash with decommissioned military aircraft from the war and Raitz chartered a DC3, a converted Dakota with 32 seats, for £305. He worked out that he needed to sell 350 tickets to break even. He gave up his job, rented a room above the Olde Snuffe Shope on Fleet Street, and started Horizon Holidays, the first 'package holiday' business, selling not just the transport, but the entire two-week experience, including, crucially for ration-book Britain, all meals. And that meant meat twice a day. 'Plentiful food at the club' was the key phrase used in the first brochures.

He had just a few weeks to sell his tickets, which were priced at £32 10s for two weeks, including the tent accommodation and food. To most it sounded unbelievably, almost suspiciously, cheap. 'Actually, £32 was no small amount, but air fares in those days were extremely expensive,' Raitz recalled. BEA, the state-owned airline, charged £70 to Nice, the closest airport to Calvi.

The first season was not a financial success for Raitz. He had sold 50 tickets fewer than he needed to break even. But the travellers were universally enthralled by the beach, the bamboo bar, the cocktails, the dancing, the snorkelling. Next season Raitz took 450 customers, and this time they were able to stay in purpose-built, if crude, log cabins. By 1952, thanks in part to the government liberalising the air industry, Raitz was seeking out other destinations: Majorca, Sardinia, where malaria had only been eradicated in 1946, and – eventually in 1954 – Benidorm. Most of his customers had never had all that much money, but they were determined to set themselves apart from their parents' generation both in attitude and in spending habits. Frugality went out of the window – and in flew enjoyment. Mostly completely unpretentious, mostly lower-middle class or working class, these were people for whom the very act of flying abroad helped propel their rise further into the modern middle classes. They were a combination of the Sun Skittlers and the Middleton classes. Harold Macmillan believed car ownership widened Britons' horizons. How much more was this the case with an airline ticket, surely?

In 1952 the *Herald* newspaper ran a survey and discovered that half the British population took an annual holiday; of those that did just 3 per cent went abroad.[2] But thanks to the Benidorm pioneers that soon changed, and rapidly so. In 1955 those going abroad jumped to 8 per cent.[3] By 1961 there were 2.6 million holidaymakers flying abroad each year. The most recent official figures show that 36 million holiday trips were taken abroad in 2010.[4]

There were three main reasons for this rapid, exponential growth, the primary one being economic. Between 1955 and 1960 average weekly earnings, including overtime, rose 34 per cent, while retail prices rose just 15 per cent. This effectively doubled the disposable income in families' pockets at the end of each week, and much of the increase was spent on leisure. The second was technological – the clunky, uncomfortable, unpressurised DC3 planes that Raitz had used were soon replaced by the jet-engine Boeing 707 and Douglas DC-8. But the third was a great deal to do with young people and families exploring areas that their parents could never have dreamed of – both geographically and socially.

To have the money, inclination and horizons to travel abroad became an immediate sign of making it, as British hoteliers found to their frustration. Eric Croft, the director and secretary of the British Hotels and Restaurants Association in 1960, said the urge to holiday abroad stemmed from snobbery and from 'the fashionable habit of keeping up with the Jones's. It is much more impressive to be able to talk of the "pension" we found in some Mediterranean resort with an unpronounceable name, where sanitation does not exist, and where a visit to the chemist is almost a daily necessity, than to admit to having a grand holiday at a boarding house with good English food at one of our seaside resorts.'

Sir Henry Lunn Ltd in 1954 offered hire purchase for holidays, a full decade before the first credit card was introduced into Britain, making it even easier for blue-collar workers earning small wages to pay for a trip abroad. Harold Bamberg, the owner of the company, said: 'This should make buying travel as easy as buying a radio set on credit.'

Billy Butlin had promised before the war a week's holiday for a week's wage – and that was in potentially rainy and certainly unexotic Skegness. Sun Skittlers and the Middleton classes were being offered – at the peak of the boom – two weeks' holiday at a beach hotel, including flights and all food and drink, for less than a week's wages.

A suntan, a smattering of pigeon Spanish, and knowledge of the wines and herbs of Europe were now available for nearly all consumers, who could return and show off their new-found sophistication by scattering these acquisitions into conversations down the pub and dinner party food served at home. Raitz had started a revolution. He was not to know that the British, with their ability to find social distinction even in their leisure time, would engineer complex ways to ensure that holidays became strictly ranked. 'Do you turn left when you enter an aeroplane?' became the droll shorthand quip that summed up the thousand different ways to show that your holidays were smarter, classier, more refined. Tuscany or Torremelinos, cruising or camping, Featherdown farm or Florida, the Dales or Disneyland? When it comes to categorising the holiday, it is no longer the cost that really matters. It is the destination and how you got there.

*   *   *

Apart from North Korea there isn't really a country on the planet that the British do not now visit on holiday. Polar bear watching in Antarctica, walking trips in the Galapagos, a guided tour of Uzbekistan – described with some glee in the brochure as 'barren' – these are just some of the package holidays that are now available for the modern middle classes to prove they are more adventurous than the pioneers who first descended on Benidorm. Far flung is the key, and wild animals are a real bonus, though it is debatable whether one can really describe as 'wild' some of the lions in the Masai Mara game reserve in Kenya, more gawped at and photographed than Pippa Middleton.

The most recent figures show that 40 per cent of all holidays taken by Brits, or 14.3 million trips abroad, are packages.[5] But now that every country, its souks and exotic beasts, can be placed on your holiday itinerary, it is more important than ever to choose your destination carefully. One company went so far as to market its white-water rafting holidays in Slovenia and trips to see the northern lights as 'Chav Free' packages, where you would not find any Britneys, Biancas or Chardonnays. The company's tongue was not that firmly in its cheek, and it struck a nerve. People became more aware than ever that there were indeed some holidays that were lower class than others. Disney World in Florida, for all its slickness and ability to make a seven-year-old's dreams come true, is the apogee of the package holiday revolution for good or ill – highly marketed, totally branded, it guarantees a type of fun. The price is high, the food is blandly international, the setting non-existent. It is the destination of choice for any Asda Mum who can afford it and frequently cited by them as the first thing they would spend their winnings on, if they won the lottery.

Benidorm, of course, has now become a byword for downmarket, for lager louts. It is Blackpool with sun, with more high-rise blocks of flats and even more pints of beer sold. It is one of a number of holiday destinations that immediately disqualifies you as a member of the Wood Burning Stovers or Rockabillies, along with most of Florida, Magaluf, Faliraki, Tenerife, Lanzarote, Sharm El Sheik, Marmaris, Bodrum, Ko Samui, Torremelinos, the Canary Islands. Many of these places are beautiful, with stunning sand and weather – that, after all, is what made them popular in the first place – but they suffer from being almost entirely taken over by the all-inclusive package holiday companies, which buy up most of the hotel rooms and restaurants. In doing so they give their customers the security of knowing what they are going to get. But this raises the fear, among the Birkenstock sandal crowd, that they will be served eggs and chips for lunch, with brown sauce on the side.

One thing that marks out the Wood Burning Stover on holiday is a horror of being served British food. They'd rather go hungry than visit Chez Wayne's in Nice (a pub that offers up Premiership football, eggs, beans and 'English chips' from 11 a.m.). The Sun Skittlers have always been rather more relaxed about these things and enjoyed home comforts when abroad.

Dorothy Isles, a secretary, and her husband Richard, a factory foreman from the mill town of Kirkham, Lancashire, usually went to Blackpool for their one week off each year, along with most of their fellow working-class neighbours. But in 1957 they ventured on holiday for the first time not just out of Lancashire but out of England altogether, by motoring to the South of France. In *Some Liked it Hot*, a book that brilliantly chronicles the holiday memories of the post-war generation, Mrs Isles explains quite how unusual it was for her class to go abroad in the era when Raitz had only just started his package holidays. She said: 'It was like going to the moon. Nobody had ever been to France for a holiday where we lived. They all went to Blackpool. They were so worried for us, and my parents were horrified. They'd never had anyone going abroad except in a war. They made us so worried that we made a will the day before we left.'[6]

Fearful of the food in France, Dorothy took a boiled chicken with her, though it had to be thrown away by the time she got to the other side of the Channel as it had started to go off in the heat. Also in her luggage was a quantity of corned beef in tins. 'It was always in the back of your mind that British soldiers had eaten bully beef in France in World War I and survived, so we could survive on it too. And that's what we lived on until we got down to the Riviera.'[7]

My mother-in-law has always claimed, unlike her husband, to have never been a member of the working class (her own father was a chief fire officer, which qualifies her as a daughter of a fairly senior civil servant). But as recently as the mid-1980s she insisted on taking with her on the family holiday to Calpe, in Spain, just 15 miles along the coast from Benidorm, a whole separate suitcase of food. It contained a large number of tins of corned beef, Pek (a type of spam, though she insists it is a higher grade of canned meat), tinned salmon, marmalade, salad cream and breakfast cereal. This was in the days before luggage allowances. She is baffled as to why I consider this odd behaviour.

Lola Smith, from London's East End, who left school at 15 to work in the local upholstery factory, went on her first holiday abroad in 1967, to Ibiza. Before this, she was one of the many East End children who spent their summer holidays (or rather their Septembers, meaning that schools were half-empty at the start of the winter term) hop picking with their mothers in Kent. They slept in pretty basic huts and worked hard for the privilege of escaping from the city.

But by the late 60s she was earning good money, as so many Sun Skittlers were, doing piece-work in a textile factory, and had heard from friends the joy of uninterrupted Mediterranean sun. For £45 she could get an all-inclusive fortnight with her husband to Ibiza ('I didn't know how to pronounce it; I called it Ibeetza'). 'I'd never been on a plane. It was very exciting. I travelled in smart clothes, a little denim mini-skirt and jacket. The first thing I did when I got to the airport was buy a beautiful bottle of Madame Rochas perfume duty free, 200 cigarettes, watching the planes coming in, and think, "Ain't I lucky?" I felt like a film star.

'I was a bit homesick. I was miles away from my family and the East End. It was only when I got home and thought, "Wasn't it smashing, it was paradise."' This was despite the fact that the food was 'diabolical', in her view. 'It was all floating in oil. That first holiday, I ate tomatoes, packets of crisps and Nestles chocolate.'

That excitement of flying abroad was the visceral proof that this was a generation on the rise. By the time that my father-in-law took his first flight abroad to the Costa Brava in 1969 with his young family, air travel was still so exotic that holiday companies arranged for a photographer to snap families coming down the steps of a plane in their specially purchased holiday outfits (the modern habit of England rugby players wearing a comfortable track suit and flip-flops would have been abhorrent), to be presented as a special memento of their time abroad. For some time, this picture was framed on their mantelpiece.

However, while his family started to branch out in search of new destinations, new languages and cuisines (the tins of Pek were eventually abandoned), proving their Middleton class status, the Sun Skittlers have always felt more comfortable surrounded not just by British food but also by Britons when abroad.

Lola Smith has happy memories of the first couple of holidays, sunbathing on the beach in Portinatx, Ibiza. 'We were all Brits together, some of us cockneys, but we was meeting scousers, people from Birmingham. There was one guy who had his own central heating business, he was well to do and spoke well, but he sat with us all day on the beach. He was very down to earth. We were mixing more on holiday than back at home. But Brits in those days got on famously when they were together. We went for the sun and beach. We never met any Spanish. But that didn't bother me, because none of us spoke Spanish and none of us tried to anyway.'

To this day, this is one of the key attributes of a Sun Skittler. Mick, who works in a shoe factory in Northampton and describes himself as 'working class and proud', holidays frequently in Majorca. 'I love it. It's just home from home. It's safe. It's got a good police presence. I go for a week or two. I've been going for 20 years. It's lovely to hear British voices. You walk down my street at home and don't hear British voices, but over there it's all British voices. My wife can go out shopping at night at ten o'clock and it's safe; she couldn't do that at home.'

Sun Skittlers, many of whom have branched out to Thailand or Turkey, have seen the world, but not necessarily broadened their horizons.

Many of the Benidorm pioneers soon moved up to the Middleton classes as they got a little older and a little richer. For them a holiday abroad provided the treasured luggage sticker which immediately signified, stuck on to a battered suitcase, how sophisticated the owner was. Some became adventurous and were able to return to their Rotary Clubs and chat about the Sistine Chapel and the Taj Mahal. And there was one particular form of holiday which has presented an opportunity to clearly affirm this group's social ranking more than any other: cruising.

By the 1990s it had become the fastest-growing holiday sector, with bookings increasing 20 per cent every year, as Brits ever older and more affluent decided to push the boat out. At the top end there are the likes of the *Viking Helvetika*, which meanders down the Rhine with just 198 passengers learning how to blow glass and make wooden clogs, or the Paul Gauguin cruise which visits Tahiti, and has a Nobel peace prize recipient as the on-board entertainment.

At the other end are the monster ships, with 1,500 cabins and zumba classes, tribute acts to Andrew Lloyd Webber and 'an audience with Charlie Dimmock'. When the *Costa Concordia* ran aground off the coast of Tuscany in 2012, the reaction of most of the Wood Burning Stovers, after concern about the loss of life, was one of horror at the gargantuan monstrosity of the boat – the sheer scale of the vessel, the numbers on board, the glitziness of the entertainment. Did people really choose to be trapped on this floating Las Vegas for a holiday? It seemed a water-borne, rather expensive package holiday.

Only a few years previously the P&O *Ventura*, one of the company's flagships, ran into difficulty when some 'chav' holidaymakers, as a local newspaper described them, took advantage of a last-minute deal to fill the space on the boat – the passengers who had originally booked and paid a deposit having pulled out because of the credit crunch. The captain was booed, a Christmas tree was set alight, fists were thrown and two people ended up in the on-board cells. One passenger, who paid £8,000 for four people, said she heard how some had paid as little as £900 for their ticket. 'I've been on 14 cruises now and this one was definitely the worst,' she told the local press with some glee. Another complainant, when challenged about why people on a budget shouldn't enjoy a cruise, replied with breathtaking snobbism: 'Actually I expect them to go on a cheap package holiday to get drunk by a pool in Spain. Not get on a luxury cruise where you are supposed to dress well and act with a modicum of sophistication and, dare I say it, self-respect.'

The whole incident seemed to confirm that many cruises have become reserved for what my mother-in-law always dismissively calls 'Blackpool posh' – the showiest end of the Middleton classes, who have made the move up to the top, but failed to completely shake off their Sun Skittling background: too much make-up, blousy dresses and blousier hair. They can well afford to holiday in Tuscany, Thailand or Turkmenistan, but their heart is always in Blackpool. Cruising is their natural hunting ground with its love of endless petty rules, a restrictive dress code and glitzy entertainment. Snobbism on sea. John and Pauline Prescott are archetypal Blackpool Posh. He, of course, once worked as a steward on Cunard ships, serving drinks to the aristocracy – leading to hurtful jibes of 'Another G&T, Giovanni' being shouted out across the floor of the House of Commons when he rose to speak. But now, a member of the House of Lords, he likes a holiday cruise around the Caribbean on the *QM2* in the top class, where butlers unpack your luggage.

If any further proof were needed, P&O became the sponsor of the third series of *Downton Abbey*, which has replaced Sunday evening vespers as the holiest time of the week for the Middleton classes. It was a perfect commercial tie-up.

My father-in-law, 30 years before his spam-sandwich holidays to the Costa Blanca, found himself in a similar situation to John Prescott. As a young man, keen to avoid national service, he signed up to the merchant navy and joined P&O. He got to see the world a generation ahead of his contemporaries, working in the steel mills of Workington. As a Second Engineer one of the perks was hosting his own table in the first-class dining room, wearing his white mess kit. 'Once a week or so we would be sent down to tourist class to host a table. And you'd always end up sitting next to someone, maybe a decorator or some shop girls who'd saved up and were sharing a cabin, and they'd say, "Oh, isn't it so much more fun down here at this end away from all those posh nobs. We know how to really let our hair down here." And I'd always think, "No, no it's not," and dream of the moment I could escape back up to first class.'

He was working on the cruises in the last few years when its very appeal was its snobbism, its delineation of passengers into first class and tourist, and in some cases first, cabin and tourist. In the post-war years travelling in first class on the *Queen Mary* was the only way to cross the Atlantic. The future 14th Duke of Bedford and his wife, the 'deb of debs' Henrietta Tiarks, went on the *Queen Mary* as the final leg of their honeymoon in 1961. They had the state room on the ship. The idea of any current member of the aristocracy, Rockabilly or Wood Burning Stover holidaying on the *QM2*, the heir to the original *Queen Mary*, is pretty remote.

The rot set in for the cruise industry as a glamorous, genuinely upper-class holiday not when Pan Am flew the first transatlantic non-stop trip on a Boeing 707 in 1958 – which in one fell swoop created the jet set age; it was three years earlier when the Shaw, Savill & Albion line, then a big cruise operator, launched the *Southern Cross*, the first major ship to be built with just one class. In a radical move, first class had been scrapped. Everyone was welcome. Of course, there were still different sized cabins, different ticket prices and different dining rooms. But everyone could wander around the ship and sunbathe as equals.

When Cunard announced its new ship, which would end up being called the *QE2*, but went by the codename Q4, the *Observer* breathlessly reported: 'So long as England ruled the waves the class system seemed as secure on the high seas as it was at home. But the Q4 marks the final liberation of the tourist classes who ... will have the run of the ship for the first time. Cunard chairman Sir Basil Smallpiece insists that basically the Q4 is a ship without classes. The Q4, which replaces the *Queen Mary*, lets tourists get to the top without the nonsense about keeping aft of the funnels.'[8]

Egalitarian it may have been, but the *QE2* never was classless, and to this day Cunard's ships remain a hotbed of snobbism. You assert your superiority by boasting that you dine in the Grills – the restaurant reserved for those who book the largest cabins, and where the dress code is most strictly enforced. They are welcomed aboard with 'sugar-iced strawberries', and by a butler. Ruth Bale is now a reluctant member of the Middleton classes, and holidays on Cunard. 'At least you know they are going to be good,' she says. 'There are social distinctions on the boat. It is peculiar. Last time we went we were on Deck 7, and I didn't realise we had been upgraded. And we met a couple who said, "Ooh, Deck 7, you pay to sway." The higher up you are, the more you sway.' The scruffiest attire allowed in the Grills is 'Elegant Casual'. And that's only on Wednesdays. So, sixty years on from the removal of the demarcation between tourist class and first class, there are more gradations within cruising than ever before. The cooped-up environment is the perfect opportunity to demonstrate your superiority to your inferiors. In the days when those in tourist class were not even allowed to walk along the same decks as those in first class, let alone drink in the same bar, this just wasn't possible.

The one form of holiday transport that, in theory, is genuinely classless is the no-frills budget airline: Ryanair, easyJet, bmi baby and their lower-case ilk. Countesses or call centre workers, it makes no difference, you queue all the same for a notionally cheap flight (before tax and baggage charges mysteriously make it more expensive than British Airways' Club Class). Indeed I know of one Viscount who was a regular Ryanair flyer, until on a flight to Riga he wasn't allowed to check in because he'd booked his ticket under his name, but without his title – and this didn't match his passport, which had the full honorifics. 'They said to me, "Your passport says your first name is Viscount, we can't let you on." Really! This would never have happened on BA.' It is possibly no coincidence that the emergence of no-frills airlines on the travel scene combined with an obsession – on the part of politicians, especially John Major – with talking about a 'classless society' in the 1990s. And in some ways they are a great leveller: all are treated equally poorly and made to eat the same over-priced sweaty paninis.

Their success was in part down to the airlines taking advantage of deregulation of the airline industry within Europe in the 1990s, but also to a significant change in how people went on holiday. They abandoned the travel agent and sought out their own holidays – aided and abetted by the internet taking off. With so many different types of people using the same airline to travel, the real social demarcation became the destination. Pay a visit to Gatwick, Stansted or Manchester airport and you can clearly spot the radically different classes among the mass of sprawling travellers and trollies: snaking queues of stag and hen parties off to Bratislava or Budapest, in matching T-shirts, pink stetsons and Calvin Klein underwear; the second-homers heading to Bergerac Dordogne, with tans and paunches; minibreakers, hand luggage only, with moisturising cream in 100ml packets, anticipation as visible as the freshly applied lip gloss, waiting for the Porto desk to open.

And it is at Stansted that you will find the Wood Burning Stovers. As well as offering genuinely cheap trips abroad (in the era before fuel surcharges and air passenger duty), these no-frills airlines also opened up vast numbers of destinations, especially on the Continent, and far away from the traditional coastal resorts. This was, of course, partly because Ryanair's business model relied on seeking out obscure aerodromes to avoid expensive landing charges. It also meant British holiday-makers could discover vast tracts of Spain, Italy, Morocco and France that had never previously been on the tourist trail, or certainly not in the package holiday brochures – places such as Limoges, Carcassonne, Rimini, Riga, Fez and Jerez.

The queue at Stansted for Perugia – a tin shack of an airport in the pretty Italian countryside of Umbria – is full of Poppies and Georges sporting good teeth, poor hair and Bananagrams, well nourished burghers of Hampstead and Chalfont St Giles. They are the wealthier sections of the Wood Burning Stovers, off to spend the week by the pool in a villa with their children, possibly near the hill town of Città della Pieve, where they can sip espressos, buy the international *Guardian* or *Weekend FT* from the local shop and see if they can spot Colin Firth buying ice cream for his children (the actor and his Italian wife have a house nearby). Unlike the Portland Privateers, who tend to have bought their own second homes, this lot are renters, by inclination and by budget. Perugino rather than pedalos are on their itinerary. They have been forced to use a mass-market airline for their holiday, but feel a certain sense of hard-won pride in the knowledge that they have saved money and nego-tiated the hell of a 6 a.m. Stansted check-in intact.

Though they would be loath to admit it, their trips across Europe on a no-frills airline are partly inspired by Peter Mayle's *A Year in Provence*, published in 1989. A former advertising executive and writer of sex education manuals, he did what many dream of doing – sold up and moved to rural Provence, in the south of France. His whimsical tales, though occasionally lapsing into patronising descriptions of local, simple peasants, were enormously popular and cemented in people's minds that beaches, buckets and packages were *déclassé*. For a true break you need bucolic, remote and – that key WBS term – 'authentic'. If you now visit Loumarin, the small town to which he moved and where his books are based, you will be hard pressed to find a single 'authentic' local peasant or business. The shops are full of 'vintage' linen at London prices, and the workmen wear Armani, thanks to the influx of second-homers, some of the Portland Privateer crowd, able to pay their exorbitant bills.

Provence was where we went on holiday as a family, when we were deemed old enough to go abroad. As children, we managed to combine both incredibly spoilt holidays with the studious avoidance of being flash. My parents were firm believers that holidays were wasted on the young. We certainly never went abroad as toddlers or pre-school children – a key difference from the modern WBSs who take great pleasure in Isla being able to travel for free on Ryanair if she's below the age of two. From about the age of five or six, my sister and I were packed off on a British break with our nanny, so that our parents could have some peace and quiet. We would often be joined by a cousin and his nanny. One of the nanny holidays was a beach trip to Dorset, and one or two were at a caravan park on the Isle of Wight that happened to be owned by an uncle (an aristocrat who lacked a stately home, but owned various property interests scattered around the country, including this tourist destination). We had a cracking time.

When my sister and I were finally trusted to be tourists, the one thing we avoided was skiing. This is curious, as skiing in the 1980s was what the Rockabilly set did in the winter; indeed it was almost as much a badge of membership as the Hunter wellies (tick), membership of the National Trust (tick) and jar of pesto in the fridge (tick). At our private schools an organised ski trip was arranged once a year, and many of my friends would go on to become chalet girls or boys in their gap years or university holidays. But possibly that was the problem. My parents, still clinging on to the lower levels of aristocracy, were definitely a slim notch above the forerunners of Rockabillies, and for them skiing was mostly for hearty army types, which they never were, and for ever-so-slightly flashy Harrys from the 'gin and jag set', as my father called them. The idea of shared jollity grated, and skiing is a decidedly communal activity. My parents suffered from a fear, not just of English food when abroad, but the English too.

Summer was Provence, where my grandmother had bought a holiday home in the middle of nowhere in the early 1970s, an era when a holiday home in Europe was very much a mark of status, especially when it came with a working vineyard as this did. Friends would be invited, and my mother would go out of her way to warn them that it was 'terribly scruffy', by which she meant it was a crucial 40 miles from the expensive Kirs being served in Peter Mayle country and you couldn't buy any vintage linens in the local *tabac*. Because with some people the subtleties of postcodes reach even Provence. It's no different from the days of Concorde, when you would have thought that travelling faster than the speed of sound was exclusive enough. But no, British Airways ran the Premier Club, an exclusive coterie of the top 1,000 most frequent Concorde flyers, who were accorded the honour of a limo and extra-fawning service at check-in and, crucially, the prestige that came with being in the inner sanctum.[9]

Ironically, no-frills airlines only served to make these snobbisms all the more acute. Because everyone, in theory, could afford to travel pretty much anywhere in Europe, everyone had to go much further to prove that their equally cheap, equally accessible place was in fact exclusive. The snooty glances at the Manchester airport check-in, as you steer a clear path around the Faliraki stag party, is repeated across airports around the country. Nowhere were these divisions more apparent than within the higher reaches of New Labour during its early years, despite the promise that we were all middle class and could all enjoy a holiday abroad in the summer.

Kinnock and Blair went no-frills to rustic Europe; Kinnock to Tuscany and Blair to the Dordogne. At this time the Dordogne was so popular with New Labour Wood Burning Stovers that the *Guardian* newspaper was able, astonishingly, to organise a Westminster vs Labour cricket match on French soil in 1993.[10] The Labour team included Roger Stott (a Labour spokesperson on Northern Ireland), Ben Pimlott, the renowned biographer, and Jack Dromey, Transport and General Workers' Union partner of Harriet Harman. They trounced their *Guardian* opponents. By the time Blair made it to Downing Street he started to push the boat out and either stayed at Cliff Richard's Barbados villa or gladly accepted invitations from Silvio Berlusconi in Sardinia, watching fireworks light up the night sky with the words 'Viva Tony'. He had leap-frogged from WBS to Portland Privateer and all the way into hair-dyed global jetsetter in the space of just over a decade, and was now hanging out with the international plutocracy. And he was never forgiven by the rank and file WBS back in Islington and West Didsbury.

The WBS middle classes stick to Europe, preferably close to a suitably rustic town, near a pool not a beach. Of course there will have been the odd foray to India or Chile, maybe during a university holiday, possibly as part of some charitable mission building a school, just as their Victorian middle-class forebears did – though 150 years ago the public-school missionaries spent their holidays in the East End. There might possibly have been a mini-break to New York or Istanbul. But now that you can cross the globe in a day on a week's wages, it is considered a little *infra dig* to holiday in south-east Asia or the east coast of America. After all, Goa is now a favourite destination of Asda Mums along with some of the beaches in Thailand.

The Rockabillies are equally snobby about holidays, but they manage to stamp their status in a different way. Not only have they rejected package holidays, but they are just a little sniffy about jaunts to the Dordogne or the Algarve. Their favoured destination in the summer is Britain. The wealthier Rockabillies still splash out snowboarding in the Alps after Christmas, and a rugby tour with the school team to South Africa is also considered perfectly acceptable. But the rank and file, come July and August, stay at home.

This puts them in tune with an increasing number of consumers who, because of the credit crunch and ensuing recession, became, in the awful parlance of the campsite public relations executives, 'staycationers'. But holidaying at home has long been the preserve of the two extreme ends of British society. A suspicion of foreign food and hot weather has remained a defining characteristic of many who could afford, if they wished, to travel furthest afield. Anyway, the second week of August for much of the aristocracy and fellow tweed-owning classes has always been reserved for shooting grouse in Scotland – impossible to do if you were stuck by a swimming pool near Grasse. As a family we would always have left

France by the end of July, and the drive up the M1 for the 'glorious twelfth', with golden retriever, Barbours, guns, cartridges and a soggy picnic in the back was an annual ritual. This preference for home was only heightened by the growing package holiday industry, which stripped foreign travel of any sense of exclusivity.

By 1989 the middle-class backlash against package holidays was in full flight, and the *Independent*, in a thunderous editorial, revelled in a series of calamities which had hit the European tourist industry, including an outbreak of typhoid on Spain's Costa Dorada, the alleged murder of a Spanish waiter by a group of British holidaymakers on the island of Ibiza, a scum of algae on the beaches of Italy's Adriatic coast and a fresh crop of airport delays. Package holiday companies 'sowed the ground of their own destruction with their misleading brochures, cut-price rivalry for market share at the expense of a decent service, and collusion with greedy foreign developers. As new hazards are added to drunken British hooliganism, the cheap and cheerful Mediterranean package holiday looks increasingly unappealing. If this year's decline turns to slump, the developers and tour operators cannot complain if they reap what they have sown.'[11]

Robert Kilroy-Silk, who long before he became a clownish figure on the political scene had made his name as a class warrior fighting for the dismantling of segregated work canteens, hit back in *The Times*: 'The fashionable snobbery of decrying the package holiday and asserting that staying at home in Britain is best is all right for those with inherited Georgian houses in Somerset, or those that can afford to spend nine weeks in the Lake District. Most of those from the back streets of Birmingham, Bradford, Liverpool and Leeds have no such choice. These people, along with coal miners and steel workers, who produce our essential goods, were called heroes when they fought in all our wars right up to the Falklands. They were not sneered at then. Perhaps their self-appointed superiors, the arbiters of taste and their London mouthpiece, could leave them to enjoy their holidays in peace.'[12] He had a point, even if his economic analysis of 'essential goods' was way out of date.

But staying at home is not what makes a Rockabilly; it is which beach you go to. Snobbism over stretches of sand around Britain's coastline has been in existence since bathing machines protected Victorian and Regency modesty. Westgate-on-Sea in Kent banned Punch and Judy to preserve its image in 1921.[13] Morecambe was acknowledged as the place where families of factory foremen went, along with office workers. Skegness could not match Filey, and Torquay trumped Great Yarmouth.[14]

An Eastbourne family was doing better than a Hastings one, and Lytham St Anne's was superior to Blackpool.[15] Eastbourne's middle-class image was preserved by the Duke of Devonshire, who owned and planned much of the resort and refused any commercial development on the sea front.[16] Many seaside towns, in fact, split into two resorts, with one half decidedly more upmarket than the other. Cliftonville was distinctly more genteel than its neighbour Margate, for instance. These social distinctions carried on for decades after the war, with the reputations of some resorts falling or rising. Filey, once the venue of Billy Butlin's flagship resort, had lost its sheen by the 1960s. Southport was clearly at least two cuts above Blackpool. Poor old Blackpool, always at the bottom of the pile, forever condemned as a working-class destination. Now mostly visited by drunken stag parties, its only salvation – after its bid for Britain's supercasino was scuppered by politics – lies in lobbying UNESCO to be a world heritage site. The historians backing this optimistic bid describe it as 'a cultural landscape without parallel in the rest of the world',[17] as important a part of the industrial revolution as the spinning jenny. They may well be right, because no other town in Britain or perhaps the world has been so unambiguously the destination of the working class at play.

That is in part because many of the working class were traditionally very tribal about where they went on holiday, returning year after year to the same resort, staying in the same boarding house and often travelling with fellow residents. During Wakes Week various industrial towns, especially in the north west, would shut down all factories across the area for workers to have a break, which from 1938 became a paid one. It was the one time of the year you could take a holiday, indeed it was more or less compulsory. Whole streets of factory workers might stay at neighbouring digs and then stake out a joint pitch on a beach. One of them, Arthur English, said: 'You went to Blackpool to bump into people you knew from back home, so that they could see you could afford a holiday.'[18]

The hierarchy of British beach holidays exists to this day, and the miles of beautiful sand along Britain's coast appear to serve one purpose come summer: to reaffirm the social status of those paddling in its waters. Those attached to a Butlins or Pontins just don't cut it. A week at Minehead, Skegness, Prestatyn or Bognor Regis isn't necessarily cheap, but it is organised and it is enforced, shared jollity. Cruising without the views. Blackpool without the posh, reserved for Asda Mum staycationers. Billy Butlin's first camp was inspired by a terrible stay he'd had to endure at a boarding house in Barry Island. He was determined to cater for the 'mass of middle-income families for whom no one seemed to be catering'. It is now all but impossible to stay at one of these camps for a week's wages – seven nights for a family will usually cost in excess of £1,000, about double the average weekly wage. Though you do get a Bob the Builder show for the children, a Take That tribute band and a carvery every evening at the food court.

By contrast, Burnham Market in Norfolk is known as 'Chelsea-on-Sea', where two-thirds of the properties are holiday homes, mostly owned by wealthy Londoners. Bridport in Dorset is 'Notting Hill-on-Sea', Rock in Cornwall is 'Kensington-on-Sea', the neighbouring beach Polzeath is 'Sloane Square-on-Sea' and Southwold in Suffolk is 'Islington-on-Sea', according to the newspapers, whose lack of imagination in search of a catchy headline never fails to amaze. Nowhere has yet to be dubbed 'Battersea-on-Sea', but it's only a matter of time. Rock is the granddaddy of these 'on-Seas', a social magnet so strong it appears to attract the pupils of every public school of Britain and plenty of others who wish they were. The Rockabillies that descend on this small, Cornish town bray, litter, drink vast quantities of vodka and play games of rugby on the beach; they are as close knit a group as the Wakes Week holidaymakers who would stake out pitches on the Bury or Blackpool beach together. Whereas that generation would all sunbathe in their Sunday best, the young Rockabillies' uniform is Jack Wills, Joules, Seasalt or Finistere. Flip-flops, upmarket hoodies, pastel polo shirts, honeyed highlights in the hair and the ability to flick them to maximum public school effect. It is the training ground before their 'gap yahs' in Dharamsala and Tanzania.

Of course there is only a limited amount of paddling done on these beaches. The parents go to these locations to browse the antique shops, pick up crab from the fish stalls (at a considerable mark-up to their local Waitrose), and work their way through whatever is deemed that year's must-read. A game of boules effortlessly manages to convey that they are able to furnish their holiday with a little Provençal *savoir faire* while still being on this side of the Channel. Often the parents are not there at all; they let Hector, Tabitha and Badger have free run of their holiday home – which explains the terrible behaviour of many of the children. It reached a head a few years ago when the Devon and Cornwall Constabulary felt forced to crack down on all-night beach parties.

Harry Worthington, a 15-year-old Eton pupil, complained to a reporter: 'The police pick on anything we do whether it is right or wrong. We need somewhere to go at night and meet our friends. They are ruining our holiday here. It is close to class envy.'

The richest of the Rockabillies can well afford to holiday in Umbria or Corfu, but packing up their Volvo XC 90s with surf boards, a Sainsbury's shop and crabbing nets manages to indicate that this is a family that has freed itself from the shackles of Ryanair. The less wealthy Rockabillies may present their preference for Polzeath as an active decision to help the environment and have more fun at home, but in reality many Rockabillies have little interest in the museums of Europe or the sunstroke of the east.

Staying at home is not the sole preserve of the Rockabillies. And possibly the very pinnacle of staycation snobbery are the Featherdown Farms, a franchise of 'glamping' favoured by certain Wood Burning Stover elements and Portland Privateers who enjoy occasionally slumming it. It is a mystery why the travel industry is so obsessed by ugly neologisms – but glamping is supposedly glamorous camping, usually involving a Cath Kidston tent. But at Featherdown, or at the equivalent site Normandie-Safarie in France, no tents are involved. Instead, families stay in canvas-covered wooden huts which are equipped with running water, a sitting room, various bedrooms, leather armchairs, a flushing loo and – of course – a wood burning stove. A few chickens peck around, ticking the rustic box. You are even supplied with a hand-powered coffee grinder, which allows your morning shot of caffeine to be free from electric intervention. One of the brochures is brazen enough to ask: 'Who are our customers? Our target group are double-income educated families with children between 2 and 15 years old. They are high consumers who are aware of their surroundings. Our customers consciously seek out small-scale educational holidays in picturesque rural settings.'

The Portland Privateers are usually most at home in an upmarket hotel with kids' club and spa, possibly the chichier destinations in the Mark Warner brochure, where golf is offered for the parents, wakeboarding for teenage Cosima and an all-day crèche so that someone else can deal with mewling Hector. Chewton Glen, in Hampshire, and Babington House, in Somerset, are two particular favourites if they are staying in the UK. But they like the reassurance of Featherdown Farm being a branded experience, even if the weather and mud are not. At a drinks reception or gallery opening it can be slipped into conversation as easily as the name of their favoured bikini waxer.

* * *

A holiday should be a time to escape the prejudices, envy, snobbism and divisiveness of the British class system. But it is the down time, the pauses, that somehow heighten our anxieties about status: the tension as we queue at Gatwick, or pick up our luggage off the conveyor belt in Perugia; the sly glance to see if that is the different shade of Jigsaw sun dress, a matching hue of Birkenstock sandal; spotting the fellow Rockabillies heading down the M5 with buckets and spades spilling out of the Seasalt canvas kit bag in the back of their Audi A6. Are they people like us? Or people we don't want to be?

In the early days the suntan alone flagged that you had enough money and get up and go to venture abroad. Now we need to know where that abroad was, and the method of travel, and indeed whether you left these shores at all. Travel for all never did quite broaden the horizons as the generation of Macmillan and Raitz hoped. Instead, it managed to provide the perfect crucible in which to affirm your status. Those Wakes Week beaches, homogenous groups of British holidaymakers, are recreated across the country, indeed across the world – at car rental firms, and waiting to disembark the ferry. The horizons didn't widen, it was just that the sunsets got a bit warmer.

CHAPTER 8

LEISURE

Loose Women or Woman's Hour, Working Men's Club or Turf Club? Why does leisure breed a culture of being in the club or being blackballed?

On the evening of Friday, 9 December 1960, Britain heard for the first time the mournful lament of Eric Spear, played out on a cornet. Since then the same piece of music, for which Spear the composer was paid £6, has been heard more than 7,800 times. It is the opening theme tune to *Coronation Street*.

The television programme is so much part of the fabric of people's sitting rooms, like a dog-eared sofa, that it seems utterly unremarkable save for its longevity. Only *The Archers*, on the radio, has been going longer. But when it first aired more than 50 years ago it was a revolutionary broadcast, from a revolutionary broadcaster. It did something that no one had really attempted before – it put up a mirror to the working classes of south Lancashire and reflected those everyday stories back. Not for shock value, but for entertainment.

From the mid-50s onwards it had become fashionable for novelists and playwrights to dramatise the working class in an unsentimental light. But these pieces – *A Taste of Honey, Look Back in Anger, Saturday Night and Sunday Morning* – were initially plays or novels, aimed at a very small and mostly very elite audience. The working classes themselves could not find their experiences, mundane trivialities, frustrations and aspirations on the television. Harry Kershaw, who was the initial script editor and would go on to be *Coronation Street*'s executive producer, recalls that this huge group of people, 'who perform the many boring, difficult and laborious tasks which guarantee the survival of the economy', had nothing to watch when they came from work. 'And prior to *Coronation Street* they could watch until the dot disappeared into the blackness of the screen but they would never find themselves mirrored there. And then one December night in 1960, everything changed.'[1]

The idea for the programme came from a 25-year-old former child actor called Tony Warren, who was fed up trying to adapt the wartime derring-do exploits of Biggles for the small screen. 'Let me write what I know about,' he begged producer Harry Elton. So he was told he had 24 hours to come up with an idea. The title was originally *Florizel Street* (there was a picture of Prince Florizel, hacking his way through the enchanted forest to get to Sleeping Beauty, hanging on the wall outside Warren's office), but was changed to *Coronation Street* when a cleaning lady called Agnes said that Florizel sounded too much like a disinfectant.[2] The show was commissioned to run for 13 weeks.

Elton loved the initial script, but told Warren he had to pitch the show to the executives at Granada in a couple of snappy sentences. This was what Warren came up with: 'A fascinating freemasonry, a volume of unwritten rules. These are the driving forces behind life in a working-class street in the North of England. The purpose of *Florizel Street* is to examine a community of this nature and, in doing so, to entertain.'³ There was to be a pub, a corner shop and a raincoat factory at the end of the street, and a row of turn-of-the-century houses (based purely for design purposes on Archie Street in Salford), only one of which had an indoor loo. And there were to be strong characters, Elsie Tanner, all 'tit and glitter', Ena Sharples, the hairnetted harridan who held court in the Rovers Return with a glass of milk stout, and young, chippy, university graduate Ken Barlow, who didn't want to take his middle-class girlfriend to tea at the Imperial Hotel because his mother washed dishes in the kitchens there.

It was backed by Granada – the biggest of the four independent production companies that made up ITV, then just four years old – but among the senior executives there were serious disagreements about the resolutely working-class nature of it. One said that the advertisers would pull every single advert if it was screened. Kershaw said: 'There were still elements – and powerful elements – in Granada who honestly believed that no programme could be a success without a strong and obvious middle-class appeal.' The team making the show stuck to their guns and refused to write in a young middle-class doctor whom the executives wanted to live at No. 5, 'to add bloom to the show'.⁴

The *Coronation Street* crew's hunch was correct. It was not just the working classes of Britain who would enjoy the show, but a wider audience too. The critical reception was muted – with most newspapers ignoring the new serial. But within weeks it was clearly a popular hit and by mid-1961, when the remaining ITV broadcasters agreed to transmit the show, it was top of the ratings. It was helped, of course, by the fact that there was only one other channel broadcasting in those days, so the competition was limited. By 1962 the highest two shows in the top ten were Monday night's *Coronation Street* and Wednesday night's *Coronation Street*, both with over 8.5 million viewers, ahead of *Maigret* on the BBC, and Val Parnell's *Sunday Night at the London Palladium*, *Emergency Ward 10* and *Double Your Money* over on ITV.

One of the few fans in the national press was the *Guardian's* television reviewer Mary Crozier. Within months, she said, it had 'won an all-classes and all-places audience. Nothing quite like this has happened before in television. Who would have thought that the Northern accents, so accurate and so unlovely, the drab little street, the corner shop, the Rovers Return, and the day-to-day small happenings of the street's families would cast such a wide spell? It looks like it could run for ever.'[5]

Just one month before *Coronation Street's* début the obscenity trial for *Lady Chatterley* had concluded, a landmark event for Britain's cultural landscape, which many see as the start of the Swinging Sixties. When the prosecuting barrister Mervyn Griffith-Jones asked a witness if it were the kind of book 'you would wish your wife or servants to read', he was rightly mocked for his pomposity. But he was merely stating a certain truth: masters and servants consumed a different culture in 1960. But this was before *Corrie* came along.

Many of the middle classes would pretend that they had never seen it. 'We were the TV equivalent of those ladies and gentlemen who carried around their James Bond novels in *War and Peace* dust covers, and who only admitted to watching documentaries and the odd play,' recalls Kershaw.[6] But it was just not possible for a show to be that popular without attracting a wide base of viewers. Warren said: 'We had become fashionable, and rumours came North that Peers of the Realm were descending twice weekly to the Servants' Hall for a quick peep.'

This was certainly true in the household in which I grew up. Publicly, the culture on show in this five-bed west London house was one of leather-bound Georgian volumes on the bookshelves, oil paintings on the wall and albums of Purcell trumpet concertos. But most of the culture that was actually consumed, especially when there were no guests, was television, and specifically *Coronation Street*. My father, a regular at the Royal Opera House, supporter of the British Library and son of an Earl, is addicted to it. His relationship with the show is almost longer than his one with me, having watched it religiously for the last 35 years. Indeed, since our first Betamax video recorder in 1980 he has hardly missed an episode. While sitting, in black tie, watching *Così Fan Tutte* at Glyndebourne, or being given a private tour of the Hermitage Gallery in St Petersburg, he can only truly relax if he knows the Sky+ box is catching the events at Weatherfield. It is a love affair that baffles and infuriates my mother, but it was one of the very few interests he shared with his adolescent son and daughter.

As children, my sister and I were allowed to stay up to watch *Corrie*. For a while, my bedtime was 7.45 p.m. and I was always sent upstairs during the half-time ad break, while my older sister was allowed to stay till the end. This must have wreaked havoc with my sense of continuity, but it meant that I would drift off to sleep with the sound of the closing credits filtering through the floorboards. I have loved it ever since, though my fondness for the show has faded considerably in recent years.

It was only when I wrote a tribute to the programme for the *Telegraph* on the occasion of its 50th anniversary that I got round to asking my father what on earth attracted him to it. It

245

turns out he was introduced to it by one of our nannies, who for the first few years of our life – before we were sent off to boarding school – lived with us on the top floor of the house. She'd watch it after getting us ready for bed, and my father would pop into the 'television room' (upstairs from the strictly-no-television drawing room) to say goodnight and he'd linger; he became hooked. There we would all be, Linda, the nanny, two young children, and my father, who in those days would often be either getting ready to go out to a dinner party or hosting one himself, huddled around the 12-inch set watching Hilda Ogden or Rita Fairclough.

The soap opera had triumphantly brought the different classes of Britain together – not on screen, but as an audience. Television is unique in this way. No other art form or leisure activity can unite the nation simultaneously, because no other platform is so ubiquitous. Just 1 per cent of British households do not own a television.

There never really had been a national culture in Britain; culture divided along regional and class lines. There were hints of it during the Festival of Britain in 1951, an event which has in retrospect taken on mythical significance. Yes, it was a splash of futuristic colour for grey, ration-book Britain, and an amazing 10 million or so visited the event. But it was not for everyone. As Michael Frayn, the playwright, wrote at the time, it was visited by and aimed at 'The radical Middle Classes – the do-gooders, the readers of the *News Chronicle*, the *Guardian* and the *Observer*, the signers of petitions, the backbone of the BBC. In short, the Herbivores.'[7] The carnivores mostly stayed away, or visited but were not impressed. But the funeral of George VI in 1952 and the following year's coronation of Elizabeth II were the two great catalysts that spurred the buying (mostly on hire purchase) of televisions, and the medium has gone from strength to strength.

Since then, royal pageants and soap operas have competed for the highest viewing figures on television and brought the nation together like no other event. When Ken wed Deirdre in 1981 on *Coronation Street*, 24 million tuned in – more viewers than ITV attracted two days later when the Prince of Wales married Lady Diana Spencer, though plenty more watched on the BBC. The Diamond Jubilee concert in June 2012, with Princess Anne and the Archbishop of Canterbury tapping their feet to Jessie J and singing along to Rolf Harris, appeared to be the final apotheosis of this knitting together. The Queen herself told the members of boyband JLS that she had watched them on television while eating her supper before attending the second half of the concert. In fact, she called it 'dinner',[8] further proof that vocabulary and what you called your evening meal were no longer class delineators. And it was television that appeared to have been instrumental in destroying class barriers and creating a shared experience – with the background of the audience and the performers irrelevant in the face of entertainment.

But though the second Elizabethan age has certainly seen a blurring of class distinctions, with the arts and entertainment playing a key role, we are further than ever from a classless culture. The regional divisions have mostly dissolved, not least with the proliferation of differing accents on the radio and television and the growth of provincial art galleries, theatres and museums. But whether you turn to ITV or the BBC to watch a royal event, or now Sky, is a decision still pricked by class. *Loose Women* or *Woman's Hour*? Wimbledon centre court or Wimbledon greyhound stadium? National Trust or National Lottery? We think much of this is a question of taste, money, or possibly a generational thing, but the books you read, the newspapers you buy, the sport you watch, the shape of ball you hit or kick or throw at the weekend, the entertainment you consume, the YouTube video clips, quiz nights, book clubs, working men's clubs, gentlemen's clubs: they are all things still influenced by class.

*　*　*

The UK spends a greater proportion of its GDP on leisure and pleasure than any other Western country.[9] And in the last 30 years or so there has been a considerable increase in the consumption of culture – in its widest possible definition. The National Lottery, which started in 1994, not only encouraged a vast swathe of the country to gamble, who previously had never done more than have a flutter on the Grand National, but it also poured £8 billion into funding the arts, giving us more options than ever before about how to entertain ourselves. The Government, for official statistical purposes, has a pretty hazy concept of leisure and culture, deciding that singing in public, watching a street performer, going to the circus or attending a salsa class counts as 'engaging in the arts'. At least it has the good grace to exclude karaoke. Under this loose definition, three-quarters of the country has 'engaged in the arts' in the last year.

This wide variety of culture, from visiting a library to a trip to a stately home, from reading a book to watching an Asian dance event, is of critical importance to sociologists. Though I have talked a lot about consumer companies using Acorn, Mosaic and their own databases to analyse the social make-up of their customers, there have been two long-standing official methods of splitting the population of Britain into different classes. The Office for National Statistics examines the employ-ment status and the job that the head of the household performs. More of that later. The other method is the one which most people will have heard of: A, B, C1 and C2, D, E, with the first group of three used as shorthand for 'middle-class' and the second group of three as shorthand for 'working class'.

This six-group categorisation has been in existence for more than 50 years and was originally developed by a body called The National Readership Survey. It has been used relentlessly since then by various newspapers and magazines to find out more about their readers, which advertisers they should chase and which competitions will work. The six groups, from A, 'higher managerial, professional', down to E, 'casual, lowest grade workers, those dependent on benefits', may loosely be based on the employment status of people, but they were aimed at finding out about these people's culture – what they did in their spare time, away from work, whether they turned to the football pages or society columns, whether they tuned into *Mrs Dale's Diary*, the original radio soap, or the Third Programme. The Survey still exists, and the current question-naire runs to 73 pages, and asks about 30,000 people every few months everything from whether they have taken out a loan of more than £5,000 to how many minutes they use a mobile phone every day, which supermarket they shop in, and which radio, television, magazine, newspaper and internet sites they indulge in, how long they consumed them for and which bits they remembered.

The biggest clients of the NRS survey were originally the newspapers, which, despite their diminished role in Britain's culture, remain defined by the class of their readers. Red-top, tabloid and broadsheet are terms that are meant to describe the size and colour of the paper they are printed on, but in reality they are shorthand for the social status of their customers. Possibly the best analysis of the different British national papers was conducted by the peerless *Yes, Prime Minister* television show in a 1987 episode. Jim Hacker, the Prime Minister, says in a typical bout of frustration: 'I know exactly who reads the newspapers. The *Daily Mirror* is read by people who think they run the country. The *Guardian* is read by people who think they ought to run the country. *The Times* is read by people who actually do run the country. The *Daily Mail* is read by the wives of those that run the country. The *Financial Times* is read by people who own the country. The *Morning Star* is read by people who think the country should be run by another country. The *Daily Telegraph* is read by people who think it is.'

Sir Humphrey, his chief civil servant, then says, 'And Prime Minister, what about the people who read the *Sun*?'

Bernard, Sir Humphrey's assistant, chips in: '*Sun* readers don't care who runs the country as long as she's got big tits.'[10]

Today only a little over a third of the British population read a national newspaper. Back in the 1950s, newspaper circulation ran at the equivalent of every household reading one and a half national newspapers each day. But though the papers' readership base is shrinking, newspapers still influence the class debate – both in how they describe various social groups and in how readers of different classes shelter under their mastheads. It is a virtuous circle, endlessly reinforced by the writers of the articles, the pictures of various celebrities that appear, the readers that this attracts and the advertisers that chase after those readers, the editorials that chase after the advertorials.

Take the *Daily Telegraph*: 88 per cent of its readers are ABC1, which explains why so many of its adverts are aimed at the Middleton classes and Rockabillies: Everest driveways, Neville Johnson bespoke furniture, 15-day Scenic Tours to the Jewels of Europe, British Airways, the RSPB and John Lewis washing machines. Its readership is far more closely aligned with the customer base of Saga and Lakeland, the kitchenware shop, than to any particular political party.

The only newspaper to have more upmarket readers, nine out of ten of whom are ABC1, is the *Financial Times*. Monday to Friday it is a staid round-up of global financial events. But at the weekend it shows its true colours, with its magazine, *How to Spend It*, which has become a bible to Portland Privateers, who lap up its columns dedicated to cigars and philanthropic giving. A recent gift guide section included a palladium and buffalo horn chess set costing £3,800 and a collection of tequila glasses from the celebrity jeweller and PP pin-up boy Theo Fennell. A snip at £18,000.

The *Sun*, on the other hand, attracts a readership that is 64 per cent C2DE. It is not pure working class, in the strictest sense. And it's not just those that are looking for big tits. In fact, 42 per cent of its readers are women. What the tabloid has done is to reinforce the prejudices and aspirations of its readers more successfully than probably any other newspaper. They may have started off as working class, and most of them still define themselves that way, but the paper's core readership, the Sun Skittlers, are triumphant members of the modern consumer classes – the first generation to buy their council homes; Benidorm pioneers, tasting the delights of foreign travel; bingo, betting and National Lottery players. Ask a Sun Skittler why they always buy the *Sun*, and they'll answer 'It's the cheapest one available' or 'It's a bit of fun.' They do not have strong affiliations with the paper's editorial policy, they just know it's the one for them.

The *Sun* newspaper in its current format was launched in 1964, five years before Rupert Murdoch got his hands on it. It was ostensibly a Labour-supporting paper, but its readership, as its first editorial spelt out, was the new post-war generation who were 'rising in status'. It stated boldly: 'Steaks, cars, houses, refrigerators, washing machines are no longer the prerogative of the "upper crust" but the right of all. People believe, and the *Sun* believes with them, that the division of Britain into social classes is happily out of date.'[11] But, of course this was not to be so.

The *Sun* failed to break down class barriers. Indeed, to its critics, it has helped reinforce class divisions by championing a certain type of working-class culture, by mischievously whipping up resentment of any form of elite – be it academic, artistic or political. One of the most frequent adjectives it uses is 'posh' – a word which appeared 2,592 times in the last year, more than seven times a day. It's not just because it is short and punchy (tabloids have very narrow columns, and long words are a luxury). It is a word used more frequently than almost any other of the snappy tabloid terms such as slam, evil, blast, curvy, daft, axe. About the only word that is used more often, but not by much, is 'sexy'. The preponderance of 'posh' underlines the paper's obsession with class – the Government is full of 'arrogant posh boys', David Cameron's nickname in the paper is 'posh Dave', a £1.5 million town house is 'posh', caviar is 'posh nosh' (but Greggs pasties are not), *The Apprentice* is full of 'posh guff', girls who go to a boarding school are 'posh birds', Selfridges is a 'posh store', Brasenose

College in Oxford, Cameron's alma mater, is 'posh', indeed Oxford is 'posh' and students who go to Cambridge are 'pampered posh planks'. The Royal Opera House is 'posh' and events held there are 'swanky'.

The *Sun* is not the only one to do this. Both 'middle class' and 'working class' are alive and well as descriptions on Fleet Street, even if the BBC is sometimes coy about using such potentially judgemental labels. The *Sun* used the term 'working class' 245 times in the last year, compared with 151 times for 'middle class'. Over at the *Daily Telegraph* and the *Daily Mail*, unsurprisingly, the ratio is exactly reversed. At the *Mail* 'working class' was used 185 times but 'middle class' was used 416 times; at the *Telegraph*, the term 'working class' was used 357 times, 'middle class' 822 times. The *Mail* and the *Telegraph* are very different in tone, but both know their readers recognise and understand class as a meaningful description, and that almost all of their readers would, if given the option, describe themselves as 'middle class'. In the world of the *Mail* home owners are middle class, graduates are middle class, families are middle class and frequently hard-working too. Most people with A-levels are middle class and to be applauded. Cocaine addicts and shoplifters are to be ignored, unless they are middle class, and then they are to be treated with a special scorn reserved for traitors to their class. But the key thing that all newspapers do is to fudge the term 'middle class'. It is very rarely used as a descriptor of someone earning the median UK salary, namely those whose pay is £24,000 a year. The Duchess of Cambridge, employers of au pairs and those in the 40 per cent tax band cannot, in all reasonableness, be described as middle-income. The *Daily Mail* in 2012 even ran a front page headline, 'Soak the middle class', after the Liberal Democrats suggested a policy of raising taxes for those earning more than £50,000.[12] In the eyes of the *Mail* all these people are middle class, and by that they mean 'people like us' or, in the case of the Duchess of Cambridge, 'people we'd like to be'. But none of them are middle-income. In fact just 10 per cent of the population earn over £50,000.

But the one paper which is obsessed more than any about class is the *Guardian*, which used the term 'middle class' 1,185 times in the last year and 'working class' 864 times. Unlike the *Mail* and the *Telegraph*, it does not use the term 'middle class' as a synonym for 'our readers'. It has a cagey relationship with the middle classes, who are often bracketed in the same sentence as 'suburban', 'overwhelmingly white', 'smug' or 'ponces'. But then *Guardian* readers do like to lacerate themselves. What most *Guardian* readers are is Wood Burning Stovers. Modern herbivores. Diametrically opposed to Sun Skittlers.

For many, the *Sun's* mocking tone when it comes to 'posh' culture is pretty harmless fun. But for some, the endless sneering is symptomatic of a wider malaise. Anthony Smith, the head of Magdalen College during the Laura Spence affair, has spent much of his career either working in or studying the broadcast media. He told me: 'Until Murdoch and ITV the British working class had a culture of self-edification, which included an awful lot of self-education. My family read the *News Chronicle*, a liberal paper, and the *Daily Herald*, a labour paper, and the *Reynolds News* on a Sunday, produced by the cooperative movement. These were all newspapers that implied that nothing was too good for the workers. They didn't debase the culture of the working class as the *Sun* does. Murdoch tried to tell you in his newspapers, "You didn't really want all of that stuff. All that social and educational aspiration was humbug" – that's what it told you. It thought it proved it, and in proving it, it debased the culture of Britain.'

Is the *Sun* to blame for this? I'm not sure it is. But it has successfully reflected and fuelled the habits and pleasures of its readers, and that doesn't often include the reading of novels, visiting the theatre or listening to music. A quick glance at its adverts would quickly show you that one of the main pleasure activities of Sun Skittlers is one they share with the old ill-educated aristocracy: horses and gambling. The Queen's passion for the turf – and her clear lack of ease with the arts – is arguably one of the reasons she has enjoyed such strong support throughout her reign from the traditional working classes. They share a similar outlook when it comes to culture. Most of the traditional aristocracy have never been particular fans of the arts, apart from possibly the visual arts – and that's because many of them were brought up with lovely pictures on their walls. But the theatre, dance and opera are predominantly a Middleton class or Wood Burning Stover activity.

Betting is a resolutely class-based activity. Official figures show that the most likely people to spend money on fixed-odds betting terminals, scratch cards, slot machines and horse races are the unemployed. You could partly explain this away by saying that those without any income are desperately trying to strike it lucky. But the Gambling Commission has studied the socio-economic backgrounds of those that have taken part in any form of gambling or betting in the last year, and the willingness to place a fiver on some hopeless nag is more than a simple question of money, or lack of it. Bingo is played most frequently in the areas of the country that are most deprived, people with university degrees are the least likely to bet, and the group of workers who bet more than any other are 'lower supervisory & technical occupations'.[13] This is not the lowest grade, which is 'semi-routine and routine occupations', but it contains an awful lot of Sun Skittlers.

You are very unlikely to find a Wood Burning Stover or Middleton class in a betting shop. Nor in a working men's club. One of the defining features of most of the modern middle classes – across the spectrum – is that they do much of their socialising in each others' homes. This trend has been fuelled by a number of factors: the wide availability of 24-hour alcohol and 'party food' from the supermarkets, the recession curtailing entertainment budgets, and the resurgence of 'event television' on a Saturday and Sunday night. The Sun Skittlers, however, are the last group to keep up the traditional working-class habit of communal socialising out of their own homes, especially in their local pubs or working men's clubs. Drinking at home was something many miners, dockers and factory workers never used to do. Mick McGlasham, a 62-year-old former miner from Bowldon in the north east of England, ended up being secretary general of the working men's club movement. But despite his elevated status, and a holiday bungalow, to this day he finds it uncomfortable drinking alcohol at home.

'I never drank in the house; in my part of the world in the north east very, very few people drank in the house. You did your drinking where you did your drinking – in a club.' Why? 'Drinking in the house has never appealed. I would drink tea with my meal.'

The clubs, a bit like the unions, have suffered a catastrophic decline in membership. Back in the 1970s there were over 4,000 clubs with about 6 million members; there are now

2,169 clubs with barely 2 million members.[14] Most of the
decline has come about because of a radical change in the
leisure habits of many of the working class, and indeed the
millions who have willingly or unknowingly entered the ranks
of the modern consumer classes – all of whom are relaxed
about drinking at home. Supermarkets, who back in the 1970s
offered a paltry selection of alcohol, have in recent years
consistently slashed the price of beer and spirits in order to
bring in customers – in turn, fuelling the decline of pubs and
clubs.

The collapse of the manual industries has also played a part,
of course – many of the clubs were closely associated with
particular collieries or factories. But there is an argument that
the closure of the clubs themselves, with the shutters coming
down at a rate of one a week, has been in a small way responsible for the decline in the working class. They were the main
venue, outside of the workplace, where a sense of community
was fostered, certainly a male camaraderie; they laid on trips
to the seaside, they hosted comedy and talent nights, they
organised sports on a local and national scale, with the bigger
clubs able to turn out at least two football teams. McGlasham,
a classic Sun Skittler, says: 'Years ago you could go into the
club and see your community there. But the new style of people
nowadays who can order a takeaway, and at home have a
television and all the things that go with it and the cheap alcohol – that's the problem.'

But despite the calamitous decline, many clubs do cling on.
And they do so in the face of a Shiraz-swilling political elite
that has banned smoking in public places, and the rise of television, which now provides cheaper, more reliably high-quality
entertainment than the local committee can put on down at

the club. The smoking ban has devastated many working-class venues. Back in the early 1950s smoking was cross-cultural, with non-smokers just as likely to come from the working-class as from the middle class. If anything working class men smoked slightly less than those better off.[15] Back in 2004, the then Health Secretary, John Reid, was derided for saying the only enjoyment for a single mother living on a council estate was having a cigarette. But the figures show that he had a point. There has been a massive sea-change and 28 per cent of manual workers now smoke, compared with just 13 per cent of non-manual workers.[16]

Kevin, a factory foreman, whom I met propping up the bar of his working men's club, is defined by his leisure tastes far more than his job. At home he watches the television (it's a £1,000 flat-screen from Tesco, the one object he'd rescue from a burning fire before anything else), but otherwise he's a club man. He's the captain of the club's skittles team and he says with a misty-eyed pride: 'It's my life down here. I come here virtually every day.'

Leisure is taken very seriously at the clubs that still flourish. There are nearly 2,000 national trophies to be won each year in competitions that encompass the following: bowls, pigeon racing, Queen of Clubs, chess, whippet racing, dancing, singing, dominoes, bagatelle, phat, whist, golf, shooting, glamorous grandmother, angling, cribbage, snooker, shove-halfpenny – and skittles. No wonder there is little time for many of the Sun Skittlers to sit down and read a book.

This group do wear their lack of education and reading as a badge of honour. They want their families to want for nothing, but that doesn't always stretch to the library. Mick, a shoe factory worker and loyal working men's club member, is astute enough to realise that a university education, something he lacks, is crucial. 'It's very important my grandkids go to university. I hope it'll make a difference and they'll get better paid than myself. I've done better than my father. I was brought up in a council house. The fact I own my own house means I've done better than they achieved, and I want them to go one better.'

But when I asked him about the books he read, he said with a hint of a boast: 'I've never read a book in my life.'

The lack of books in people's homes has been leapt upon by the Wood Burning Stovers as a great social crisis in modern Britain. A recent study found almost 40 per cent of those aged eight to 17 live in homes with fewer than 10 books. When this was reported the figure was invariably contrasted – with much hand-wringing – with the 85 per cent of those aged eight to 15 who owned a games console and the 81 per cent who had a mobile phone.

The *Evening Standard* newspaper in 2011 kick-started a campaign – fought with the same zeal as if it were abolishing child labour in Victorian times – to rid Britain of the 'Argos catalogue family'. It reported a teacher's story of a nine-year-old boy who'd been asked to bring a book from home to share with his class. He brought the catalogue, saying: 'It's the only book my family have.'[17] The paucity of paperbacks in the household was given added potency by the fact it was from Argos – the bible of all things Hyphen-Leigh: gold Nan bracelets, Gordon Ramsay health infusion grills, zumba fitness DVDs and walnut jewellery boxes with peek-through arched windows. The story would not have had quite the same piquancy if the only book the family had was a White Company catalogue. Argos, worried about the image this story gave them, pulled off a masterstroke by giving the boy over £500 worth of books. The scandal was presented as one about literacy. It was really one about class. There is still a section of society for whom books are 'middle class' and therefore not for them.

The one group for whom reading is very much for them is the Wood Burning Stove brigade. And they like to show it, with stacks of Penguin classics resting against their sitting room walls as proudly as a Portland Privateer's Damien Hirst spot painting. Of course a book-lined sitting room is all very well and good, but it is not public. You can only trumpet your membership of the Wood Burning Stove class to those lucky enough to be invited to your tasteful home with black-and-white photos of Lysander on the wall, and Penguin classic mugs on the open shelves in the kitchen, alongside the jar of Puy lentils. A far more effective class signifier – both being portable and pretty cheap – is the sturdy, green canvas book bag sold by Daunt bookshops, the last major chain of independent bookshops left in the country and situated in the smartest postcodes in London. These bags are so ubiquitous at certain bus stops and train stations, slung over the arms of their *Guardian*-reading owners, that I sometimes wonder if Daunt bookshops have sold more bags than books in the last five years. Every fibre of its canvas being gives off an odour as redolent and evocative as the smell of Monmouth Coffee's Kochere Ethopian blend brewing on the Moka pot. 'All our bags are fair trade and are made by re-wrap, a not-for-profit organisation working with co-operatives in India,' explains the website. Short of rubbing themselves in organic Palestinian olive oil, there are few things that are likely to excite a Wood Burning Stover more than fair trade cotton scratching against their shoulders.

One would have thought reading had remained a constant pleasure since time immemorial, or at least since the advent of cheap paperbacks. But it has exploded in popularity in parallel with the growth of the modern consumer classes. The Wood Burning Stovers more than anyone are behind the astonishing rise in book clubs and book festivals in recent years. Back in 1983 there were just three book festivals in Britain; there are now more than 350, and a government report suggested that about 2.5 million adults have either been to a literary festival, listened to a talk by an author or attended a book club in the last year. These are not the exclusive preserve of *Guardian* readers – that just wouldn't be possible with the paper's diminishing readership of not much more than 200,000. Wood Burning Stovers are not fiercely loyal to any newspaper; many read the *Telegraph*, which sponsors the most famous book festival of them all: Hay. Plenty read *The Times*. What marks out a WBS are not just the books, book bags and book festivals they spend their money on, but a real desire to consume intellectual roughage. They desperately feel that the quality of public discourse has declined in recent years, exacerbated by a dumbed-down media (they spend a lot of time tutting when reading the papers, and occasionally howling at the radio as another presenter is unable to use 'fewer' and 'less' correctly). And they believe that dragging Margot, Evie and Jago to the Stoke Newington Literary Festival children's afternoon, or pitching their Indian shakir tent in a field near Hay, will satisfy this itch. This also manifests itself in their passionate attachment to Radio 4, seeing it as the last bastion of civilisation. The archetypal Wood Burning Stove pleasure used to be Mornington Crescent, the spoof game on *I'm Sorry I Haven't a Clue*, whose rules (or lack of them) were designed to exclude anyone foolish enough to stumble upon it by accident. Aggressively abstruse, it swiftly allowed those within the magic club to feel smug for having gained membership; the rest were left baffled and drifted off to Tony Blackburn on Radio 2. The new WBS favourite is *In Our Time*, a less puzzling but an unapologetically erudite radio discussion programme hosted by Melvyn Bragg, which attracts 2 million listeners, something a television programme on Daoism or the Pharaoh Akhenaten could never hope to achieve. In an age when more than four out of ten adults are university graduates and you can buy Birkenstock sandals from Debenhams, Wood Burning Stovers cling to any culture that can still differentiate them. Melvyn provides that life raft, even if the half-hour programme is often even more difficult to comprehend than an Ikea flat-pack instruction booklet printed in Mandarin.

For those who find three academics arguing over William Hazlitt a bit too challenging there is another form of intellectual stimulation that is guaranteed to attract the WBS gang: quiz night. It is a leisure activity that has mushroomed from something a handful of people did down the pub to a mass entertainment undertaken by millions every weekend. And it is not confined to Wood Burning Stovers; Rockabillies, competitive by nature, love a quiz night almost as much as tickets to Twickenham. Indeed, the perfect evening for many a Rockabilly would be the Caversham Lawn Tennis Club quiz night (fancy dress optional) or the Abingdon Rugby Club quiz (chilli jacket potato included in the entry ticket). These quizzes are invariably organised in the name of charity, but really they are an excuse to drink beer and for people to affirm their compatibility.

My children's primary school's annual quiz is a notoriously competitive evening, and the parents who attend are as representative of the school intake as the British political party leaders are of the population – not at all. BBC producers and City lawyers, who live in £1 million houses, fight tooth and nail to recall Usain Bolt's 200 metres record and the capital of Laos. The conversation over the warm Pinot Grigio veers between which Oxford college you attended, the shortage of pasta at the local Waitrose and our rising annoyance at the quality of coffee served in the local park café. Walking into the event you would have absolutely no idea that the school had a mixed intake with many of the children entitled to free school meals. The parents of these children are nowhere to be seen. The school does its best to cement the community, but parents' natural inclination to group themselves together along patterns of consumption and leisure is difficult to overcome.

The activity that comes closest to being truly classless – or rather appeals to many different classes – is football. About 30 million tickets to either a Premiership or league football match were sold last season, returning the sport to the popularity it enjoyed in the 1950s, though a great deal of those will be repeat visits by season ticket holders. About 700,000 attend on a given weekend. And it takes up a large amount of print and air time. The fact that it appeals equally to Sun Skittlers and Portland Privateers is an amazing turn of events and reflects how the leisure industry (and it is an industry) has boomed in the last two decades while becoming gentrified and commercialised. Football, in the snobby prep school I went to, was often referred to by us as 'yob-ball', or 'Kev-ball', even as we attempted our best Keegan keepy-uppy skills. Some of us had posters of our favourite team on our prep school dorm walls, and one or two might possibly have ventured to a match with their fathers, but they were the exceptions. Football was to be played, not watched. Indeed, the public school I went on to did not play football, which was not unusual among many of these establishments. Rowing, cricket and rugby were the main sports, and fives, racquets, athletics, swimming and hockey were the minor ones. This anti-football attitude felt by many of the middle classes was exacerbated by the pre-Taylor Report reputation that most football grounds had in the 1970s and 80s: violent, thuggish dens into which no self-respecting broadsheet-reading John Lewis customer would dare venture. Growing up in Chelsea, I lived just a 15-minute walk away from Stamford Bridge, and at one point the deputy chairman was an uncle. But to suggest going to a match on a Saturday afternoon would have been akin to squirting a dollop of salad cream on top of my Jersey Royals.

The participation in different sports has always been split along class divisions. Hence the particular bile reserved for class warrior John Prescott photographed taking the afternoon off work (when he was meant to be running the country) to play croquet. Croquet! He might as well have been caught quaffing Gin and Dubonnet off the back of a polo pony. He was clearly meant to have been playing skittles or darts. Or football. To not appreciate football, or 'working-class ballet' in the words of Alf Garnett, is now tantamount to declaring class war. All 22 members of Tony Blair's cabinet named football as one of their interests in *Who's Who*.[18]

Sport, with its frequently arcane rules (devised on the playing fields of Victorian England's public schools), does a brilliant job of making its participants and spectators feel insiders or outsiders. Those who tune into *Test Match Special* on Radio 4 Long Wave are dialling into a special club, with its own code and language. But even within individual games exclusion can be rampant. Cricket has to this day struggled to completely shake off the snobbism that saw scorecards subtly, but clearly, delineating public-school amateurs and working-class professionals by whether their initials came before their surname or after. The annual gentlemen vs players cricket match was not abolished until 1962, a move applauded by Fred Trueman, the indisputably working-class Yorkshire lad who wasn't allowed to go to grammar school because his parents couldn't afford the uniform. He called it a 'ludicrous business'. But then his view might have been coloured by the announcement made over the tannoy at Lord's in 1950 about his Middlesex contemporary: 'Ladies and Gentlemen, a correction to your scorecards. For F.J. Titmus, please read, Titmus, F.J.'[19]

It's not just cricket. All clubs and sports do this to a certain degree. George Davies, the founder of George at Asda, nearly became a professional footballer. He scored for England boys against Scotland and carried on playing serious semi-professional football throughout his late teens and his twenties. He was a Bootle Grammar School boy but he made quite a few friends from the smart north-west public schools – Sedburgh and Repton – through playing golf. 'Golf wasn't middle class then, it was upper class. Eighty-five per cent of my pals were from public school and you should have seen the way some of the mothers of these chaps treated me when they found out I went to Bootle Grammar School. First thing, you'd go to their house and I can remember one friend saying, come and meet my mother and father. And I can remember knocking on the door of the drawing room and I just knew they thought I didn't fit in and shouldn't fit in.'

Despite these endless slights he was invited by these same boys to join Liverpool Ramblers, one of Britain's most distinguished amateur football clubs. But he was blackballed. Why? 'Because I didn't qualify. They said that the restriction was for Arthur Dunn league players, a public school league.' A few years later, when he was starting to make a success as a businessman, he was invited by a work colleague to join the Ramblers. Davies explained that he had already been blackballed once and it really wasn't worth the humiliation of trying again. 'A year later I became captain of the whole club. And you know what? I was the major speaker at the 125th anniversary dinner a few years ago.' His lack of ill-will towards the club that had initially snubbed him is classic Middleton class behaviour – a willingness to forgive all slights ('doors to manual') as long as they are eventually allowed into the inner sanctum.

Nick Hornby's book *Fever Pitch* must take some of the credit (or blame) for breaking down the class barriers at the turnstiles to football grounds, but the main reason has been money – the astronomical increase in ticket prices, the flood of Sky's broadcasting fees, and the resulting influx of star foreign players and rising levels of comfort for those in the boxes. It's not just the prawn sandwiches now; if you spend enough money you can treat yourself to Poached Loch Duart Salmon with a cucumber salsa or peeled king prawns with garlic aioli from the 'Platinum Buffet' at the Emirates Stadium. And it is here you will find the Portland Privateers, who love nothing more than spending an afternoon at a high-profile sporting event sipping expense-account-funded Kronenbourg (at Old Trafford, the Emirates or Stamford Bridge), champagne (Wimbledon), John Smiths (Twickenham), Pimms (Lord's). They are sports fans, but they are above all events fans. I was lucky enough to be invited to an evening of athletics at the

London Olympics and was seated behind a row of clients of Aviva, the insurance company. Portland Privateers to a man, wearing TM Lewin pastel shirts and black brogues, they appeared more interested in the beer and their smart phones than the track and field. During the final of the 200 metres, starring Usain Bolt, two of them watched the event, not with their own eyes, but on the screen of their iPads, which they held up to record the race.

It's not just sport. Book festivals (not the Privateers' natural hunting ground, but you can spot them at Hay in the private houses rented out by Barclays Wealth to ensure their guests don't have to sleep under canvas), blockbuster art shows, ambitious triple-bills at the National, Chelsea Flower Show, Henley, Goodwood, Garsington – once upon a time many of these events were part of 'The Season', the curious loose amalgamation of drunken sporting and art gatherings that took place in spring and early summer for debs and debs' delights to meet each other and for their parents to confirm their patronage of all that made Britain great. But the modern season has been hijacked by the new elite, the Portland Privateers and the companies they work for, who invariably sponsor the preview or gala night. As they sip Laurent Perrier rosé in the corporate hospitality tent they could be anywhere – Glastonbury or Glyndebourne – the champagne is more or less the same, and so too the gossip and clientele. Indeed the loos in the VIP Winnebago section of Glastonbury are a great deal more fragrant than those found at Glyndebourne. It is not about the event itself, it is about being seen at the event and having something to chat about, something to show on your iPad, which you whip out during the next round of mini-burgers and asparagus *en croûte* parcels at the following week's gathering.

Football may get all the plaudits as the class leveller, but there is one leisure activity that can claim to match it in popularity and possibly breadth of appeal: the National Trust. It has an amazing 3.8 million members and boasts of being Britain's biggest membership organisation, three times as large as Unite, the country's best-supported union. It is gaining members almost as quickly as the unions, the working men's clubs and bingo halls are losing theirs; in recent years it has been recruiting one new member roughly every minute. Last year 17.7 million tickets were sold to National Trust properties. To get a full picture of the appetite for stately homes and scones for tea you need to add to that 17.7 million figure all the tickets sold to visit a non-National Trust garden or property, because the real blockbuster piles – Woburn, Chatsworth, Beaulieu, Blenheim, along with all the Royal Palaces – do not belong to the Trust.

To many, the enthusiasm that a great mass of the country has for a nicely clipped yew hedge, Georgian chamber pot or royal tapestry is utterly baffling. And there are those within the organisation who fret about their customer base not being wide enough, and that it fails to attract enough inner-city customers. The similar organisation, English Heritage, even conducted various focus groups about a possible name change after concerns had been raised that the word 'Heritage' was putting off potential visitors for being 'all too middle class'.[20]

But spending a day out at Oxburgh Hall, Dunham Massey or Heysham Head is something that unites many Asda Mums and the huge, silent swathe of Middleton classes, those who have embraced all the trappings of a 'middle class' (as defined by the newspapers) lifestyle, without any of the hand-wringing. The history is all well and good, and so too the maze (or even the maize maze) for their children, but they love most of all the tea room and gift shop. At some places this is taken to extremes. Woburn has its own Antique Centre, where you can buy a £3,350 Georgian mahogany tea table; Chatsworth has seven separate shops – take a bit of Chatsworth home with you with a Chatsworth Interiors scent diffuser, or order a piece of bespoke garden furniture from the Chatsworth carpenters. If you go to Blenheim Palace, Vanbrugh's masterpiece in the Cotswolds, there are plenty of visitors inspecting the library or the Sèvres porcelain, but they are outnumbered by those snapping up the 'Below Stairs' range of gifts, including the Butler's scented candle which has the aroma, the box explains, of 'waxed wooden floors and a freshly laid fire in the butler's pantry', or the Valet's clothes brush made from scented pearwood and ideal for cashmere, or perhaps a House Maid's lampshade brush. This is the British class system, as seen through *Downton Abbey*-tinted spectacles, packaged into neat little £14.99 boxes. For a long time there has been a complaint that Britain has been turned into a heritage theme park; well, this is its final apotheosis. And this is how millions choose to spend their weekends. Intriguingly, there is no 'Above Stairs' range.

Much of this lust for master–servant heritage enjoyed by the Middleton classes is fuelled by television. Most of the Middleton classes are fully aware that in the space of just a generation or two they have climbed upstairs from the servants' hall and through the green baize door to enter the ranks of the modern consumer classes. And there is enjoyment to be had in watching, from the comfort of their Sofa Workshop armchairs, with a glass of M&S sauvignon blanc in their hand, the troubles of those yet to make it through the door.

Downton Abbey is adored not just by this class, but by the proper aristos and Rockabillies, who love nothing better than to try to spot historical inaccuracies, the class lapses ('Oh dear, Nigel Havers really should know how to hold a gun') and laugh at how impossibly enlightened the Earl of Grantham is towards his servants – all the while failing to leave the money out for their Bulgarian cleaner coming on Monday morning. The Wood Burning Stovers can't stand its premise – agreeing with the historian Simon Schama that the programme is a 'steaming, silvered tureen of snobbery'[21] – but are frequently caught engrossed in it, though they claim to watch it only ironically. *Downton* is of course the latest in a long line of period, class-based dramas that have been lapped up by nostalgic viewers: *Upstairs Downstairs, The Forsyte Saga* (described by one critic as '*Coronation Street* for the middle classes' and so popular churches moved the timing of their Sunday evensong to avoid a clash) and *Brideshead Revisited*. As with the newspapers, these shows manage to confirm our prejudices, regardless of whether we are above or below the salt. It's not just dramas. It would not be an exaggeration to say that the majority of the greatest of all TV comedy in Britain has been class based. From the *Frost Report* sketch with John Cleese, Ronnie Barker and Ronnie Corbett ('I look up to him because he is upper class ...'), to *Hi-de-Hi!, Fawlty Towers, Blackadder, The Good Life, Dad's Army, The Likely Lads, Auf Wiedersehen, Pet, The Royle Family, Steptoe & Son, Only Fools and Horses, Hancock's Half Hour, Reggie Perrin, Alan Partridge, Till Death Us Do Part, Keeping Up Appearances, Peep Show, Fresh Meat* – all of these to a greater or lesser degree win their laughs by playing on the tension between classes and mocking the very British sport of social climbing. While the casual racism of the

Black and White Minstrel Show and the sexism of Bernard Manning have completely lost their appeal in the space of a generation, these class-based sitcoms are just as popular as ever, and are endlessly repeated. They only work because we fully understand the social tensions being lampooned.

Those in charge of our TV programming, especially at the BBC, are happy to use class for laughs on screen, but spend a disproportionate amount of time concerned about the class of the viewers. *My Family*, once Britain's most popular sitcom, was axed by the BBC because it was 'too middle class', according to its star Zoe Wanamaker. The characters – a dentist and charity shop worker living in a large family home – certainly were, but does that necessarily mean its audience was? Despite the working classes shrinking in size and relative importance to the economy of Britain, there is an obsessive fear that they are not being seen on screen. Or if they are being seen on screen they are being mocked in *Shameless* or by characters such as *Little Britain*'s Vicky Pollard, created by public-school-educated comedians.

Television from its very inception has been obsessed by which classes were watching and who was excluded. Television was born in the radio age, when there was the Light Programme, the Home Service and the Third Programme – and the powers that be were explicit in their hope that families would progress up the ladder from band music and *Round the Horne* on the Light Programme (which was rebadged Radio 2 in the 1960s) to the serious news on the Home Service (later Radio 4), all the way to the sunny uplands of Benjamin Britten and Samuel Beckett plays on the Third Programme (which became Radio 3). Like the supermarkets with their Value, Ordinary and Finest ready meals, culture can be segmented too. But the segmentation did not encourage cultural aspiration, it only served to keep the majority of classes in their own little groups.

The really big class split was the introduction of commercial television in 1955. When the Conservative government two years previously had suggested an end to the BBC monopoly, their proposal was supported by 60 per cent of the country. But many of the great and the good, including the author E.M. Forster, William Beveridge, the father of the Welfare State, and the National Union of Teachers fought hard against the proposal. Beveridge said television should be employed 'to make men more intelligent, to be better in their judgement of entertainment, music and everything else'.[22]

Lord Reith, the founder of the BBC, said commercial TV was a 'maggot ... introduced into the body of England'.[23] But ITV was not to be stopped, despite the best efforts of *The Archers*, which on the night of ITV's début responded with a grisly death. Grace Archer was the sacrificial lamb, burnt to a crisp in a barn fire, while a toothpaste advert played on the television screens. The *Archers* spoiler pulled in 8 million listeners. The *Manchester Guardian* gave her a suitable send-off: 'She was loved, and millions know/That Grace has ceased to be./Now she is in her grave, but, oh/She's scooped the ITV.'[24]

There was immediate suspicion and disapproval of the prize money being offered on many ITV shows, such as *Take Your Pick* and *Double Your Money*, hosted by Hughie Green, which offered a possible prize of £1,024 (about £21,000 in today's money). One early critic complained that in *People Are Funny* contestants were subjected to 'various indignities and then are consoled with a washing machine or a wireless or a bunch of pound notes'. But ITV was a resounding success. It had won over the great swathe of the working classes, many of whom felt there was nothing for them on the BBC.

But for nearly all of its existence ITV has not been able to shake off the sense that though it caters to the working classes much more effectively, it has also – through its brash razzmatazz and chucking about of prize money – failed to encourage aspiration within those viewers. *Coronation Street*, just a few years after its launch, was derided, in a public debate held in Lancashire, as 'the abomination street', portraying northerners as 'peasant morons' and 'creating in people the feeling that perhaps there was something to be said for their own drab existence'.

People tend not to remember that *Brideshead Revisited, Auf Wiedersehen, Pet* and the original *Upstairs Downstairs* were ITV shows, and instead the channel is seen as the home of Jeremy Kyle, *The X Factor, The Price Is Right* and *Loose Women*. These are all firmly Sun Skittler or even Hyphen-Leigh shows and are all derided for celebrating the worst type of anti-aspiration culture that concerned the herbivores of the early 1950s. To this day some Middleton classes just won't watch ITV, too harsh a memory of the working-class homes from which they have graduated. Ruth Bale, who grew up in a council estate in the 1950s, said: 'I never watch ITV. I just don't. Looking back, my parents certainly watched ITV; they watched rubbish, really very working-class taste. My mother loved *Take Your Pick* and *Double Your Money*.' The stain of ITV's original commercial origins just can't be washed away after all these years. And equally, Asda Mums feel far more at home with ITV than with the BBC – the real litmus test being whether you watch *BBC Breakfast* or *Daybreak* while getting the kids ready for school. Asda Mums just don't watch the

273

BBC show. 'It's far too boring. You need to have a giggle in the morning, not listen to politics,' said one. But *Daybreak* always gets the thumbs up. 'It's more light-hearted and they have fashion, and more things I can relate to,' said Vikki, one of the Asda Mums I met in Bootle.

For quite a long time Sky, which launched with its 'squarials' in 1989, overtook ITV as the object of hatred for Wood Burning Stovers. The satellite dishes themselves were seen as an eyesore and proof that the inhabitants lacked taste and class, and were only interested in sport and trashy soaps imported from America. Many residents' associations fought to ensure that Sky didn't enter their street. In the early 1990s its director was forced to defend its output. 'Sky One is upmarket. ITV is the downmarket channel, while we have a young and affluent audience. This is not council-house television.'[25] But many thought he protested too much. Indeed, many of its first customers were Sun Skittlers, with money in their pockets thanks to owning their own homes, and a desire to treat themselves. Now over half the population has Sky. It is an obligatory monthly outgoing for Portland Privateers, who have a Sky HD box in their kitchens as well as their home cinema rooms. For them, the £50 a month full sports package is as essential as Bupa dental care.

Ironically, 20 years on from its launch many Wood Burning Stovers will reluctantly admit to being rather keen on Sky, which now gives away a £50 M&S voucher for those who sign up. They like its dedicated Arts channel, broadcasting highlights of the Hay Festival and the ballet ('It's just like BBC 2 in the old days'), and Sky Atlantic, home to *Mad Men*, the slick US drama. The fifth series of the programme, aired in 2012, was watched by a mere 98,000 viewers. It was lavished with attention by all the Wood Burning Stover newspapers and magazines, but just a third of 1 per cent of all the households in Britain actually watched it. That, of course, didn't worry this particular elite. As one leading *Guardian* columnist said: 'In an odd, and clearly snobbish, way I'm rather pleased with the small audience. I like the fact that the masses don't like *Mad Men* because, presumably, it is too sophisticated.'[26]

Back in 1960 the choice was stark – BBC or ITV. There are now more than 600 different channels, all showing programmes for the 'masses' or the 'sophisticates' and the hundreds of different gradations in between. TV didn't make culture classless, it just did a very good job at creating hundreds of different programmes that appealed to the hundreds of different classes.

* * *

A few years ago a young reporter was interviewed for a job on the *Telegraph* business desk. He was asked by the city editor at the time, who was known for being a bit spiky, why he thought he'd be good at the paper. The eager applicant said: 'I'm very clubbable.' To which the editor replied: 'What, like a seal?' He didn't get the job.

Clubbability – though not the seal variety – has been a trademark of Britain at play for decades, from Pall Mall gentlemen's clubs, through tennis and golf clubs, Women's Institutes, Rotarians and Soroptimists to bingo halls and working men's clubs. Nearly all of these attract their members from a particular social class, some from a ludicrously narrow one at that – it's part of the appeal. In the 1960s there was a club at Oxford University called the Snuff Committee, the purpose of which was to take snuff and drink port. Membership was by invitation only; the sole stipulation was that one had to be the son of a landowner.

Many of these clubs are slowly dying out, most notably working men's clubs, though a recent analysis of the House of Lords found that 45 per cent of peers were members of a gentleman's club such as the Garrick Club, Carlton Club or White's. And modern-day gentlemen's clubs – the private members' bar such as Soho House or Home House – are a flourishing business thanks to the Portland Privateer clientele, however hard these clubs try to ban bankers or anyone wearing a suit.

Culture, in its widest possible sense, is meant to be the antithesis of these clubs. The beauty of coming together, disparately but simultaneously, to watch an hour of television, visit Chatsworth's gift shop, take in an Andrew Lloyd Webber show or discuss a novel can break down social barriers in a way that no social engineering can hope to achieve. But class is never far away. Our daily newspapers, pop music, plays, books, National Trust cream teas, sport – these are all, in part, about belonging to a club. It is about understanding the rules and sharing the same experience, of excluding outsiders. Of being part of the 98,000 who watched *Mad Men* last night, of having a recording of Usain Bolt on your iPad, of turning your nose up at *X Factor* but adoring *Strictly Come Dancing*. And despite many valiant attempts to lessen Britain's clubbability, the urge still remains.

However, one thing is certain. Despite our hugely different leisure habits, we consume culture like never before. After the war one tenth of people's spending went on leisure and relaxation. This more than doubled over the next 50 years to reach a quarter of people's spending.[27] The average family now spends more on 'recreation and culture' than on food and drink or on clothes. For all the long hours modern Britain toils, we are no longer the working classes but the leisure classes. But if this is so, we need finally to turn our attention to how we earn our living. And find out whether how we fund this consumption plays any role in defining who we are.

CHAPTER 9
WORK

'So, what do you do?' Does the nature of your work have any bearing on whether you are working class or not?

Susan Shaw came home from work on the evening of 26 March 1973 and, showing the front page of the *Evening Standard* to her daughter, pointed at the picture and said: 'Who's that?' Tania, the two-year-old, said: 'Mummy.' Susan then settled down to an evening of ironing, only briefly glancing up to catch herself on the nine o'clock news. She had, as she said, 'arrived'. For a brief few weeks in 1973, during a time when some of Britain was being rocked by IRA bombs, she became one of the country's most talked-about women. The cover of the *Economist* that week featured her with the headline: 'By Jove, she's done it.'[1] By Jove, she had. But the source of her fame was, to modern eyes, faintly ludicrous: she had merely gone to work.

On that day in March she became the first woman ever to walk, as a member, onto the floor of the London Stock Exchange, the beating heart of the City of London. There were six women who joined the illustrious institution that day, but by a quirk of timing Susan beat the rest by a few hours. All of the women were already fully fledged stockbrokers, but had been denied the ultimate badge of status: being a member of 'The House' as it was called. Until that moment it had been, quite literally, an old boy's club. You had to be voted in, with a sponsor and a seconder; talent was not a requirement. Who you knew counted for far more than what you knew or what qualifications you may have held. The country's centre of commerce, its money-making engine, was a closed shop. The rules of the stock exchange did not explicitly bar women, but every time a woman had applied to become a member, they had been voted down. One particularly fusty member, when asked why they shouldn't join, said the lack of female loos made it an impossible notion.

Susan, along with many, saw the arguments against joining as 'absolutely ridiculous. There were loos back in our offices. And there were public loos up in the visitors' gallery,' she says. Another female applicant pointed out that if they were caught short they could always dash down to the loos at Bank underground station.

The atmosphere, not just in the stock exchange but in much of the City, was straight out of the prefects' common room of a pre-war public school. Susan, ten years before her day of triumph, had started her career in the City as a glorified tour guide, in charge of the visitors' gallery in the exchange – a glassed-off balcony overlooking the trading floor, which in the mid-60s looked not that different from 40 years before. It still boasted many members not only in bowler hats but a clutch, including Government brokers, who still wore top hats to work. 'Oh, it was very public school. When I first joined the stock exchange gallery there were debs' delights on the stock exchange floor,' she says, referring to the young, eligible, occasionally titled men whose main purpose in life, as we saw earlier, was to track down a 'deb' to marry. This involved attending two or three cocktail parties and balls every evening, and fitting in a bit of light work around their hectic social life. 'They would come up during lunchtime to our little sitting room in the gallery and flop down, exhausted from a morning's work. They were probably blue button clerks attached to their uncle's or father's firm, and that was how they joined the City. It's what you did.

'You'd get lots of ragging and teasing. On a dull day, someone would be reading the newspaper, and another person would light it from underneath. Lovely, jokey sort of things. None of it was malicious.' A waiter rang a bell at 3.15 in the afternoon, which signalled that smoking was allowed on the floor of the exchange. It was known as the smoking rattle. Not everyone thought the ragging was so innocent. A female member, who joined a couple of years after Susan, remembered the culture of schoolboy nicknames: 'I was the Night Nurse, there was Sweaty Betty, Super Bum, the Grimsby Trawler, the Road Runner, Stop Me and Pick One. They were very cruel. Stop Me and Pick One was because she had acne. You had to have broad shoulders and a good sense of humour because you would be the butt of a lot of jokes.'[2]

It was perhaps not that surprising that a culture based on that of Eton, Harrow and Winchester, with their nursery food, ragging and regimented uniforms, was so prevalent in the City. After all, many of its workers had come straight from public school to work there. Not that many bothered with university. A sociological study conducted in the mid-70s of senior workers in the City found that four-fifths had attended a fee-paying school. At the time the chairmen of the so-called Big Four banks were: Sir Archie Forbes of Midland, who was a Scottish chartered accountant; Sir John Thomson of Barclays, who had gone to Winchester and Magdalen College, Oxford, and was a member of the Jockey Club and a Lord Lieutenant of Oxfordshire; John Prideaux of NatWest had joined the family merchant bank of Arbuthnot Latham straight after leaving Eton; while Eric Faulkner of Lloyds had, after Bradfield College and Corpus Christi, Cambridge, joined the private bank Glyn Mills.

Lord Poole was asked how his bank, Lazards, had managed to avoid being affected by the crash of 1974, when various small banks went belly up. 'Quite simple,' Poole answered. 'I only lent money to people who had been to Eton.'[3]

The lack of women was not only a sexist conviction; it was a comforting reminder of their Victorian public schools, all-male institutions, save for the matrons. As one City worker, who ended up running one of the City's biggest institutions, told me: 'Back then the only woman you really ever saw either served you your lunch or was your secretary.' The symbolic victory of Susan and her fellow female workers was not just a victory for their sex; it was an important class milestone. The rise of the consumer classes, the package holiday takers, the bread machine bakers, was just not possible without the emergence of two-income households.

Susan Shaw is an unlikely revolutionary. She lives in Barnes, in an impeccable house filled with family pictures in silver frames, and serves coffee in a little cafetière along with a plate of two-finger KitKats. Most of the women who joined that day were middle class, and slightly embarrassed about rocking the boat. Their unofficial leader was Muriel Wood, who was then 55, and had started her career in the City in 1925 as a typist. Like many people, her career was given a boost by the war, when she ended up running the office, owing to lack of available staff. She had lodged a number of requests to become a member from the mid-1960s onwards, and each had been turned down. Without being a member, they could all operate as stockbrokers, manage clients' money, place orders to buy and sell shares. But they could not become partners of their firms. They did not think they were fighting a feminist cause. Mrs Wood said at the time: 'I am very anti the women's lib movement. You cannot ask people to have confidence in you if you behave irresponsibly. They have let our sex down very badly.'

By 1971, though, just a few months after Germaine Greer's seminal feminist manifesto *The Female Eunuch* had been published, the matter was taken up by Parliament, and the Council of the Stock Exchange became increasingly concerned. They were pushing hard to allow women in, and another vote was taken, but again it was defeated. To this day Susan, now in her 70s, is slightly baffled as to why there was such intransigence, with each of the votes going against female membership. 'If you can get into a man's head, maybe you can tell me the answer. It had been like that always, and they thought it would never be the same again. They felt comfortable in their own skin on the floor. They could put up with women in the office, that was another matter, but not on the floor.'

Finally, via the back door, they were allowed in, but only because the London Stock Exchange had agreed to a merger in 1973 with all the regional exchanges in cities such as Birmingham, Liverpool and Manchester. These exchanges already had female members, so London's no longer had a leg to stand on. 'It was a bit of a damp squib, in the end,' concedes Susan. So she, and another five women who had applied in the previous year, found that their membership was reluctantly waved through.

On the day itself, a Monday, she was nervous, with 'knees like jelly'. Her boss, Richard Bradshaw, who had championed her application, suggested they get the ordeal of walking onto the floor of the House over with as quickly as possible. So she, by accident, beat Muriel and the other four by a couple of hours. 'I do feel very sorry about that.' At 9.30 a.m. she became the very first woman to step onto the floor of the London Stock Exchange. 'I didn't know what to expect. But actually it was amazing. People suddenly came up and shook my hands, and said, "Welcome, welcome" and "Well done", and I got kisses on the cheek from someone I knew.'

A year later there were 52 female members. Thirty years later there was a female chief executive of the London Stock Exchange.

* * *

Susan and Muriel's victory was hailed as the breaching of the final bastion of privilege. The Civil Service and the Army had both abandoned the concept that you could obtain a position either with a cheque or because of who your father was. British industry, or what was left of it, was headed by grammar-school boys or even those that had started life on the shop floor. But the City was still class-bound. A well-meaning merchant banker at a staff Christmas party, on hearing that one of his typists lived 'on an estate in Romford', replied, 'How splendid. Do you keep horses there?'[4]

A brief glance at the City now suggests that the women's victory was not just one for their sex, but a class victory too. Stephen Hester, the chief executive of the Royal Bank of

Scotland and the fattest of the fat cats, is a comprehensive-school boy from Yorkshire. Stuart Gulliver, the head of HSBC and a rival in the 'pooch with paunch' stakes (his bonus in 2011 was £5.9 million, even after he had handed back £1.9 million because the bank had been involved in a mis-selling scandal), went to grammar school in Plymouth; his mother worked in the local dockyard. The Bank of England Governor throughout most of the 1960s was Lieutenant-Colonel George Rowland Stanley Baring, 3rd Earl of Cromer, offspring of the famous banking family, Barings. The Governor for the last decade has been Mervyn King, grammar-school boy and son of a railway driver. Most of the biggest City firms are now owned and headed by Americans or Swiss. The colour of your money, not the stripe on your old school tie, is what counts. And this apparent transformation has been reflected in radical changes that have happened across offices, factories, pits and trading floors.

But while the coal mines, steel works and typing pools are diminished to almost nothing, this does not mean the working class has been eradicated. Far from it. The work that goes into being working class has merely changed. And for all of the barriers that have broken down in the specialised billionaires' club – Old Etonian Nat Rothschild is no more stinking rich than comprehensive-school drop-out John Caudwell, the mobile phone magnate – many workplaces have failed to fully open themselves up to workers of all classes. Some professions, notably law, have successfully broken down barriers to entry for ethnic minorities – there are a disproportionately large number of black and Asian barristers compared with the overall population – but have failed to break down class barriers. There are still some jobs where it is easier to enter if you went to public school, Oxbridge and come from a well-connected family.

The job you do has always been very important, as a marker of status. How you answer the 'So what do you do?' question at dinner parties is something that has tied up the dinner-party classes in knots for decades. And for the non-dinner-party classes, one's trade – especially in an era when there were jobs for life and a decent pension – was a key part of one's make-up. I believe that for a number of reasons, not least the death of the job-for-life, work is no longer the most important factor in determining one's class. But in the eyes of officialdom it is. How you earn your money defines your social position. The Office for National Statistics – whose data are used to determine various key pieces of government policy, from the quality of medical care you will receive to the number of teaching assistants at your school – spends a great deal of time working out what social class we all fall into. And its starting point is always your job. At the very top are chief executives and elected officials such as MPs, and at the very bottom are leisure park attendants, shelf stackers and window cleaners. Which is odd, as my window cleaner's last holiday was in Barbados.

It all goes back to the Victorian era, possibly the golden age of the detailed, bureaucratic and thoroughly nerdy desire to classify anything that moved and plenty that didn't: insects, fossils, diseases, servants and their masters. There was a growing awareness that mortality rates were directly linked to social class. Statisticians started to allot occupations to different categories, based on various industries. Then, at the start of the 20th century, a statistician called C.H. Stevenson formed the belief that it was not necessarily income that explained the lower mortality rates of wealthier people, it was what he called their 'culture', which for him also included knowledge of health and hygiene issues.[5] The key was the skill of your job, not necessarily the industry you worked in. The classic model of five social classes, with professionals at the top, followed by managers, then skilled work, then partly skilled, with unskilled manual work at the bottom, is the creation of C.H. Stevenson and remained pretty much unchanged between the 1920s and the 1990s. There was the odd tweak as the nature of some jobs changed. In 1960 airline pilots were promoted from class III to class II (boosting the Middleton family's rise up the social scale); and in 1961 postmen and telephone operators were demoted from class II to class IV. It was only a decade ago that a more thorough overhaul was undertaken by the ONS, which incorporated employment status – whether you were salaried or a contractor, whether you worked for a large organisation or a small one. The most up-to-date classifications include 42 different sub-categories, and they distinguish, for example, whether you are in agriculture as an employer, as an 'own-account' worker, as a semi-routine agricultural labourer or as a routine labourer. In other words, the 21st Earl of Moray, owner of vast tracts of farmland in the northern Highlands, is given a completely separate status from one of the Latvian temporary workers employed to pick parsnips on his estate; in the original classifications they would have come from the same 'agricultural class'.

Then within the 42 sub-categories there are about 600 specific job groups. Butchers, bakers and (sadly, no candlestick makers) chefs all fall into group 543: food preparation and hospitality trades. Even at this specific level the flaws immediately become apparent. Is Jamie Oliver, father of Poppy Honey, Daisy Boo, Petal Blossom and Buddy Bear, worth over £100 million, scourge of turkey twizzlers, hero to Asda Mums and Rockabillies alike, really in the same social class as the local butcher? Well, actually, no. Because he employs lots of people he'd be in group 122, restaurant and catering establishment proprietor. But despite the hundreds of different sub-categories, it is a very crude way of defining people. The most senior QC, owner of a pile in the country, a magnificent cellar of claret and an expensive second wife, is in the same class as a junior barrister, just qualified, who thinks a night out at Strada is a bit of a treat. David Linley, nephew to the Queen, who sells £9,250 photo frames from his carpentry shop, is – or was before he became an international Portland Privateer brand – a carpenter, in the same class as Perry (named after Como), the chap who put up the bookshelves in our north London home.

Possibly the most acute problem with the classifications is that no one in modern Britain is prepared to call themselves upper class, and certainly not those in class 111, chief executives and senior elected officials. This is clearly nonsense, as the astute historian Arthur Marwick argued many decades ago. Those at the very top of the pile – high court judges, members of the Government, senior civil servants, chief executives (basically the top 1 per cent) – were upper class in his eyes. And yet the three most recent prime ministers have described themselves as being 'middle class, and my politics were in many ways middle class' (Blair), coming from 'an ordinary middle-class family' (Brown) and belonging to 'the sharp-elbowed middle classes' (Cameron). They all have shrunk from admitting that getting the very top job in the country makes them automatically part of the elite, and therefore upper class.

And the old-fashioned definition of what constituted the upper classes – those who didn't need to work – no longer really stacks up. Most aristocrats now work, be it the 7th Earl of Rosslyn and the current Viscount Nelson, both of whom are police officers, or the Earl of Pembroke, who until recently worked for that arbiter of middle-class style, Conran Design. Even the stinking rich aristos spend considerable time and effort working out how to squeeze more income from their estates. And the less rich ones, especially, are forever trying their hand at B&B, organic tea rooms, antiques fairs on their back lawn, corporate bonding days in the deer park, anything to pay for the leaking roof and inheritance tax. Their children, who traditionally could be relied upon to loaf and do little but snort their inheritance up their nostrils, appear to have acquired an appetite for graft. Edward Spencer-Churchill, son of the Duke of Marlborough, is a director at a private equity business which owns various downmarket retailers; Lord Freddie Windsor works for J.P. Morgan; and Arthur Mornington, heir to the Duke of Wellington, toils for Charterhouse, another private equity house.

And most plutocrats such as Sir Philip Green or Lakshmi Mittal – owners of serious amounts capital and labour, and clearly upper class by any Marxist definition – spend most of their time glued to a Blackberry or a spreadsheet, even if it is aboard a luxury yacht moored offshore. Britain has never had so many über-rich, but not that many of them are idle.

The other major flaw is that these ONS classes do not really recognise families as a unit, only the status of the main bread-winner, the 'head of the household'. This seems very unfair on Susan Shaw and her generation. Their victory helped raise not just the status of their sex, but also the entire social standing of their families. Indeed, it is not an exaggeration to say that this generation of working women is responsible for the great-est surge in the middle classes Britain has ever seen. It was their money and their purchasing decisions which dragged so many working-class families higher up the ladder.

It was not until after the war that the 'marriage bar', which banned certain women from returning to work after they were married, was lifted. When workers at the Peek Frean biscuit factory in Bermondsey – the first to make the bourbon biscuit in Britain – were interviewed in 1955 as part of a study, it was found that 'what most of the women wanted was an opportunity to earn money to raise the standards of living of the family as a whole'.[6] One filing clerk, interviewed by Mass Observation in 1957, said: 'We have been able to afford a nicer home because of my work; we can buy all sorts of extras or a holiday.' In a letter to *Women's Own* in 1955, a Mrs V. Norman of New Malden wrote: 'The most cherished addition to our home is our baby son, now growing up a placid, happy little soul. This is partly because I am not a harassed housewife, thanks to my labour-saving devices – none of which we would have been able to afford had I left my job when we were first married.'[7] To deny working women, and their role in the growth of the consumer society, a proper place in the classification of social classes, because they are not usually 'head of the household', seems odd.

However, what the official classification does do, in its own dry and flawed way, is highlight that there are some high-status jobs and some basic jobs, with countless gradations in between. We may not agree that street cleaners, leisure theme park attendants and lollipop ladies have the very lowliest jobs in Britain today, and that those of chief executives, army officers and advertising directors are among the very best. But we'd all know at which end of the ladder they should be placed. And the National Statistics Socio-economic Classifications, through the sheer variety of jobs that they list and code, hint at the idea that certain workplaces – regardless of the hierarchy within those occupations – are full of Boden-wearing, latte-drinking Waitrose shoppers and some are full of New Look-wearing, *Closer*-reading Asda Mums. In that respect, classifying all barristers together is a meaningful exercise. Find me a barrister, however junior and poorly paid, who regularly shops at Brighthouse.

So what is a posh job, and what is a working-class job? This is so difficult to pin down, because of the seismic changes that have happened to the British economy over the last two generations. Back in the 1950s most Britons, when it came to work, were working class. And that meant manual work. And those who weren't were usually sitting at a desk. The shift from being a country whose money was made from manufacturing to a service economy is well documented. But it is worth giving some basic statistics to show how dramatic these changes have been, because they come hand in hand with the rise of the consuming middle classes. Back in 1954 there were nearly 9 million people who worked in manufacturing, with over 1.8 million of those in textile manufacturing, involved in everything from lace, millinery and fellmongery to rayon, jute and woollens. There were 791,000 coal miners and 228,000 who worked in shipbuilding. In contrast, there were 466,000 in insurance and banking, just 78,000 lawyers and a mere 53,000 who worked as hairdressers and manicurists, the ultimate service economy job.[8]

The most recent figures show that manufacturing workers have fallen to 2.63 million, with just 87,000 in the textile industry; there are no longer official figures for how many shipbuilders there are, but it is certainly less than a tenth of the number back in 1954. How many coal miners are there? Just 6,020. That's not enough to fill the stadium of Burton Albion Football Club. The service side of the economy is considerably larger, indeed ten times larger than the manufacturing side. The catering and hotels sector accounts for 1.7 million workers – three times the number back in 1954; insurance and banking employs over 1 million; and there are now 281,000 lawyers. Those working in call centres top an astonishing 1 million, make up 3.5 per cent of the entire workforce and constitute one of Britain's biggest 'industries'.[9] And there are now about 100,000 hairdressers plus an unknown number of manicurists (sadly, the ONS no longer lists them separately, but with over 1,400 nail bars in Britain there may even be more manicurists than miners). This means there are now a greater number of people cutting hair than making clothes and textiles in Britain. And there is now the same number of advertising and marketing employees in Britain as there were domestic servants back in 1954.[10]

These profound changes, however, do not in themselves explain why there is a romance about the old manual labour jobs, and why the modern working-class jobs – those in the fast-food industry, or call centres – are so despised. This complete disdain for today's low-skilled jobs was highlighted in the row over the Government's welfare-to-work scheme in 2012. The idea was simple. People aged between 16 and 24, who had been unemployed for more than three months, could voluntarily work at a number of leading companies such as Tesco, Burger King and 99p Stores. Admittedly the jobs were basic entry-level ones and the work was unpaid, but the participants continued to receive their Jobseeker's Allowance. The company would benefit from the free labour, the worker would gain some limited experience and – more important – get used to the rhythm and habit of work. Many companies, not least the supermarkets, complained that too many school leavers failed to grasp the basic concept of turning up on time and looking either a boss or a customer in the eye. Critics said that the scheme was outright slave labour, and when it emerged that participants who dropped out might lose their benefits the howls of anguish turned to barricade-mounting from the home-made bresaola on sourdough brigade.

The then Work Minister, Chris Grayling, was forced onto the attack: 'The critics are job snobs. The *Guardian* newspaper publishes stories attacking big retailers for offering short-term unpaid work experience placements for young people. But that same *Guardian* newspaper advertises on its website – yes, you guessed it – short-term unpaid work experience placements for young people. The BBC's *Newsnight* joined in the attack on big retailers offering unpaid work experience. And on the BBC website? Yes, you guessed it again – an offer of unpaid work experience placements. It's time we put an end to this hypocrisy.'[11]

His point was a valid one. The complaints mostly came from Wood Burning Stovers – from the comfort of their desks with an Apple Mac on top, and a spare sachet of soy sauce in the top drawer. The scheme was far from perfect, and the Government's claim that half of the participants went on to find proper employment after finishing the scheme was not strictly true. In fact, half stopped claiming benefits at the end of their placements – a slightly different matter. But Grayling was right to say that there were job snobs out there. Few critics aimed their fire at Oxfam, Shelter or Mind, the charities that took advantage of the scheme. Most of the bile was reserved

for Tesco, Burger King, TK Maxx and BHS and the like –
consumer companies that not only served those low down the
social scale, but employed them too. It was another case of the
denigration of McJobs, those basic, repetitive, unskilled jobs
mostly in the service and retail industries that have become the
staple of the modern working classes. Miners were glorious
and noble labourers; their burger-flipping grandchildren have
become objects of pity.

It is a debate that has been raging for some considerable
time. Tony Parsons, professional champion of the working
class, writing in 1998, after McDonald's announced it was
creating 10,000 jobs, said: 'Mrs Thatcher left the traditional
industries out for the dustmen. It has been over 20 years since
working-class kids learned a trade. Perhaps that will all change
under Tony Blair. Let us hope so. Because the alternative is an
army of young, unskilled people earning £3.50 an hour in
burger bars ... Once upon a time the British built shops and
cars. Now we build cheeseburgers.'[12] Since then McDonald's
has nearly doubled its workforce.

Possibly the nature of the brands and the products these
companies produce – 99p goods and processed patties of beef
– has something to do with it. A Sainsbury's check-out girl is
not accorded the same level of scorn, despite doing exactly the
same work as her equivalent across the road at 99p Stores.
And there is still a belief, perpetuated by those who define
themselves as working class, that manual labour carries greater
value than working in a shop – though those who have worked,
standing up all day, behind a supermarket fish counter will
know it is a tiring way to earn a living. The world has moved
on. Britain does not make very much, but it does consume an
awful lot, despite the recession squeezing people's spending

power. There are millions of people needed to service that consumption, and many of these jobs are unskilled, unglamorous and lack prospects.

Those that most mythologise the glory of hard, dirty manual work are those who joined the workplace before the advent of computers and call centres. The Sun Skittlers, who ended up at the local factory, digging roads or painting and decorating, never had the option of sitting with a headset on and trying to deal with the angry customers ringing up about being overcharged on their gas bill or lack of broadband, with no option of taking a loo break unless it has been scheduled. Britain's first ever large-scale call centre only opened in 1985, when Direct Line employed 63 people to answer phones in Croydon. Call centres have become modern factories – offering repetitive, exhausting, unskilled jobs to those who leave school with no prospects, or with plenty of qualifications but no luck.

Another reason why so many people despise these modern working-class jobs is that they are very poorly paid. This was not always the case. Some traditional manufacturing, mining or factory jobs came with a decent amount of money at the end of the week. In 1954 the average weekly wage of a miner was 245s 11d,[13] or the equivalent of £36,300 a year in today's money – well above the average wage. As the *Manchester Guardian* pointed out, many miners at the age of 30 were earning as much as a solicitor or an accountant of the same age. 'From the coalfields have come orders for new cars beyond the reach of the modest suburban motorist, who runs a prewar model without any help from his firm. Small cars costing between £600 and £700 are the most popular, but there have been orders for expensive sports cars and for at least one saloon costing nearly £1,000.'[14] And this is for a year when only one out of every five households in the country owned a car.

The 1950s, 60s and much of the 70s also saw factory workers fund their newly consumerist lifestyles thanks to the practice of 'piece work', with employees paid by the finished article, not by the hour. Lola Smith, an East End girl who'd left school at the age of 15, went to work in the local furnishing factory as an apprentice machinist. The pay was £2 a week, and she had to stick at the apprenticeship for at least three years before she stood any chance of moving on up. 'But apprentices do not earn what piece workers did. And so as soon as I could I left my apprentice to go into piece working on men's trousers. And I was earning as much at 16 as a married woman. It was about £6 a week in the mid-50s.' Arthur, the cycle factory worker in Alan Sillitoe's 1958 novel *Saturday Night and Sunday Morning*, earns £14 a week, about £640 in today's money.

In short, manual work paid. And it still does to a certain extent. The average weekly wage in the mining and quarrying industry in Britain today, among the very few who still do it, is over £900 a week. It is over £500 a week in the construction industry. But it is a mere £220 a week in the accommodation and food service sectors – chambermaids, waiters, burger flippers and pizza toppers.[15] Official statistics show that waiters, bar staff, hairdressers and kitchen assistants have the four worst paid jobs in the country, all paying – for full-time workers – a median wage of less than £12,500 a year.

One of the defining features of these low-paid McJobs is the lack of union representation. Beauticians, hotel porters, laundry workers and domestic cleaners, all earning less than £15,000 a year, are rarely members of a union. Even among workers in retail, the country's largest private sector industry, who technically have their own shopworkers' union, membership is pretty patchy. Indeed it has been argued, by the likes of Owen Jones in his thought-provoking book *Chavs*, that the decline in union membership itself has been a cause of the collapse in the working class, or certainly in its conditions and pay. The reliance on part-time and temporary, non-unionised workers has certainly not helped wages, and has most probably damaged the sense of camaraderie that existed in many factories and dockyards. Back in 1954 well over half of the UK's workforce were members. Now it is about a quarter of the workforce. Those who are in a union are now more likely to be a white-collar Whitehall civil servant than a blue-collar, tabard-wearing, supermarket checkout operative. About half of public sector workers are still unionised, but just 15 per cent of private sector workers are. And the worst paid are the least unionised.[16]

For many, being part of a union is no longer about the solidarity of their fellow workers but about providing a safety net for when they are made redundant or when their pensions are under threat. The simple link between the working classes and the unions has been severed. I know plenty of Old Etonian members of the National Union of Journalists and Oxbridge graduates who are placard-waving members of Unison. And they gladly employ non-unionised domestic cleaners (cash in hand) to hoover their Habitat rugs and scrub the downstairs loo of their three-bed terraced homes in Wandsworth.

What is less clear is whether the decline in the union movement, the collapse in the dockyards, steelworks, mines and textile factories of Britain has in itself diminished the aspirations of the so-called working class. There is a feeling that the recession of 2009–12, whose after-effects have been felt longer and harder than any recession in living memory, has sucked the hope out of many workers. But I think it just exacerbated a long-running despair that these McJobs were not just poorly paid, but came with no substantial pension, in a way that the previous generation's manual work did. The working classes used to stand a realistic chance of a comfortable retirement, earning enough to own their own home and finish life substantially better off than they started it. The fact that the average home now costs eight times average wages – compared with four times back in the 1950s – has made this almost impossible. Unemployment, and the wave of new immigrants who have come into the country, especially from eastern Europe, and taken many of the manual jobs has merely added to the resentment.

One of the defining features of the Sun Skittlers – though not all the traditional working classes – was a reluctance to climb high up the employment ladder. They may have aspired to own their own home and enjoy a holiday abroad in Majorca, but a desire for promotion up the ranks to management level was something that filled many with horror. Kevin, a foreman in a cardboard box factory whom I interviewed, is fairly typical. 'The machine I am on, I've been on for 35 years now. Making the cardboard, from the paper, cutting it. I don't get bored.' He's been foreman for 25 years, a position which puts him in charge of nine men, and he's been on the same machine that he started his career working on. 'I wouldn't want to go the next step up the ladder. No, no. I wouldn't want that responsibility. Money is not the issue. Job satisfaction is what matters. At the moment I am in charge of one machine. If I was a shift manager

I'd be in charge of ten machines. I am quite happy with the position I am in. You've got to work in the environment to know why you don't want to push yourself no further.'

This acceptance of one's lot, and a reluctance to work one's way to an apparently better position, was highlighted by Richard Scase in his 1972 survey of manual workers. Of those whom he asked, 93 per cent said class existed, and 70 per cent said they were working class. Workers were resigned to a long slog, with little aspiration to change their circumstances.[17] Much of the desperation can be explained by the grim economic circumstances of the time, an echo of the recent financial crisis which has engendered a bleak outlook among many workers. Mark, an unemployed scaffolder, told a recent survey: 'I don't even know if the phrase working class even means anything any more. Where's the work? It's all gone to other people, and there's nothing we can do about it.'[18]

If it's tricky defining exactly what a working-class job is, it's not that much easier pinning down a middle-class one. It used to be any job that required a degree, but now that 45 per cent of school leavers go to university there just aren't enough 'middle-class' jobs to go around all the graduates. Which explains why so many university leavers end up in call centres. But there are still a handful of jobs with the snob factor, and there always have been. Job snobbism has been in existence for decades. My father, on leaving school after failing his A-levels, went into the army. As an officer, of course. That's what you did if you were an unacademic aristocrat or shabbistocrat in the mid-1960s. A generation before, many of the men would have worked on the family estates, or gone into the family business, but by this time the country houses had been knocked down or sold off to hotels, and many family businesses had failed to survive. Agricultural college, land agency, estate agency, minor stockbroking (an ability to hold your after-lunch cognac was considered a far more important skill than any acquaintance with spreadsheets) and the army were the main occupations this class fell into at this time. He joined the Life Guards, one of the smartest, if not the smartest, of all the regiments. Why? 'It was my father's regiment.' Of course. He is one of the least martial men I know (though quite a good shot), so it was unsurprising that he left after six months, having acquired nothing but a habit of cleaning his shoes every single day (it was a morning ritual while the breakfast cafetière was waiting to be plunged, when I was young), and a refusal to be seen carrying any bag in public, save a briefcase. It is a trait he holds to this day, much to the annoyance of my mother. He then became an art dealer, an emerging Rockabilly glamour job in the 1960s along with advertising, public relations, glossy magazine journalism, photography and being a wine merchant.

These class distinctions remain, though in a less extreme from, with a whole host of industries staffed almost exclusively by certain groups of people, sharing the same tastes. Public relations, publishing, television production, advertising – however lowly your job in these industries might be, you are almost certainly a particular type of middle class, probably a Wood Burning Stover or a Rockabilly, in a way that a manager in a wholesale business – one of the ONS's highest-ranking classifications – is unlikely to be. This is because so-called creative industries pay very poorly at the bottom end. Entry-level journalism and advertising pay less than what a full-time street cleaner gets, and yet most of the work is based in central London. More than that, most employers expect you to have completed some form of unpaid work experience. So the only way you can possibly afford to work in these jobs on leaving university, even if living off Tesco Value baked beans in a bedsit on the Holloway Road, is with parental help. This is what makes these jobs so suited to the Rockabillies. Girls in tweed gilets from Joules can bounce into their Covent Garden offices, where they work for a public relations agency representing the restaurant industry, flick their hair, grip their Caffè Nero skinny latte and be unconcerned that their weekly pay packet won't cover their lunchtime sushi bill.

Charity dinners now frequently offer a week's work experience as one of the auction prizes, so that Daddy can help Florence boost her CV points while she's on holiday from Newcastle University. The Conservative party, at a fundraising ball, managed to raise £3,700 by offering up a week's work experience at *Tatler*, the only monthly magazine where the manes of its readers, and indeed its staff, are glossier than the pages it is printed on. It's the Rockabilly bible, devoured by those wanting to find out the latest inside gossip on Prince Harry's love life. One union leader, Michelle Stanistreet, attacked the auctioning off of work experience places: 'Such a disgusting practice simply perpetuates privilege and inequality. Is this what is meant by the Big Society – only the wealthy need apply?'[19] It's certainly hard not to wince at wealthy parents in black tie bidding against each other to secure the best CV points for their children. But it is merely a formalised, and modernised, version of what the aristocrats and wealthier Rockabillies have done for decades – ensuring their heirs spent a month or two learning about finance at the family stockbroker or accountant. It still goes on, with a smattering of young aristocrats working for investment banks and property companies on the understanding they will eventually take over the family estate with a working knowledge of a rental yield and an interest rate swap. The companies themselves, despite their ruthlessly meritocratic image, to this day enjoy a bit of aristo-dash in their boardroom – certainly the aristocrat's family cash invested in the latest project. Nearly all those little resource and mining companies, listed on the London Stock Exchange, that have sprung up in recent years – pumping gas out of Bulgaria or gold from under the Urals – have a Viscount or Earl on their board of directors to impress potential clients.

Work experience placements have become the latest battleground in the class war that has been exacerbated by the Coalition government, whose desire to improve social mobility is always undermined by that Bullingdon Club photo and calling policemen 'plebs' – allegedly. The placements manage to be – when they are a week at a glossy magazine auctioned off to Martha and Mungo – a conspiracy to keep the Rockabillies at the top of the class ladder. But when they are a month at McDonald's or Tesco for out-of-work Kayleigh or Aaron it is a conspiracy to keep the Hyphen-Leighs at the bottom.

Work experience plays only a part in gaining access to these jobs. The real passport to some professions is an Oxbridge degree and, in many cases, a private school education, as we have seen in an earlier chapter. But what makes many of these jobs 'middle class' is not the public school and Oxbridge background of many of those starting out in these professions – though that plays a significant part. It is also the money paid out in salaries. Money is important as an immediate and crude marker of status, and for its ability to furnish these workers' homes, children, wardrobes and fridges with a Portland Privateer or Woodburning Stover lifestyle.

These modern middle-class jobs may start off paying peanuts. But they still offer the prospect of modest riches to come, of just about enough to pay for a deposit and a mortgage on a flat, just about enough for a two-week holiday in Bouches-du-Rhône, regular Friday lunchtime trips to Wagamama and tickets to the Hay Festival or a new play at the Manchester Royal Exchange. It's tricky to completely divorce the consumer products from the job that funded those purchases.

Money never used to be a class issue. If anything, people who earned filthy amounts of cash were rather looked down upon by the old aristos, unless they went on to buy themselves a country house with a good stretch of fishing, to which all the old aristos could be invited. Unless, in other words, they did a passable impression of being members of the aristos themselves and fully assimilating themselves, as all good Middleton classes have done in the past. Even then, there was a fair degree of suspicion about loud money-makers. *Nouveaux riches* – or 'noovs' as we called them at school with much glee – were regarded with far more scorn than the working classes, with 1980s entrepreneurs such as Alan Sugar, Richard Branson and Maurice Saatchi all failing to win full favour with the elite. They may have been awarded titles, but that didn't make them aristocrats. Graham, now Lord, Kirkham, the adopted son of a miner who went on to found the DFS sofa chain (the biggest sofa retailer in the world), showed how it should be done. After he floated his business on the stock exchange, netting himself over £100 million, he celebrated by buying Gainsborough's *Peasants Going to Market* for £3.5 million. He couldn't resist the joke.[20]

In those days there were only ever a handful of businessmen who could earn enough to snap up an Old Master simply to provide a good punchline to a tale. In the last few years there has been so much money made in the City that thousands upon thousands of workers have been able rapidly to enter the ranks of the Portland Privateers. They have done this not over a lifetime in the City but in as little as a decade or 15 years at the coal face. The money started to pour into the City in the run-up to the Big Bang – the epoch-changing event in 1986 that deregulated the banking industry and allowed American investment banks to come in and snap up old British broker-ages. And save for the merest pause for breath as various insti-tutions crashed ignominiously in the wake of Lehman Brothers' collapse, it hasn't stopped. The Big Bang was important, not just for the City, but for the wider culture it ushered in; it has filtered down to many companies miles away from the Square Mile. After the event, directorships replaced partnerships in nearly all City banking and stockbroking firms. As Philip Augur, in his excellent *The Death of Gentlemanly Capitalism*, argues: 'Whereas candidates for partner shared the liabilities and rewards of the firm and were screened closely for suitabil-ity, the criteria for directorships were less closely monitored. The title of director proliferated and with that came a devalu-ation in its status. Status was dethroned and cash became king. Young brokers had nothing left to go for but a bigger bonus.'[21] This quest for cash was egged on by the rise of the professional headhunter, a new breed of über-job that emerged in the mid-1980s, along with the mega-bucks management consultant and the super-star interior designer. They were souped-up middlemen who went on to earn more money than either of the parties they brokered for. It was that sort of decade, and a true sign that the service economy had usurped the manufacturing one.

Workplaces a generation ago tended to be extremely hierarchical, with one's status denoted by a myriad of little signs and symbols. It was not just the top hats worn by the senior staff, the bowlers of those one rung beneath them, the brass nameplate on the office door or who you called Sir and who you didn't. At Marks & Spencer's old headquarters in Baker Street, London, one could tell the seniority of the director whom one was visiting by the thickness of the carpet along the corridor, which became ever plusher as it neared the chairman's imposing office. Lola Smith eventually quit her machinist job in the East End to work in the City – as a silver-service waitress at a large insurance firm in the 1980s. The chairman, directors and managers all had their separate dining rooms, with separate bars where you could order your gin and tonic before lunch. The Raleigh bicycle factory had 15 different staff canteens, one for each rank of worker, from directors down to the most basic shop-floor workers.

These antiquated methods of attributing status lacked subtlety, but they rewarded aspiring workers. They have now all but been replaced by pay and bonuses, except in a handful of modern workplaces which attempt to mollify overworked staff with free ice cream, as they do at Google's London headquarters, or stunts such as 'duvet days'. The result is that the gap between an average wage and the top wage has become ever wider. In the City the gulf is becoming absurd. In 1983 Smith Brothers, the stock jobber firm, posted record profits and the chairman was on a £105,000 yearly salary. This compared with an average salary of £5,902 a year.[22] In other words, the chairman of one of the very top City firms was earning 18 times the average British salary. Nowadays top bosses – those running FTSE 100 companies – earn on average £825,000 from their basic salaries. This is the equivalent of about 36 times the average British wage – a simple doubling in relative terms within a generation. But that's before you get to the all-important bonuses and share options, which push up the average FTSE 100 boss's pay to an eye-watering £4.7 million.[23] This is 221 times the UK's *average* wage.

Even if you dismiss these salaries as the pay packets of an infinitesimally small number of people – indeed, just 100 individuals in charge of Britain's 100 biggest public companies – take a look at the thousands of anonymous City workers, shuffling off to their desks in Bishopsgate or Canary Wharf. The average bonus for an investment banker at RBS, including the most junior back-office worker, was £22,941, which is £1,000 more than what an average worker in an RBS high street bank branch earned in a year. We know from official tax returns that there are at least 350,000 people who earn a (declared) income of more than £150,000 a year, the majority of whom work in the City. This area of London has helped create the Portland Privateers, not just because of the money it has fed their way, but because it has become so estranged from the rest of Britain.

Retail banks and merchant banks used to be cousins. One was the traditional branch found on the high street, and was where you went to obtain a mortgage and deposit your savings; the other was in the City, and lent money and advised companies. Workers in one would understand what the other did, more or less. Now they are a world apart. There is a mischievous tale (reported in *Private Eye*) that when Barclays hired Marcus Agius as its chairman, on a basic salary of £751,000 a year, from the investment bank Lazards, he had to be taken into a Barclays branch at the weekend and shown how to use a cash machine. He had previously obtained all the cash he needed from his secretary who got it on his behalf, and had never before stood in front of an ATM.

This gulf between those with jobs in, or related to, the City and those outside it is most clearly exemplified by the bonus culture, a culture that almost entirely fuels the Portland Privateers' attitude and way of life. It explains why, despite their apparently lavish lifestyle, many in this class feel as if they are living on the edge, more squeezed than Miliband's squeezed middle, their income barely covering their outgoings. In some years their bonus will be a mere £15,000 and their children's private education may be in peril; in other years it will be enough to buy outright that holiday cottage in Burnham Market or Bracciano. It is a culture that breeds insecurity and discontent. I have never once met a banker happy with the bonus he received. On the very day that Nick Leeson, the rogue trader, brought down Barings Bank, 67 staff were due to be paid a bonus of £250,000 each. That was the justification for his actions, he claimed. 'The biggest crime I am guilty of is trying to protect people and ensure that the bonuses they expected were paid.'[24]

Golden handshakes, golden handcuffs, golden parachutes – none of these has lost much glitter during the financial melt-down that hit the markets in 2008. Aviva handed its new UK chief executive a bonus of £45,000 in 2011 for just one month of work as part of a £4.25 million welcome package.[25] The former chief exec of Barclays, Bob Diamond, got his pesky tax bill paid by his shareholders. A 'culture of entitlement' was a phrase brandished during the riots of 2011 to explain the violent and acquisitive behaviour of the looters, but it is fair to say that many in the City, and its related industries spread across the country, also possess an entitlement culture.

* * *

Susan Shaw said that she would always love the smell of the City, but she returned a few years ago and couldn't help but feel the atmosphere had been poisoned by the levels of excessive pay. 'I personally feel it's very wrong. The difference to me is the awful amount of risk taking, much more than we ever did in my day.'

Investment bankers, fund managers, derivatives traders, corporate lawyers, management consultants, commercial barristers – these people's jobs do not in themselves denote class. What makes these occupations so synonymous with the Portland Privateer class is both the money that comes with the job and the belief among many of the workers that this money can be used, indeed should be used, to reward themselves with the best coffee, car, basement conversion and education for their children.

Since 1954 the real disposable income of households – as in the amount of actual money left in their pockets after paying tax, and taking into account inflation – has steadily risen. Most of us, every year, steadily got richer and had more money to buy things. We may feel miserable about the state of our finances following a long and deep recession, but we are still richer than our parents, and a great deal richer than our grandparents. There have only been very rare years when the money in our pocket has not swollen in real terms. In fact just four: 1976, 1977, 1981 and 2011.[26] This simple economic fact has driven the fundamental changes in how we have

307

lived our lives and defined ourselves. Two generations ago we just had less money to spend. It's only when we have spare cash in our pay packets that we can start to be defined by what we spend it on; before that time, how we earned our pay packets had to be a more important aspect of how we saw ourselves.

Another key change to working life since the 1950s has been the considerable shortening of it. We now spend far less of our life at a desk, or on a production line. People are entering the workplace far later, because of the increased time spent in education, and are living far beyond their retirement age thanks to improvements in health. Between 1951 and 2000, the number of Britons aged 65 and over rose by about 70 per cent, yet the average age of retirement fell rapidly.[27] And although the recession forced many pensioners back to work, only 3 per cent of them are in full-time employment.

This shortening of the working life and lengthening of retirement, of course, is causing serious policy issues for politicians around the world and will continue to do so for years to come. But it leads to an unmistakable conclusion: if far less of your life is spent at work, and far more of it at leisure, down the supermarket, on holiday, work must become a less important factor in defining yourself. More than this, the nature of the work we do colours how we see ourselves. Britain is a service economy, which means many of us are in the job of selling and marketing brands and status, from Tesco Value baked beans right the way up to the financial services industry, which is now all about 'brand equity' and 'adding value'. The success of Britain, in economic terms, rests on us continually buying more of these services, on trading up to the better brand, cruise ship or ready meal.

Class is no longer what we do with our hands nine to five, it is what we do with our wallets at the weekend. How that money arrives in our wallets must play a part, but how we define ourselves and how others view us mostly comes down to the weekly drive to the local retail park, rather than the daily trudge to the factory.

CONCLUSION

In the general election of 1951 Winston Churchill made an explicit attempt to appeal to housewives still dealing with ration books: 'We are for the ladder. Let all try their best to climb. They are for the queue. Let each wait in his place till his turn comes.'[1] It was a swipe at the new Welfare State but also an appeal to something everyone understood at the time: social aspiration.

I am no sentimentalist yearning for a return to the glorious 1950s. This was the decade that for all its exciting jet age possibilities was also grey, drab and hard work for millions of families on rations and weighing up whether it was worth spending two weeks' wages on their first washing machine or television. It was a country riddled with snobbism, where your accent and choice of vocabulary marked you out, where an exam you passed or failed at the age of 11 determined so much. But what this era did suggest was that life would get better, that there was a ladder you could climb to help you achieve a better position in life than your parents had done.

Since then most of us have climbed. How much the politicians really helped in this endeavour is debatable. Right-to-buy was a transformative piece of legislation, but left those who were unable to take advantage of it in a worse position than before, stuck in an ever-decreasing pool of devalued council homes. The establishment of a comprehensive education system and the dismantling of state-funded grammar schools have improved standards of literacy and numeracy, but the effect has probably been to kick the ladder away for many rather than allowing us to climb higher. One of the consequences of pushing more pupils into higher education is that Britain is now awash with students holding degrees of limited value, unable to find graduate-level jobs. And those who most benefit are those whose parents are willing to pay for a premium brand of tutor or a Taste the Difference postcode.

In fact, social engineering, through major legislation and tinkering with the tax system – even down to VAT on Greggs' pasties – has become the default ambition of all governments in recent decades. A desire to 'level the playing field' and create 'equal opportunities for all' is something that unites parties across the spectrum and will offend no voters. Churchill won the election of 1951, but his defence of capitalism is deeply unfashionable now. Even Conservatives promise to end 'excellence for the few'. A generation has been told that everyone is a winner, and no one a loser, that a 2.1 from the University of Bedford is equal to a 2.1 from Oxford, that we are all 'colleagues' or 'executives', we're one nation and we're all in it together.

Most people don't believe any of this tosh and have an in-built discernment. They can feel the heft of something. They resent being told by the political elite – the modern upper class – what they should and should not aspire to. And most do aspire.

The old rigid class system, based largely on birth and education, has been dismantled mostly thanks to the private sector and personal endeavour. The credit should go to the consumer companies and their customers. More than anything it was the supermarkets, for the first time offering self-service and a wide selection of goods; it was the package holiday companies, flying Brits abroad not to fight a war but to soak up the sun; it was the department stores, offering a dazzling array of labour-saving devices to free householders from back-breaking house-work; the television, broadcasting rich and enriching dramas; clothing chains that allowed shop girls to dress like debs, and dukes to dress like dustmen. These were the real agents of social change – fuelled by cheap oil, the microchip and the outsourcing of production overseas. The revolution, in turn, shifted Britain from a manufacturing economy into a service one, an economy which now revolves around 'adding value' to our lives and lifestyle.

For most of us the revolution has been a good thing. Even those at the very bottom of the socio-economic pile, those in 'High Rise Hardship' or 'Inner City Adversity', now enjoy a lifestyle which in the mid-1950s would have put them firmly in the middle-class category. Beveridge's five evils have not been fully slain, but for the great majority want and squalor are a distant memory. Bread in a toaster, *Daybreak* on the television, putting on a cashmere jumper from Primark, taking the kids to school in a Renault Scenic – these are morning ritu-als for many, and none of them particularly luxurious.

The pernicious recession, whose roots lie in the queues outside Northern Rock in 2007, has put a severe dent in many people's pockets and increased unemployment. But people's wallets are still fatter than back when Wimpy was opening its doors for the first time, and the dole queue is shorter than during the era when Hampstead was fighting its battle against

McDonald's and the London Stock Exchange was defending itself against women.

But this relative security and luxury has come at a price. The companies enabling our more comfortable and enjoyable lifestyle have, partly by accident, partly by design, perpetuated a version of the class system. By endlessly categorising us, by segmenting us into different groups of customers, they encouraged us to see the world as one made up of value, ordinary and finest; of freeze-dried, cafetière and Nespresso; of the Light, Home and Third.

In the summer of 2012, Tesco's chief executive, Philip Clarke, announced that the company would start to tailor its website to individual customers, based on the data the company had collected from its Clubcard loyalty scheme. You may think online retailing is truly democratic – anyone can buy anything from anywhere – but even here categorisation is rampant because the companies know your postcode, your willingness to spend and your Mosaic or Acorn social grouping. They even know whether you are more likely to buy Finest chicken Kievs on a Thursday, or frozen turkey twizzlers on a Tuesday, as their loyalty cards track every single purchase. Clarke said: 'Today we're in a new era of retailing – the era of mass personalisation. Mass – because digital technology has given everyone the opportunity to communicate with companies and organisations everywhere. Personal – because communication is one on one, and thanks to data we now have, a retail offer can be tailored to reflect an individual's tastes, lifestyle, income.'

So those customers, when they log onto the website, will be shown different selections of products based on their propensity to buy fresh peaches or tinned, orange squash or freshly squeezed orange juice, tuna in a tin or salmon in a dill and cream sauce. It is a sophisticated and more thorough version of internet cookies – which track where you have visited online and then flash adverts for your favourite brands when you are on another website. This time around, however, Tesco is tracking what you buy in the real world and then offering you a personalised version, based on your habits, when you log on. Your search for 'pesto' could bring up a whole separate set of results from your neighbour's search, with one of you being offered fresh basil and lovingly grated parmesan, the other a jar of basic stuff with cashew nuts rather than pine nuts (oh, the poverty).

The companies are horrified if you suggest to them that they are encouraging stereotypes or building up class ghettos; they argue that they are making it easier for customers to find what they want. Their response to anything that makes you raise your eyebrows is: 'It's customer demand.' They are often right. But by segmenting they are undertaking a systematic version of the 'choice editing' that Habitat and John Lewis pioneered back in the 1960s when they sought to banish 'frightfully provincial' retailing. It is a hugely profitable exercise, and one that makes for a more satisfying shopping experience. But it undoubtedly cements different social groupings. If you already live in a deprived postcode, without access to a decent supermarket or primary school, and you then log onto the internet only to find it is promoting cheap, basic goods, how will you know what is at the top of the ladder?

If you live in wealthy, second-home-owning Burnham Market, is it any wonder you get the latest outlet of Joules? Or that the most recent branches of Waitrose have opened in Stratford upon Avon, Highbury, Gerrards Cross, Alton or Muswell Hill?

We have been willing participants in this conspiracy, especially as the great recession of 2009 took hold and ate away at people's disposable incomes. It used to be about keeping up with the Joneses; it is now about being different from the Joneses. And buying Heinz ketchup with balsamic vinegar, popping into Wagamama with the kids and a day trip to Blenheim are all part of the game. When money is tight it is harder than ever to distinguish oneself from the crowd, and many don't want to do it in an obvious way. Which is why the companies that have really flourished in the age of austerity are those that ruthlessly target a particular socio-economic group and give them exactly what they want – especially those at the extreme ends of the ladder. Some great successes of 2010 to 2012 have been Waitrose, especially with its cunning Essentials range, John Lewis, Jack Wills, Boden and Mulberry, as well as Iceland, Aldi, 99p Stores, Poundland and Brighthouse. Being all things to all people rarely works, which partly explains why Tesco and Marks & Spencer have struggled so much in the last couple of years.

And this great class conspiracy perpetuated by these companies is not something we should necessarily fight. If we aspire to the idea of social mobility, we must also embrace a world in which there is Ryanair, Featherdown Farm and Butlins; televisions with E!, BBC One and Sky Arts; and homes with Glade plug-ins, Jo Malone smelly candles and hyacinth bulbs. Many of us now express our fortunes through consumption, whether we realise it or not. And we need a full range of outlets in order to demonstrate our rising, or falling, fortunes. The distinctions between whether you are an Iceland shopper or a Waitrose customer are probably less harmful than those that decided whether your initials came before or after your surname. A world of scratchy flannels, of 13 ounces of meat a week, of being blackballed, of always feeling an outsider, of mocking glances when you called lunch 'dinner' or pronounced the 'd' in Cholmondeley ... of getting it wrong.

Being judged for how you spend your money, rather than how you earn it, seems to me to be progress of some sort.

Fifteen years after the tweed suit incident on the night of the 1997 general election, I realise that my father was right. And not just that I looked a bit of a mess on a hot and sticky night. The details of status matter to some people an awful lot. Sometimes it is just good manners to turn up in what your host wants, even if you think your style is being cramped. The actress Patricia Routledge, herself a daughter of a 'high-class gentleman outfitter', expressed it most neatly when she described playing Hyacinth Bucket, one of the great sitcom figures of the 1990s, and the archetypal snob: 'She's an absolute monster and I enjoyed playing her enormously. But I had to find out what made her tick. Coupled with [her social pretension] was her aim for everything to be right and to be the best. Which is a good thing.'[2]

Snobbism, and the desire to trade up and furnish one's lifestyle with the trappings and markers of a better life, is not a bad thing. It may in fact be a good thing. It has, I hope I've shown, been one of the most powerful drivers of social and economic change in Britain over the last two generations: of the decline of the working men's club and the rise of the trendy wine bar, of champagne overtaking pale ale, of Dyson vacuum cleaners and iPads replacing the Breville sandwich toaster and the radiogram. We may regret these changes and see them as a symptom of a society corrupted by consumerism. But snobbism is the engine oil that can keep the cogs of social mobility turning. Especially in an age when there is less money about, the need to distinguish oneself from the millions of other 'middle classes' is a powerful one.

Most of us are now, indeed, middle class, from the Viscounts upset with Ryanair for getting their titles wrong to the Asda shoppers feeling embarrassed about the brand of nappies they buy. But that does not mean we are classless – just that there is a huge variety of different consumers sheltering in the middle, trying not to get crushed or squeezed. Britain will never be truly classless. We enjoy the climb up the ladder too much.

NOTES

INTRODUCTION
1 *Guardian*, 24 September 2012
2 *Daily Mail*, 23 May 2012
3 *Guardian*, 9 December 1960
4 *Desert Island Discs*, 1 September 1996

CHAPTER 1: FOOD
1 *Daily Mirror*, 13 June 1975
2 *The Grocer*, 25 February 2012, p. 54
3 Helen Chislett, *Marks in Time: 125 Years of Marks & Spencer*, p. 148
4 Andrew Rosen, *The Transformation of British Life, 1950–2000*, p. 18
5 Andrew Rosen, *The Transformation of British Life, 1950–2000*, p. 19
6 Humphrey Carpenter, *A Great Silly Grin: The British Satire Boom of the 1960s*
7 'Not with a Banger but a Wimpy', *Observer*, 8 November 1959
8 'Storm in a Milkshake', *The Times*, 6 August 1992
9 Miriam Akhtar and Steve Humphries, *The Fifties and Sixties: A Lifestyle Revolution*, p. 107
10 *The Fifties and Sixties*, p. 26
11 Office for National Statistics, *Annual Abstract of Statistics*, 2010
12 *Daily Telegraph*, 7 March 2009
13 Digital Spy

CHAPTER 2: FAMILY
1 David Kynaston, *Family Britain 1951–57*, p. 563
2 *Daily Telegraph*, 11 January 2011
3 *Family Britain*, p. 153
4 Owen Jones, *Chavs: The Demonization of the Working Class*, p. 18

5   *Family Britain*, p. 525
6   Dominic Sandbrook, *Daily Mail*, 20 November 2010

CHAPTER 3: PROPERTY

1   David Cannadine, *The Decline and Fall of the British Aristocracy*,
    p. 644
2   *Ideal Home*, p. 123
3   Duke of Bedford obituary, *Daily Telegraph*, 28 October 2002
4   John, Duke of Bedford, *A Silver-Plated Spoon*
5   Tory manifesto, 1951
6   'The End of the Affair: Implications of Declining Home
    Ownership', Andrew Heywood, Smith Institute, 2011
7   Miriam Akhtar and Steve Humphries, *The Fifties and Sixties: A
    Lifestyle Revolution*, p. 56
8   Quoted in Owen Jones, *Chavs*, p. 34
9   Quoted in *The Fifties and Sixties*, p. 59
10 Quoted in David Kynaston, *Family Britain 1951–57*, p. 137
11 *The Fifties and Sixties*, p. 61
12 Lawrence James, *The Middle Class: A History*, p. 434
13 *Family Britain 1951–57*, p. 57
14 Andrew Rosen, *The Transformation of British Life, 1950–2000*,
    p. 131
15 'The End of the Affair: Implications of Declining Home
    Ownership', Andrew Heywood, Smith Institute, 2011
16 *Daily Mail*, 14 November 2008
17 *The Sunday Times*, 13 November 2011
18 'Breakthrough Britain: Housing Poverty', Centre for Social Justice,
    p. 5
19 'The End of the Affair: Implications of Declining Home
    Ownership', Andrew Heywood, Smith Institute, 2011
20 'Super-gentrification in Barnsbury, London', Tim Butler and Loretta
    Lees

CHAPTER 4: HOME

1   *The Times*, 5 October 1966
2   Office for National Statistics, *Family Spending*, 2011
3   *Daily Mail*, 8 February 2011
4   Deborah S. Ryan, *The Ideal Home through the 20th Century*, p. 95

NOTES

5   Bill Bryson, *At Home: A Short History of Private Life*, p. 372
6   Dominic Sandbrook, *White Heat*, p. 691
7   *The Times*, 9 October 2008
8   Terence Conran, *The House Book*
9   Lawrence James, *The Middle Class: A History*, p. 533
10   *Desert Island Discs*, 29 April 2011

CHAPTER 5: CLOTHES

1   Ian Jack, 'Five Boys, the Story of a Picture', *Intelligent Life* magazine, Spring 2010
2   Paul Fussell, *Class: A Guide through the American Status System*, p. 172
3   Eric M. Sigsworth, *Montague Burton: The Tailor of Taste*, pp. 66–69
4   *Montague Burton*, p. 46
5   *Montague Burton*, p. 89
6   *Montague Burton*, p. 89
7   Quoted in David Kynaston, *Family Britain 1951–57*, p. 674
8   Miriam Akhtar and Steve Humphries, *The Fifties and Sixties: A Lifestyle Revolution*, p. 41
9   John Lewis Partnership archives, McAnally memo 7.11.55
10   John Lewis Partnership archives, RE/3476 1.6.70
11   John Lewis Partnership archives, 13.1.58
12   *Evening Standard*, 1 November 2001
13   *Living etc*, October 2012

CHAPTER 6: EDUCATION

1   *Guardian*, 24 May 2000
2   *Times Educational Supplement*, 18 August 2000
3   *Daily Mirror*, 29 May 2000
4   *Evening Standard*, 26 May 2000
5   *Daily Mail*, 27 May 2000
6   *Memories of Kidbrooke School, 1954–2005*
7   *Desert Island Discs*, 12 March 2006
8   *Guardian*, 23 April 2004
9   David Kynaston, *Family Britain 1951–57*, p. 504
10   *Family Britain*, p. 141
11   Andrew Rosen, *The Transformation of British Life, 1950–2000*, p. 68

12 NFER Teacher Voice omnibus survey, February 2012
13 *Daily Telegraph*, 25 April 2001
14 *Family Britain 1951–57*, p. 141
15 Institute of Social and Economic Research, February 2012
16 *Daily Telegraph*, 15 February 2012
17 Letter to the *Spectator*, 26 May 2012
18 *Guardian*, 26 April 2012
19 *Daily Telegraph*, 6 October 2012
20 Sutton Trust, 'London is the Capital of Private Tuition', 28 September 2012
21 *Daily Mail*, 29 August 2011
22 *Today* programme, 30 May 2012
23 *Standpoint* magazine, March 2012
24 *The Times*, 14 March 2012
25 Sutton Trust, press release, 14 August 2012

CHAPTER 7: HOLIDAYS

1   Roger Bray and Vladimir Raitz, *Flight to the Sun*, p. 2
2   *Flight to the Sun*, p. 34
3   David Kynaston, *Family Britain 1951–57*, p. 671
4   Office for National Statistics, *Travel Trends*, 2010
5   Office for National Statistics, *Travel Trends*, 2010
6   Miriam Akhtar and Steve Humphries, *Some Liked it Hot*, p. 84
7   *Some Liked it Hot*, p. 95
8   *Observer*, 9 April 1967
9   *The Sunday Times*, February 25, 1990
10 *Guardian*, 30 July 1994
11 *Independent*, 7 August 1989
12 *The Times*, 18 August 1989
13 Lawrence James, *The Middle Class: A History*, p. 566
14 D.R. Thorpe, *Supermac: The Life of Harold Macmillan*, p. 384
15 *Supermac*, p. 384
16 *Some Liked it Hot*, p. 16
17 *Guardian*, 27 August 2010
18 *Some Liked it Hot*, p. 21

NOTES

CHAPTER 8: LEISURE

1 H.V. Kershaw, *The Street Where I Live*, p. 47
2 Tony Warren, *I Was Ena Sharples' Father*, p. 58
3 Daran Little, *The Coronation Street Story*, p. 8
4 *The Street Where I Live*, p. 20
5 *Guardian*, 27 June 1961
6 *The Street Where I Live*, p. 49
7 Quoted in Lawrence James, *The Middle Class: A History*, p. 429
8 *Daily Telegraph*, 6 June 2012
9 'Cultural Attitudes and Attendance', Arts and Business, p. 120
10 IMDb memorable quotes, *Yes, Prime Minister*, 'A Conflict of Interest', 1987
11 Dominic Sandbrook, *White Heat*, p. 61
12 *Daily Mail*, 24 September 2012
13 *British Gambling Prevalence Survey*, 2010
14 Working Men's Club and Institute Union Limited, Annual report and accounts, 2011
15 David Kynaston, *Family Britain 1951–57*, p. 174
16 Cancer Research UK, based on ONS general lifestyle survey, 2010
17 *Evening Standard*, 31 May 2011
18 *Daily Telegraph* blogs, 21 May 2012
19 *Family Britain 1951–57*, p. 137
20 *Sunday Telegraph*, 1 January 2012
21 *The Daily Beast*, 16 January 2012
22 Lawrence James, *The Middle Class: A History*, p. 431
23 *The Middle Class*, p. 429
24 *Family Britain 1951–57*, p. 507
25 *Guardian*, 13 July 1993
26 *Guardian* online, 28 March 2012
27 *The Middle Class: A History*, p. 558

CHAPTER 9: WORK

1 *Daily Express*, 31 March 1973
2 David Kynaston, *The City of London, vol. IV: A Club No More*, p. 425
3 *A Club No More*, p. 514
4 Philip Augur, *The Death of Gentlemanly Capitalism*, p. 34

5   'Official Social Classifications in the UK', David Rose, University of Surrey, 1995
6   David Kynaston, *Family Britain 1951–57*, p. 577
7   *Family Britain 1951–57*, p. 579
8   Office for National Statistics, *Annual Abstract of Statistics*, 1955
9   Contactbabel
10 ONS, Annual Abstract of Statistics, 2011
11 *Sunday Telegraph*, 19 February 2012
12 *Daily Mirror*, 5 January 1998
13 ONS, *Annual Abstract of Statistics*, 1955
14 *Manchester Guardian*, 16 August, 1954
15 ONS, *Annual Abstract of Statistics*, 2010
16 Owen Jones, *Chavs: The Demonization of the Working Class*, p. 155
17 Arthur Marwick, *British Society since 1945*, p. 172
18 *Independent on Sunday*, 26 June 2011
19 Journalism.co.uk, 14 February 2011
20 *Daily Telegraph*, 11 January 2003
21 *The Death of Gentlemanly Capitalism*, p. 106
22 *The Death of Gentlemanly Capitalism*, p. 22
23 *Daily Telegraph*, 12 June 2012
24 *Guardian*, 13 July 1995
25 *Daily Telegraph*, 22 March 2012
26 ONS, *The Impact of the Recession on Household Income, Expenditure and Saving*, 2011
27 Andrew Rosen, *The Transformation of British Life, 1950–2000*, p. 114

CONCLUSION

1   David Kynaston, *Family Britain 1951–57*, p. 33
2   *Desert Island Discs*, 8 August 1999

ACKNOWLEDGEMENTS

I am indebted to a number of people and organisations that have helped me with the research for this book, many of whom gave up a considerable time either to be interviewed or to track down an elusive piece of information. Others have just made suggestions. All have been invaluable. Any errors are all my own.

I would particularly like to thank: Cathy Chapman and Liz Williams at Marks & Spencer; Jonathan Rae at CACI; Craig Inglis, Helen Dickinson, Amy Shields at John Lewis, and particularly Judy Faraday, who opened up the John Lewis Partnership archives for me; Sir Terence Conran; Matthew Riches; Alice Lythgoe-Goldstein and Julian Edwards at Which?; Nick Agarwal, Leah Watson and Jo Newbould at Asda, as well as Suzanne, Vikki, Michelle and Kizzie at the Asda Bootle focus group; Barry Slasberg and Mick McGlasham at the Working Men's Club & Institute Union, along with Kevin, Mick and Steve at the Kingsley Park Working Men's Club; Elizabeth McLaren and David Bradbury at the Office for National Statistics; Jonathan Black at Oxford University careers service; Dawn Collins at Ipsos Mori; the staff at the British Library, particularly those at the newspaper archive at the Colindale reading room; Robert Opie; Richard Hyman; Jill McDonald and Dionne Parker at McDonald's; Steve Buck;

Anthony Smith; Lola Smith; Ruth Bale; Susan Shaw; Kayleigh Goldie; Hayleigh Pain; Gavin Casey; George Davies; the Earl of Portsmouth; Rita Clifton; Katrina Bates; Lady Clementine Wallop; Victoria Wallop; Alex Sowerby; Jane Sowerby; Helen Sowerby; Lady Anna Thomson; Jo Dickinson; Scott Wadlow; Kira Philips; Saul Dibb; Hamish Thompson; Tim Philips; Anthony Bale; Andrew Wille; Hugh and Claire Davies; Amy MacLaren; Matthew Moore; Merope Mills; Joan Moynihan; Tim Hyman; Victoria and John Pratt.

Three online sources have been particularly useful: Measuring Worth, the Sutton Trust and the BBC Desert Island Discs archive.

I have leant heavily on a small number of historians, notably Dominic Sandbrook, David Kynaston and David Cannadine. I would urge anyone interested in post-war social history and the change in the class structure to seek out their works.

This book was written during a 15-month period when I worked across three separate departments of the *Daily Telegraph* – and though it was written during my spare time a number of editors have been particularly supportive, notably Richard Fletcher, Jonathan Sibun, Kamal Ahmed, Liz Hunt and Maureen O'Donnell. I would also like to thank Martin Beckford and Graeme Paton who read large chunks of the book and made invaluable suggestions.

This book would not have happened without the help of my agent, Veronique Baxter at David Higham, and all at HarperCollins: Iain MacGregor, Hannah MacDonald, and especially my editor, Elen Jones, who has been excellent at dealing with a first-time author. Thank you also to Steve Dobell for his careful copy-edit.

ACKNOWLEDGEMENTS

I know it is very *déclassé* to thank one's parents in public, but Lavinia and Nicholas Wallop have been, as the book made clear, a lifelong and bottomless source of information. They have never complained about me, once again, dragging our family life into the public domain. John Sowerby, my father-in-law, has also endured months of questioning and his contributions provide not only the backbone, but the inspiration, for the book.

Finally, and most importantly, I need to thank my wife, Victoria Sowerby, who has gone way beyond the call of duty, wading through endless drafts of the book. All the while, she has brought up our four children, unaided, as I worked on this project in what was meant to be family time.